Pelegrine: A Holographic Journey

By

LiLo Hoco

In memory of my mother 1909-1989

Author's Note

All the characters and events in this book are entirely fictitious and no resemblance is intended to any event or to any real person, either living or dead.

Acknowledgements

Whatever the weaknesses of this book, they would have been far greater without the kind help of friends. In particular, I would like to thank Solveig Dutkewych, Loreley French, Bernard Platt and Yvette Spitz for their direction, assistance, and guidance. Special thanks should be given to Gerlinde Sanford who helped me in many ways, especially her faith in my being a writer. Their recommendations and suggestions have been invaluable for this book.

LiLo Hoco
San Miguel de Allende, Mexico, 2009

Copyright © 2009 by LiLo Hoco
ISBN 978-0-578-00490-7

Prologue

Reasons for writing this story

I wanted to tell the story of a heroine, a female *picara* in the tradition of the male *picaro*—the rogue, the observer, the tragic cog in the wheel—who has a hard time learning to accept the nature of her drives and energies that propel her own destruction. She cannot let go of something even if it hurts her and settles for a subtle form of abuse surfacing in various co-dependent disguises. On the other hand, she has had a colorful and eventful life that she always narrates to somebody somewhere. Eventually, she got tired of the same stories. So she wrote them down for nothing more than a compelling tale. Perhaps? But maybe she wrote her life so that she would be able to visit her history only as a neutral spectator and not as a suffering patient, eternally shedding her skins.

Title, Themes and Style

The title *Pelegrine: A Holographic Journey* suggests a progression that links both the content of her life and the way her life actually proceeds, as does the first page that moves across time periods.

Pelegrine is a never-ending picaresque adventure story about a girl looking for ways to grow up, to find herself by herself. She persistently hovers on peripheries that pledge permanence. She searches and leaves her country of origin even, connecting to promises and disappointments, all of which continue to lead her on endless journeys into a thousand brave futures. I call it a holographic journey because the readers can chose how to read the deeper psychological implications of the narrative--what angles to keep as their preferred interpretations.

The holographic style changes, as does the interaction with the rational segments of her life. At one point, as she begins her first serious relationship with a woman, the story proceeds extremely chronologically. It may be assumed that the relationship with Pontiac Wingo represents a settling down, a grounding in Pelegrine's life, and that her explorations for the most part, become more structured and meaningful after that. The character of Pontiac Wingo, the most important female influence in her life, is not only to throw light on her Gertrud Stein/Toklas type relationship, her teacher-mentor connection but also, above all, celebrate her first and most significant genuine commitment to another human being. The rest of the book actually follows this chronological barometer in conjunction with Pelegrine's relationships.

The story addresses crucial issues in a woman's life who had to grow up practically all by herself not only as a baby and small child, but, seemingly, forever, having to discover what she knows by simply watching how others do it. She learns to rely on herself drawing from her emerging levels of confidence while she encounters never-ending confusions. As she finds herself, she comes less and less to rely on the stories, traditions, and styles she has formed through relationships with others, but on a form that she herself has created, based on continual experimentation.

The whole journey appears to be a reassessment of past experiences and styles in conjunction with the present, making an ongoing connection between the two, which helps Pelegrine to find out more about herself and her desires. It thus seems that until she really begins to explore herself by herself, as she does in the end, she relies solely on constructions of herself through the constructs of others.

Readers will also have questions about the narrator. There is one place in the novel where Pelegrine herself, wanting to take over narrating her own story, interrupts the narrator. In the end she succeeds because she no longer needs the intermediary mouthpiece, some one else's voice, once she has learned to live with herself the way she is.

Similar to the narrative interruptions, Pelegrine's indecisive reconsiderations of her sexuality transpire when she begins wishing for a male companion. There is very little in her experiences that might make this desire seem plausible, except as a negative reaction to the women with whom she had had relationships. In fact, her perceptions of the differences—men being "bold, adventurous, easy-going and possessing a definite physical advantage which envelops them like a protective cloak"—are not very convincing, for these are qualities that Pelegrine, too, as a woman has. That is part of what she has to discover.

There are also indications of bisexuality in her relationships, but in the end, she prefers more androgynous validations for sexual encounters rather than an over-simplified dichotomy describing a man and a woman in only their reproductive pursuit.

In many ways, Pelegrine's experiences challenge many contemporary theorists, and urge them to question the notion of theory without having evidence of experiences to back them up. Most of all, Pelegrine's story begs for diversity in feminist theory; for all its intricacies and dilemmas, no woman will have had a life like hers, yet in the structure we will all find commonalities. Perhaps this combination of an academic reading with the "real" life, of the juxtaposition of theory with praxis, presents a major accomplishment of this novel.

Structure

Not chapters but 305 channels propel this subjective documentary, and creative biography. The channels, which randomly seem to be triggered by an invisible satellite expose different story lines—similar what one may experience when engaged in aimless channel flicking, looking for something interesting on TV. However, here we are not dealing with different TV channels, but rather with only <u>one</u> station that happens to have more than one program--<u>one</u> person with more than one "movie." We are channel flicking through a person's life. The style will echo the complexity of stream of consciousness prose. But this very appropriate technique in actuality grew out of and, really, symbolizes the character's personal, once "illiterate," combustible, uneducated, restless and attention deficient self.

Some channels are very short—some are longer. The narrative also bounces between poems and letters. This fluidity of form between grammar and syntax goes hand-in-hand with the capricious shift of content because it also simultaneously reflects the volatile grammar of the character's intellectual and emotional development. Not every story angle is painted and pursued in detail. Some of it is left to the reader's imagination to fill-in the holograms.

There are three sections, each with its own subsections. The sections are divided from one another both chronologically as well as, and perhaps more importantly, stylistically.

Section 1

In the first section, Pelegrine's life before meeting Pontiac, the structure is truly holographic. The narrative slips form one time period to another without leaving the reader confused. The style is minimalist yet vivid, giving just enough description without being overwhelming to evoke the scene clearly in the reader's mind.

Section 2

The second and longest section, which spans from Pelegrine's meeting with Pontiac, falling in with Werra, then Rosemarie and then Yarrow is somewhat different in style and structure. The holographic structures subside in favor of a more traditional chronological account. Here the style changes from mainly third person narrative to numerous first person letters and journal entries. The reading at this point may not be quite as easy but does maintain the quality and technique of the prose from section 1.

The correspondence between Pontiac and Pelegrine reflect both tenderness and foreshadowing. The tone, however, in this section is becoming decidedly negative. Not many happy times, encounters and feelings are described—especially with Werra, Rosemarie and Yarrow. In fact, so few are described that it should make the reader wonder why Pelegrine attempted to hang on to these relationships for such a long time. Some readers may actually find themselves wanting Pelegrine to get it over with and move on—except with Pontiac. In fact, it may never be completely clear even to Pelegrine why exactly she left her. In hindsight, there are speculations. But these are just conjectures of older and wiser eyes. The story only wants to unfold a breathtaking chronicle of an intense journey rather than explain it.

The frequent disclosures of discord may perhaps signify that there truly were very few good times and the report is accurate as stated. Some readers may be left feeling no sympathy whatsoever for Werra, Rosemarie or Yarrow and, at times, may become impatient even with Pelegrine. Not much conclusive information is available to indicate what it was that compelled Pelegrine to hold on and stay. We must also not forget, who is telling the story and, thus, it may become clear why she did what she did. Who knows?

Section 3

The third and shortest section evolves gradually from the second. Pelegrine moves from suicidal despair through self-discovery to healthier insights and hopeful directions. The style here is still mostly chronological with a few exceptions—as when her memories peek through on their receding trajectory as seen, for instance, in Pelegrine's inventory of her total penis encounters. There are also many descriptive, rather lyrical passages in this section. They range from a very graphic shitting scene at her snowed-in cabin in the New York Adirondacks to a turbulent camping trip to the Outer Banks of North Carolina. By gradually removing herself from the magnifying glass, her numerous expressive observations point to her next venture—scrutinizing other people's noteworthy lives. Her focus has expanded from the self to the other.

> *The origin of philosophy does not lie in astonishment, as Plato and Aristotle taught, but in despair....*
>
> *Things I write here are what I shall no longer talk about; they are the shavings thrown off by the plane as it shapes the day's work.*
>
> **Cesare Pavese**

Pelegrine:
A Holographic Journey

Channel 1

When Pelegrine arrived in America, she was overwhelmed because she could not enter the harbor of New York because there was such a thing called a hurricane and she didn't even know the meaning of the word and needed a dictionary she didn't own. So the ship circled for twelve hours before the girl set foot on solid land after rocking eleven days on an autumn sea. After all, her nineteen-year-old life began with the adventurous guts of a girl with three suitcases, a bicycle and a first pair of skis from her mother on her fourteenth birthday. The big red secret. Up till then she was tying cut-up inner tubes around boards to her soggy boots. Skiing that way was just a little fun. Her stomach smashed on the toboggan, three people straddling her back and only Pelegrine's feet scratching and carving ice, to steer the sled into a barbed fence, tearing to pieces her fur coat and the rabbit once more, ripping a big hole into her inner thigh, was a little more exciting. And all the children screamed after her while Pelegrine ran home as fast as she could, rags and all. And her mother, she was very pissed and yelled even more than her fellow injured. The five-year-old girl escaped down the cellar steps and the furious Mom picked-up a stale loaf of bread and hurled it angrily after the girl. Good thing, she missed. A deep, fleshy wound glared at her. Little white hamburger dots stared into her face. The torn-off sleeves and missing pockets made her feel more miserable than when she actually hit the piercing wire minutes ago. There was no such thing as stitches, a doctor or attention. Till today a caterpillar-sized wad decorates her memory of an injury never tended to.

Channel 2

When Pelegrine was fourteen, her poor and struggling mother traded cabbages and eggs back and forth until she had what she wanted. This time a pair of skis. And Pelegrine should not find them. A difficult situation, especially since the girl was thin, limber and wiggly like a spiral. To keep her out of trouble and away from big, conspicuous presents was not easy. It almost worked. Christmas Eve crept slowly into the afternoon. Fidgety Pelegrine dropped a needle and down she crawled, under the chair and under the bed. She saw nothing. No needle but something new bumped into her head. Real skis. She soon forgot why she was where she was, squeezed under the bed. Because suddenly she saw only the end of her strapped feet onto boards that never really moved right. Five years later, these red twins would cross an unknown ocean with her. She wasn't sure why she went so far. She left not much behind, only an invitation to perpetual gloom.

Channel 3

Kurt, her landlady's son wanted to marry her and if she had, Pelegrine would have two children and would have learned child bearing, keep her mouth shut and maybe acquiesce to the world around her much better. She will never really know what kept her from going into the housewife-mother trap. Instinct? Restlessness? Desire for adventure? For sure, life there was relentless and hard. No heat in the room she rented from his Mom. A stove, yes. But after the giant coal bags were dragged-up the one-hundred-seventeen steps, she didn't feel like lighting them. Especially since with each coal burning away, the sack shrank only to be lifted upstairs again and again. The stuff just burned too quickly and barely gave-off any heat and after coming home from work at ten at night, there was no way she would squat down and light the fire and go to bed freezing, anyway. She ended-up buying a heating lamp and hid it in her closet. She briefly plugged it in when she dressed and undressed. There was a crisp glimmer of warmth. Pelegrine had to hide the lamp because the stingy landlady Mom didn't want to spend money for her tenant's unnecessary electricity.

Channel 4

And the job, too, was a drag. Pelegrine was working as a medical assistant, receptionist and verbal punching bag for an ancient gynecologist, a hero in her town, since she was famous for super human efforts at any hour of life, delivering lots and lots of healthy babies in the middle of the night. She never failed to scream at the young girl patients who came to her too late while bleeding from burst vaginal pipes. These girls were hard to save. Pelegrine didn't really understand what was going on. In spite of her dislike for the gruff old bitch, Pelegrine actually admired the old doctor woman. For some weird reason, the girl craved her attention and wished that the old lady would like her. Since Pelegrine dared to talk back to the goddess, the screaming matches between them were their only conversations. For Pelegrine, attention starved, as she was, this negative connection was better than none. Pelegrine once admitted when she was a lot older, that she probably loved the old woman, but had no way of interacting appropriately with her and her own feelings.

Channel 5

Such an adverse connector stirred in her life already when Pelegrine was in the sixth grade and experienced her first devastating crush on her biology teacher. An uncontrollable passion consumed Pelegrine who memorized chapters from the textbook so that she could recite them for her teacher. She even offered to spend her whole summer in the city to be a companion to Mrs. Sonnenschein.

"I won't go home. I want to stay with you, help you, carry your things and just be there," announced Pelegrine desperately as the school year was drawing to a close.

The teacher graciously acknowledged the offer, said it was sweet and actually acted as if she was a little flattered by the silly schoolgirl. But Pelegrine's dream could not be fulfilled. She wasn't in total control of her life. She was only eleven. She somewhat had to obey the few adults that managed to dodge in-and-out of her life. She was essentially a street urchin with a loving Mom who would miss her, but actually too late, if something really had happened. It was forever up to the little girl to stay out of trouble, to protect herself. If she waited to be rescued, there was no one to rescue her because no one kept tabs where she was or what she was doing. Pelegrine really didn't know what those feelings were called that she felt for this teacher. She knew for sure that she liked her sooo much and would have done anything for her. This feeling she later classified as her first crush and genuine emotional engagement. Such an "engagement" she should come to know more than once in her life.

Channel 6

At fourteen when she became an apprentice in a drug store, Pelegrine promptly adored her young beautiful supervisor, Moni. Every night Pelegrine wrote letters to Moni into her diary. Moni was older and wiser and very gentle to Pelegrine who often followed Moni home because she invited her in for tea and company with the parents. Pelegrine longed for those warm moments of attention. At the shop where Pelegrine and Moni worked was a lecherous boss. He always put expensive candy into Pelegrine's white work coat, hanging over night on a hook in the dark hallway. In the morning she reached into chocolates with precious fillings. And later in the day, he stupidly asked her suggestive questions, which she didn't want to answer. He wanted to know if she wanted a better career one day and be sent to a special training school by the company. He was curious to see how she reacted. She did like the sweets but rejected the future with which Mr. Derwisch tempted her. She smiled and thanked him for the gifts and asked him to stop. One Monday afternoon, Moni hurriedly grabbed Pelegrine's wrist, dragged her down to the cellars where they stored denatured alcohol, acetic and hydrochloric acids, waiting to be siphoned with a kinked hose into customer containers. She whispered to go and look at Derwisch's face and come back. Pelegrine returned in split seconds and eagerly wanted to know why he had this gouge. Moni held up her long red nails and growled,

"With these I scratched the bastard's face. Let his wife ask him where he got the scars. The asshole pushed me against the wall in the darkroom, kissed me, fondled my breasts and dug his fucking fingers under my skirt. I let him know how much I wanted his fat dick."

Moni sighed deeply and exhaustedly flopped down on a stack of Kodak paper. Pelegrine hated Derwisch now even more. Not only was he courting her in such an offensive way, but also molested her beloved friend.

Channel 7

Unfortunately, Moni transferred and moved to another town. Pelegrine couldn't follow her right away, not until her training was over and at eighteen, she intended to join Moni and share an apartment and live with her. But nothing ever happened the way she planned it. One month before her apprenticeship contract expired, the boss grabbed Pelegrine and pressed his horny body into hers, also in the darkroom where pictures were drying under infrared lamps. Pelegrine marveled at the big key bunch poking her thighs. And she fought hard to escape his swollen, slobbering lips. She slipped and banged her head against a sharp edge. In the dim light she screamed and lounged to the door, ruining the photographs of all the customers. She ran without ever stopping, down the corridor, out the store into the streets. Her white coat tails were the wings of a falcon careening to the police station, filing her case and pressing charges against a fifty-year-old bull posing as a boss. The officer dutifully recorded her story, took a picture of the scarred head and dismissed the juvenile.

It was a year later before Pelegrine had a notice to appear in court. She went with mother and sister and her story, still burning fiercely in her heart. Mr. Derwisch appeared with a distinguished looking lawyer who was constantly approaching the bench whispering to the judge. Pelegrine was telling her story without the visual aid of a freshly injured head but a memory, crisp with immediate pain. She recollected and reiterated the story she told the police officer. But nobody seemed to listen or care. The court clerk took notes. The judge nodded and gaveled the dismissal of the case because of lack of evidence. With his entourage in tow, Mr. Derwisch swished out leaving a tail of foul odor behind, while Pelegrine and company stayed unvindicated and defeated in their peasant seats.

"As always, injustice, money and political expediency rule. The people and their children don't matter. Only the kings have traded places with butchers, child molesters and bureaucrats. I might as well have lived in the last century," Pelegrine grumbled.

Channel 8

After she completed her training and because she had exposed the genital interests of her boss, she did not receive a proper letter of recommendation, only a piece of paper, verifying her dates of employment, nothing else. Her qualities and her trade school achievements were undiscussed, thus hampering her growth in the profession of a licensed druggist with her own white coat and her own druggist pin showing a scale with mortar and pestle. It would be difficult to find employment after an apprentice has nothing but dates in her portfolio. Only because she opened her mouth and complained of unwanted sexual advances made by an authority in charge of minors in the Europe of the early 1960's, Pelegrine's first employment record reads as if she had worked for three years without merit. She was denied an essential document, necessary to succeed on a journey to become a master druggist. She trekked to England to learn English instead and upon her return to her country, worked in the mountains and later in Vienna as a receptionist, instrument washer, and dictation taker for a renowned woman gynecologist. Only one small incident should become significant later.

Channel 9

When Pelegrine was almost 19 and her friend Franzi was 17 and their mutual friend, Amalia, a lot older, around 50, at least, the three became a nest. They would go out together Saturday nights into the wineries outside Vienna. They pretended they were a family, mother and daughters. It was a funny disguise and the men they met believed it. All three liked the lie and never stopped laughing when they were telling it and others seriously accepted the fraud. Franzi's real mother was happy that she hung around with Pelegrine because she worried about her daughter. Apparently, she did not really trust her and wanted Franzi protected in the company of girlfriends instead of boys. Franzi was alluring and a coquettish charmer, not only with boys. She rolled her pretty gray eyes just as fast at Pelegrine as she would at the guys from the next table. After one of those outings, the fake family threesome staggered to the last street cars and, finally, through the early morning lights of the sleeping city. After they parted from Amalia, Franzi wanted Pelegrine to stay with her that night. They agreed and quietly crept in the door and tried not to awaken her parents. Then they barely undressed and both slept on Franzi's single bed. Nothing unusual. Except, this particular evening they had been very affectionate all night long and especially silly and embraced each other casually an awful lot. Actually, nothing really unusual either. European girls touch easily, hold hands when walking and are, generally, physically closer. But today the closeness did not stop. And when the girls were lying in bed, a little drunk and giggling, Franzi suddenly kissed Pelegrine on the mouth and slipped her hands under

Pelegrine's under panties sticking her finger inside her. Pelegrine did not move. She pretended she did not notice anything. But notice she did. Every second, especially that Franzi had super long fingernails which actually were hurting her. It was also clear that she did like the advance. But she would not admit that out loud, ever. She only lay motionless, frozen and stunned. In the morning the girls avoided eyes and never touched upon that subject. Only Pelegrine wanted to be with Franzi constantly now, hoping that another such moment would come. It seemed to her that Franzi played with her, because she would make a few hours available every now and then, but departed abruptly and always too soon. Then suddenly, out of the blue, she declared one day that she was marrying a fellow she had just met. Pelegrine was profoundly hurt. She tried to visit the ever-harder-to-come-by Franzi until she just decided to go away very far and forever.

Channel 10

The deep admiration Pelegrine felt for the lady doctor fit into her history of lost and unfulfilled loves. At the doctor's office, she learned a lot of Latin terms for the dictations she had to take describing the diagnosis of the patients. God help her if she misspelled a word. The old lady was furious and impatient to no end, would scream at petrified Pelegrine and patients alike and everybody wondered what they were doing back again after having been whipped with words. Cäcilia, the illiterate but kind housekeeper sneaked a little soup or a piece of cake to hungry Pelegrine, hunched-over her handwriting, trying to spell "curettage," hoping the buzzer would stop calling for her, hoping she would have to go to the labs and deliver blood and urine samples. On these trips she enjoyed the daylight, the sun and the tiny warmth, before she returned back to that cruel office, that cold room at night and to that life, period. When the witch would let her go home after twelve working hours, her bicycle tires had difficulties in the dark, ten-o'clock-night not to get swallowed by the streetcar tracks between the fat and aging cobblestones. But she wobbled home and endured the frozen winter nights. She dreamed of another world and another life. Somewhere. The year before she sojourned to England as an au pair. There she met Tommy, her British fiancé, waiting to embrace her in New York, if the hurricane ever died.

Channel 11

As her seventeenth year fizzled out, Pelegrine planned to move to Linz where Moni was waiting. Pelegrine was to start her first real job after completing her apprenticeship. Two weeks before leaving for Linz, she bicycled to a small cafe in Gmunden on the Traunsee to have a good-bye glass of wine with her old school friend Erika who was on her way to London to perfect her English. Pelegrine did not want to lose Erika whom she had known throughout her school years. The two girls became more and more depressed and crushed themselves into a tormented hysteria, long before the actual departure. These tears had Pelegrine pedaling home furiously who had made up her mind instantly that next day she would contact Erika's employment agent to find a family in London for Pelegrine also. Suddenly, Pelegrine, too, wanted to learn English. Her little school English was not enough because she only learned it by rote and not by choice. The entire class spitefully refused to curl their tongues in order to slide out perfectly shaped, round and soft English *r's* like liqueur-filled chocolates. There was only one single girl in class that did it right. And she sounded weird and stupid as the only person in the huge class room producing authentic *r's* and *th's* and not guttural hisses coming from angry rattlesnakes. All girls spoke English with a heavy German accent. And on purpose. Because it was the only cool thing to do. *Ze vindo is offer zere.* Not rounding their tongue and lips to produce sounds like that prissy girl who pronounced her words even better than the English teacher. This model pronouncer was treated like an impostor and outcast. No wonder that silly Pelegrine did not acquire useful English skills. But now decided she needed some, only to follow her girlfriend, Erika.

Pelegrine overwhelmed her compliant mother with her instant decision that she was leaving for England in two weeks. At this time she didn't even have a contact, a contract or a ticket to go. The powerless mother reluctantly consented,

"What? Why? If you think so. I don't know. But all right."

And the long wait before the fast goodbye began. The agency answered rapidly, found her a family but failed to send Pelegrine's travel ticket. Pelegrine used her savings and off she went. Arriving late at Victoria Station, a tall, skinny bird-eyed man bent down to her, stammering,

"Are you Miss P-P-e-l-e-g-r-i-n-e?"

"How in the hell, did he figure me in the hordes of thousands?" Pelegrine wondered. But then she looked pretty stupid and lost and it was probably written all over her that she needed to be found. She nodded and followed him silently. She stepped inside his car and sank back wondering about the signs saying, "Keep left." She intensely translated each word. She knew that `keep' meant *to hold* something in your arms like a baby or a log. Clutching it.

"What are they clutching in the left arm? Beats me."

And the house black and big and the woman, his wife, nice and pretty with gray eyes and black hair, looking like a female Montgomery Cliff. Pelegrine liked the way she looked. Even though she turned out to be bitchy and selfish. She greeted the strange girl and placed two raw eggs into her hands. Pelegrine did not understand a word she was saying. After Mrs. Canterbury disappeared, Pelegrine kept standing in the chilly kitchen air with her coat still on and two British eggs in her cold hands. She guessed that it was meant for her to either boil or fry these eggs to put something into her stomach. She scrounged around and found the frying pan and approached the stove. The words "on" and "off" were a new problem. She tried the knobs and instantly had a live vocabulary lesson. As a matter of fact, she had live lessons from then on, especially with their six-year-old, wild and unmanageable daughter, Alexandra, called Assia. The little tyrant enjoyed Pelegrine's speech handicap and ran away from her only to be chased to get dressed with a tie around her neck, which her mother had shown Pelegrine how to manipulate while lying in bed. She was too lazy to rise before noon. So she asked for a diaper, one of those big old cottony things. And she said,

"Look, Pelegrine. Over, under, over, through. Here, voila. Now go and let me sleep."

Trying to straddle that girl monster to practice 'over, under, over, through' was making Pelegrine sweat. But learn. And fast she learned to speak. So fast that after a week she knew how to scream, "Shut up." And even tell the mother that she had never made toast in her life. That is why she brought it cold. The toaster was the first thing Pelegrine had turned on when she got up. Her efficient mind invented a hierarchy of chores. And when the lady of the house rang the bell three hours later, Pelegrine did not realize that she now had cold toast, cold bacon and lukewarm eggs joining the chilled orange juice on the tray. She entered the master bedroom, wobbling the tray to a table, opened the curtains, and flopped the tray on her stomach. Then Pelegrine ran her bath and while she bathed, Pelegrine made her bed and if the sheets were sticky with white goop, then they had to be changed. Pelegrine figured Mr. Canterbury must have had a wet night with his wife. She had never seen what this stuff looked or felt like. It was like dried milk with a starchy texture. She had only heard it described from Erika's descriptions of her escapades with Karli squirting his ejaculations on her stomach. And giggly Erika reported all that to curious Pelegrine. Altogether, Pelegrine didn't feel very happy there. She was a glorified maid and began rebelling slowly and subtly. She refused to wear white aprons or serve from the left during dinner parties. She would always forget, on purpose. And when she protested and declared that she wanted to leave, the Mrs. raised her pay by a pound and gave her two afternoons off instead of one. Trusting Pelegrine agreed but later left anyway, only to encounter another marvel--Lady Astor, notorious for not paying her girls. She ran through them like napkins.

Channel 13

The job seemed intriguing. No kids, no cleaning and time to go to school. Only answering the telephone, the door and bringing orange juice to the Lady's bedside at ten in the evening just after the lady maid had undressed her, combed her hair and braided it into a long tail for the night.

The cook was the only kind human contact Pelegrine enjoyed. She had two bun-like braids twisted in cups over each ear. The old woman lived in the basement and saved her money under a mattress. Pelegrine sometimes ran errands for her or fetched a taxi to go to the hairdresser with the Lady and waited. Pelegrine always enjoyed trips outside the Hyde Park luxury prison. Even though Pelegrine's life was not full of labor anymore, she was incarcerated with not enough time to spend outside the lavish ten room flat. After her English language classes, she had to return home immediately, and on her one day off, she had to be in by midnight, and not a minute later, such as once when it was five minutes past. The Lady waited up for her, shouting her hollow, "Pelegrine" through the walls. The girl stiffened and entered and listened to the reprimand, but decided to talk back and accuse her of being inhuman and old and mean and not deserving of those many young people that had been there before and suffered. The old lady almost choked. No one had ever, ever spoken to her this way. "Out, to bed," she belted. And Pelegrine staggered to sleep.

From then on, life became unbearably oppressive with one exception on the day when the cook asked her to go to the butcher and buy a big piece of meat she called a rump roast. Happily, Pelegrine agreed to run out into the sunshine. But when she wanted to pay the butcher she must have been running and jumping too hard because she had lost the money. Grief struck, she ran back home and under tears told the cook there was no meat, no money and no pay until next Friday, which would not cover the price of the lost meat anyway.

And the dear old saint went to her basement and from under the mattress pulled out a bill and said,

"Go, run, love. Get the meat."

That day Pelegrine went to church after the butcher's. She had to thank God, because this was the first kind thing that happened to her in this bloody, cold, unlovely and foggy country. Nobody had been encouraging to her for a long, long time. She did not know that being an *au pair* was a disguise for cheap labor. She had believed that it meant house daughter, to learn the language and be part of a family. In her case, there was no such definition. There was only exploitation and hopelessness--something human beings don't like. Though the cook gave her a break this time, life at the Lady's did not get better. Pelegrine met other Austrian girls at the English school. Some were living in palaces like the Buckingham and St. James'. Each was one in a string of servants. They had strict working hours and many free ones so they could go out and have fun. Anya worked for the Duke and Duchess of Gloucester. And since Pelegrine was so unhappy at the Lady's, she decided to run away. She was afraid to quit her job officially. Astor was never reasonable about anything. By that time, Pelegrine had wired her sister in Switzerland to send travel money to return home. With the dinky salary she made, Pelegrine could never save-up enough for the entire return ticket.

Channel 14

One afternoon she had the courage to pack all her belongings into thirteen cardboard boxes, ordered a taxi, stacked the cartons on the staircase like organ pipes while the Lady was taking her afternoon nap. The taxi was waiting and she still does not know how she got all those boxes, after the string broke on several, down those steps into the cab and away, without being caught by anybody. At St. James' Palace, Anya was waiting and the boxes were stacked behind a corner and when the guard was looking the opposite way, one-by-one, the girls smuggled the cartons into the castle, up the winding staircase and into Anya's tower room where Pelegrine was to spend the next four weeks, finally seeing and enjoying London while waiting for the sister's Swiss money. Without it she was going nowhere.

Life at the palace was splendid. A fugitive, fed on stolen food, sitting in Prince Richard's marble bathtub with golden faucets and dancing in his bedroom and caressing his silken shirts, smelling his powders and perfumes, was a delight for the runaway. Every time she walked down a hallway, she had to slide behind curtains and make sure no one would see her. She was really an illegal intruder and did not want to get caught and be thrown out. It was too much fun. Like a movie.

Pelegrine frequently visited the post office, asking whether a money order had arrived for her. One day the postman said yes but had delivered it to the address of the Lady. Horrors. Pelegrine sent her girl friend, Anya, with a grandiose story that she had to leave for the continent because her father had died and to, please, hand over the money. But the old woman refused. She would turn the money over only to Pelegrine in person or send it back to the sender. Pelegrine had no choice but to bite her pride and slink to that door and ring the bell and sit in that study and listen to fancy reproaches and outbursts. She could only mumble that it had become intolerable to be there and that Lady Astor was unreachable and unbearable, and that Pelegrine had wanted to have a little fun before her year in London was over, aside from sweat and labor and grief. After a two-hour battle, the Lady reluctantly smashed Pelegrine's money on the mahogany piano and ended the ordeal. Erika, the real reason Pelegrine had come to London, could not stand the work she had to do, either. At Cook's Hospital she had to wash dead bodies and fill the cavities with cotton, all holes, even the asshole. Her *au pair* farce was over a lot sooner than Pelegrine's. Erika went back home after six months.

Channel 15

When the sister's money landed in Pelegrine's hands, off she went to Paris and hitchhiked through southern France back home to Vienna. The cardboard cartons were railroaded back. Her travel friend, Garbo, got a black eye in a Paris nightclub while Pelegrine camped out in a cemetery hiding her backpack under a holly bush. She wanted to save her precious cash and stretch it as far as possible. Frequently they ate out of cans and sometimes in fancy restaurants when lush dates invited Pelegrine and Garbo. On such evenings, they stuffed themselves beyond sanity only to meet in the bathroom sticking fingers down their throats to empty out the lobster and three desserts. They gorged themselves because none knew when the next meal would make the scene. But their stomachs did not tolerate such rich and expensive ingredients. With bloodshot eyes and a disturbed tummy Pelegrine could no longer go out dancing and had to go home to the graveyard hotel. Garbo preferred to spend most of her nights in temporary comfort and usually appeared the day after, hung-over and bruised.

Channel 16

Drinking was always a touchy spot. When Pelegrine was 12, her mother had married her fourth incompetent husband and father, an accomplished bench drinker. He had one leg that was five inches shorter. In his elevated shoe, he would sneak out on Sunday mornings to buy cigars and on the way home, have just ONE bottle of beer at the local tavern. On those days, the midday meal was waiting and the mother and the girls took turns stretching their necks out the window hoping one of them would spot the familiar figure, wobbling and limping home, at last, allowing three people to breathe easier. But there was seldom such luck.

Angrily, Pelegrine and her younger sister Zange tried to distract themselves for the afternoon. A movie, a bike ride, a walk or the radio would kill the endless hours till night, when the real prowl started. The mother looked into the various pubs where he could be glued to a bench. When finally spotting the glowing red melon head, she pleaded and begged him on her knees to go home. By then he usually was in such a good mood and ordered a glass of wine for Mom who didn't want it. The two children cowered beside her, anxiously waiting, going to the bathroom, checking the alleys, walking the streets, coming back, sitting again, waiting and waiting and drowning in smoke and stench, until the establishment threw the drunkard out. But always so late. And the next day was school.

The three women dragged the bloated husband and stepfather, prematurely retired at age 45. A slip on the ice on his way to work. In America people sue when something like this happens. They become young, "disabled" pensioners in socialist countries. Mother and children hoped he would not fall again like once when the police had to drag him home. The officers found this creature calling himself a family man grunting and farting in the gutter, unable to get on his feet. At home he often got his second wind and became belligerent wanting to get rough with the girls who soon hid in their bedroom with the key turned. But on very quarrelsome nights he would threaten to hurt the mother and that is when Pelegrine quickly snapped the key back, stuck her head out the door and screamed at the top of her lungs,

"Don't you dare lay a finger on Mom. I will kill you with the kitchen knife if you do."

On such nights he staggered to the door which snapped closed in his face. With his fat and feisty fists he banged on the rippled glass pane of their bedroom door. Once he pounded too hard and crashed the glass, cutting his hands, which sent the girls jumping out the window six feet to the ground. They ran for their lives because in his rage they believed his words,

"Wait till I get my hands on you bastards. I'll smash your heads against the wall till your brains are running down."

Helplessly, the mother tried to calm the brutish beast, while the girls cowered under a heavy sky till they found the chopping block to roll under the window. Standing on it, Pelegrine cupped her hands for the little sister to climb on her shoulders up the wall to catch the windowsill. For herself Pelegrine planted a board at an upward angle. She straddled it and slid up into the window when her sister had signaled the O.K. because the pig was snoring in his bed. Their Mom cried in the kitchen and promised the children that she would do something to end this suffering. And the children believed her. Only the hatred toward this man grew over the years. And so did the urge to get away. Especially since Mom never did throw him out. Strangely enough, later as a student of literature, Pelegrine consistently felt private pangs when encountering similar portrayals in the chapbooks that described the bloody and violent end of the legendary Dr. Faustus.

Channel 17

With the monthly ten-dollar alimony her namesake father paid plus the ten she earned at the drugstore, Pelegrine wanted to live on her own at fifteen. Next year she would earn twenty and the third year would bring thirty dollars a month for eight hours work, consisting of sweeping the floors after 6 when the store doors closed, putting oil down on Saturdays, pulling out the canvass awning in the afternoon to protect the window displays from bleaching. On sunny Sundays she also had to be available to do that, but not for extra pay. Her jobs where endlessly divided between siphoning all kinds of acids such as nitric, formic or acetic into hand-held carriers which people brought from home. She filled tetrachloride, a liquid spot remover, into small bottles, affixing pink labels that had a skull and two crossed bones painted in bold letters, warning customers that this liquid will kill if consumed by mouth. These caution labels were extremely necessary because many people brought their empty food bottles when purchasing generic poisons as opposed to their more expensive, prepackaged name brand counterparts.

On some days she would stuff naphthalene crystals into pocket-sized paper packages sold as moth repellents. The paper bags needed to be glued first into squares. Then she stamped a drugstore insignia on it. After they were filled, they were pasted shut with glue on a brush and stacked into airtight tin containers. For this operation Pelegrine usually rigged an assembly-line set-up in the back yard of the store. She liked that kind of activity out in the sun. Because she was away from all the others, away from having to wait on customers and be told to fetch acids, be screamed at when she was too slow, and, and, and. But even when she was packaging mothballs, they would interrupt, and the older apprentices would lord over her, forcing errands, just as they were forced on them. The pecking order continued.

When she was bagging bird food from fifty-pound gunnysacks in the attic upstairs, way under the sky, she loved the company of the pigeons. She did not hear the demons calling for her downstairs. She pretended she didn't hear. And if they were really serious, they had to climb the million steps themselves to deliver their requests. That's how Pelegrine got even. She had her private revenge on the law of the land that profited from child labor while exploiting their youths. But she really did literally articulate these thoughts in her head then. She only acted upon instincts of justice. Even to report sexual harassment to the authorities which still behaved like kings, long before feminist notions or American groundbreaking TV dramas invaded public conscience.

Channel 18

If her Mom would let her live on her own at fifteen, for food Pelegrine intended to eat rolls with milk. And on Wednesdays, the farmers market would yield plenty of throw-away edibles and then, if Mom would give her a bite here and there, she didn't see why she couldn't make it on her own. With the tyrant fatso stepfather threatening her life and that of her mother's, Pelegrine's surroundings had become unbearable. She remembered that she once offered after her mother's third divorce, if the woman could only wait till Pelegrine was grown, she would take care of her. But she had to wait. Because at ten it was too hard for Pelegrine. Mom didn't really take the girl seriously and laughed it off and married the beer pig instead. And even this running-away scheme, mother discouraged because Pelegrine was just too young. And Pelegrine could hardly wait till she was old enough to escape. At eighteen she left for England. And the experiences there forced her once more to return to the dreaded household.

Channel 19

In London, at the Lyceum dance hall Pelegrine met her first semi-serious boyfriend, Tommy. His ears protruded to the side and he was prematurely balding and ten years older than Pelegrine but a nice man. Not demanding. Gentle, like a puppy. He had a motor scooter and would bring Pelegrine home some nights. He was bland, kind of boring, really. He had a job as an engineer, repairing delicate laboratory equipment. A loyal boy who would follow Pelegrine's tracks for the next four years. Even as far as the Austrian mountains where Pelegrine returned from England to manage a drugstore in an old, crooked building where only the ground floor for the store and one single room upstairs were in use. The rest lay dormant and cold without heat and electrical connections. In her room she only had a rigged outlet for a lamp, a toilet outside the building and no facilities to bathe or wash. Pelegrine invented bathing facilities in the dark storage corners of the store. She bought a two-burner stove, a restaurant pot and used this rig to perform personal hygiene. On the double burner she would heat pot after pot and thus managed an occasional bath in an oversized bucket, with many sponge baths in between. The area had winter forever with insulating snow burying the building to the rooftop, covering many of the postcard windows. As long as she could keep the furnace filled with coals and stay warm either in the store or under her covers in her one room, she knew she would survive. She dashed over the icicle staircase to land in her bed. One day, Tommy decided to visit this most uncomfortable hellhole.

Pelegrine thawed-out and revived an extra vacant room under the windy rafters. She dragged an abandoned stove, wood and coals, and heated non-stop. She found a rejected mattress, dyed sheets orange for curtains and gave-up her plug-in one pot water heater for his English teas. And so he stayed two weeks and bought an imitation pearl ring for Pelegrine to consider herself engaged, even though she had never more than kissed Tommy. That he demanded. For the rest he was politely waiting. Pelegrine was mildly flattered by his attention but tolerated him rather than cared for the guy. But she did not know that. She thought he was her fiancé. They enjoyed skiing the alpine slopes and playing house in a very un-house like setting. And then he left on a transfer to America.

    He wrote diligently and Pelegrine's English was kept-alive with these letters, which she collected dutifully and bound with a blue ribbon. And it would develop that Pelegrine's uncle and aunt in California, whom she had wanted to see since she was eleven years old, declined Pelegrine's requests to visit them. They always used excuses and said they were too old for a young lively girl who needed to be among her kind. Pelegrine never understood that and realized they just didn't want to see her, even though they were her most worshipped humans other than her ineffective mother. And when Tommy sailed away and Pelegrine's frozen life never thawed and her illegal quarzlamp failed to heat her, she had enough money to board a banana freighter heading for America. Why not? The gynecologist in the big city had become insufferable together with the twelve-hour work shift, and the tight Viennese landlady urging Pelegrine and her son Kurt to tie a knot, and Pelegrine not knowing what she wanted, knowing only that living in a system where the courts did not trust the word of their children, but did promote monotonous 8-5 drudgeries, baby boom and marriage prisons in dumpling pots, was not for her. She was going on twenty and had the right to a life of her own.

Channel 20

And in reality, nothing was holding her, no career, no job, no people, no future, nothing. Not even her beloved mother. The best she could hope for there was an eventual marriage with children. A traditional yet uncomfortable direction. She wasn't born right. No real education, no real parents, no real upbringing, just an urchin on the street, lucky not to go under. Only eight grades and the apprenticeship years with 48 classroom hours in a month, 12 hours a week, all in one day, starting at eight and stopping at eight, not counting the one-and-a-half hour train ride each way. If she got to bed before midnight ere the eight-hour workday commenced, she was lucky. By the age of eighteen she was an experienced, industrialized "slave," with book learning in math, accounting, business correspondence, photography, science of color and pigmentation, chemistry, Latin nomenclature, toxicology, botany and fundamentals of cosmetics. For her final project she had three years to collect and dry medicinal herbs and label them with detailed classification according to phyla, family, and healing qualities. She sounded like a witch doctor. They required three hundred roots, leaves and blossoms. She spent most of her only free day, Sunday, digging-up plants.

Channel 21

No real parents. Only four different fathers with the real one unknown, eighteen years old and dead on Russian soil. Ironically, Pelegrine was also eighteen, when her American uncle, Albert, carelessly tossed these words over the dinner table,

"Oh, Pelegrine, you didn't know that Honigacker was not your father?"

Silence and shock. Pelegrine valiantly squirmed,

"Oh, yeah, I knew."

The man her Mom was married to for fifteen years, and divorced when Pelegrine was two, the one Pelegrine and her sister Zange would visit on weekends for eighteen years, thinking they visited their "real" Dad, wasn't real, after all. She went to Tante Josefa and demanded facts. The lady dug out a folded-in-half, yellowed, brittle photograph, a picture showing more of Pelegrine than fingernails, with wrinkles curving beside the mouth, with eyes like hers and a forehead with her hair.

"You might as well know. Even though I had promised your mother I would never tell you. But it is too late now. Your mother is no good. When your father, the one whose name you have, was at the front, the women here were alone for long stretches of time. And, of course, your mother never could stay away from anything in pants very long. They placed this young soldier into her apartment. It was customary to lodge members of the armed forces in homes that had room. There was an ongoing war on several fronts. This one was here in the homes of the lonely women left behind. I don't know much at all, except that your mother was crazy about him, that he had promised to return for her after the war, because he knew that your mother was unhappily married to a man, much older than she, and a man who did not love her. He wrote diligently from the front. And one day, his postcards stopped. We assumed he was dead. Your mother gave me this picture to hide from her present husband. Because nobody was to know about this soldier man. And since you dangerously resemble him, everyone would give her hell. Your mother gave me that picture so none would ever see it. Otherwise nobody would have believed her fabrication of you being Josef's daughter."

"Now, I know," Pelegrine thought. "No wonder they always treated me different form Zange. They all suspected my illegitimacy."

"And, by the way, Zange isn't his either. She only looks very much like him. That's how everybody fell for it."

"Who was Zange's father?"

"Beautiful Freddie, an American soldier, yours was German."

Now that was a time bomb if there ever was one. She bravely took hold of the picture and held it to her heart. Now she knew whom she favored. All these years she had wondered about her likeness. She had asked her Dad, Josef, and with him had decided that they had the same fingernails. But the sister was really the one who looked like him. Pelegrine told Zange, then sixteen,

"Honigacker is neither your father nor mine."

The girls thus realized that there were a lot of confusing histories making the rounds. They decided to spare their mother, Elli, and not tell her what they knew. They kept up the lie, visiting Honigacker and kissing him like daughters.

Channel 22

Twenty years later, Pelegrine spoke for the first and last time to her mother about her real father, the eighteen-year old German soldier, Franz Wiborny. Her Mom with a failing memory, filled-in as best she could. Thirty-five-year-old Elli had truly loved this young boy. He was athletic and jumped over the fences with legs spread like scissors. He was a tender lover. Pelegrine accepted, however reluctantly, her mother's selective memories in this regard, and now protected her from pain by not telling her that she had actually known this already for a long time.

Pelegrine had a genuinely loving mother. Elli was pure love without an ounce of practicality, only haphazard survival skills. Begging, stealing and prostrating herself for her children, she knew only hardship, unkindness and meanness from her society. For her children she only offered unconditional love, kisses and hugs. Impractical goods. Not enough skills to survive in the emotional deserts, the cold world of practical realists who worked on the Wall Streets and would never die for love.

Channel 23

Pelegrine only knew jostles from school to school. Half-lives uprooted before the spring. Kindergarten in the fast fabricated, post-war barracks, with other hungry, skinny refugee children and orphans. Grades 1-3 in public elementary school for girls, where Pelegrine wore shoes every other day, when it was her turn and not Zange's. It was the time Pelegrine remembered always being sleepy in the morning, which bothered her mother, who didn't want her children to suffer. And one morning she stopped the clock to let her girls sleep longer. Little Pelegrine furiously chided her mother for doing something like that. This was no way to protect her, she said. It made matters worse. It was shameful to have to knock on the door and ask permission to enter when all the children were seated, quietly engrossed in their work. And Pelegrine had to lie and protect her grown mother. Nobody would have accepted the real excuse, she knew. So she invented her own blame and patiently stayed after school as punishment for coming late.

Grade 4 in the local boarding school with Catholic nuns who used switches for Pelegrine's little fingers when they were not hitting the right keys and messed-up Mozart. Where the loving mother stayed transfixed to the chain link fence yearning for her child that had been torn from her by the cruel aunt who wanted a decent environment for the flee-bitten, raggedy Pelegrine. The child was ashamed of the dishelved silly woman, her mother, who embarrassed her in front of the other children, whose mothers stayed home and cooked and cleaned and were normal, not like this one. Pelegrine looked away and tried to ignore her wailing Mom stretched across the fence. She was there every day. Sometimes, when nobody was looking, Pelegrine dashed out and beseeched her mother to go home and wait for proper visiting hours, every third Sunday afternoon. But it really broke Pelegrine's heart to see her defenseless mother desperately wanting the child home, where Pelegrine really wanted to be, too, especially if the horrid husbands were gone. And softly, Pelegrine assured Elli, not to take it so hard. That Pelegrine would sneak home for a visit. Just to wait. For **what** she did not know?

Every third Sunday Pelegrine walked home and visited her Mom whom she loved more than anything in the world, but wished were more competent and could raise Pelegrine better, not needing the aunt's intermittent but extremely controlling generosity by stuffing her in a boarding school. Those were difficult Sundays. They were a perpetual temptation for Pelegrine to skip the convent and the strict order of the mean nuns.

Channel 24

The rich aunt who came with *Goodwill* clothes, presented shoes too big that needed newspaper stuffing and then still did not fit, not ever, not even today. The sometime, well-meaning aunt descended abruptly and tore the neglected child off the streets and shoved her into a boarding school where Pelegrine's mother visited the chain link fence constantly, catching glimpses of her child, she felt had been torn from her,

"Like a cub from a lion. A lion's mother would not tolerate the removal of her babies. She would punch her paw into your face, Josefa," concluded Pelegrine's child-like mother. She whispered those words in the girl's ears, who also wanted to be home with her mother. That was all she ever wanted. If only without the ever-changing uncles, the no-father husbands, the cold strangers in her mother's bedroom. Yes, if the mother had only waited. She would have taken care of her, as Pelegrine had promised.

Home, however, meant freedom from stupid, Catholic rules. Free from the cool hands the nuns were slapping fast into Pelegrine's outspoken face. She could not talk-back or chat with her girlfriends at night when the sister was pacing the bedroom slowly, endlessly up and down until everybody was asleep. No, she couldn't even creep under the dozen beds to see her friend, Verena, who was now sleeping at the far end of the room, far away from chatty Pelegrine. Pelegrine once tried a visit and inched her way, elbow-by-elbow, bed-by-bed, waiting for the passing footsteps to leave so she could continue her journey to bed number 12. Somebody must have spilled glue, jelly or honey. Halfway down the row, Pelegrine got stuck on her stomach and pajamas. And the sister must have heard the unfamiliar noise. Her feet, too, got glued before the girl's eyes. And then her face, her fingers, her nose and pellet eyes grabbed Pelegrine's ears and wrenched her out, down the long path and out the door to spend the rest of the night standing on the icy stone floor in her bare feet. A tiny flickering candle illuminated the statue of Mary and the shivering child. No sounds. Only snores and tears covered the fearful night.

Channel 25

Grades 5-7 in another boarding school, away from the fence-clutching mother. The nuns had complained of the bad image and the needless agonies. The next stop, St. Mary's Boarding School for girls in Vienna with even meaner sisters and stricter rules. The biology teacher happened there. She was the only lay teacher. There, the balcony was pissed on.

Mary and Pelegrine, best friends and thick-as-thieves, had earned the honor to stay on the balcony during mass to pump air into the organ. They alternated jumping on a board and their frail girl weights pushed it down. With air in the pipes from a slow descent and an equally slow rise, the sister was delivering Sunday's hymns and chorales to the churchgoers. The girls took turns at the board. They had about fifteen seconds for fast chats before the board had risen and needed to be pushed down again. Everything was fine until they were in the middle of whispering a joke, when suddenly their hushed and repressed laughter burst out with such force that Pelegrine peed into her pants while squatting down, creating a big puddle on the shiny oak floor. Without air from the organ, the laughter pierced through the stunned congregation. Neither of the two offenders had the strength to get-up, step on the board and continue the job. The deadly Sunday silence, their girlish giggles and the urine pond ended forever their privileges as organ pipers. They were never to go near the organ balcony again, as long as they lived. All punishments and praises were so absolute, so-never-changing-an-inch. So rigid. For the remainder of the school year, they were also to hand-polish on their hands and knees each of the 198 pews, pray two rosaries a day, alternately kneel on split firewood and dried peas for 1/2 hour every day, before breakfast and after supper, while facing the Madonna. This was only January.

They could also, under no circumstances, fraternize or be seen together. They were not even allowed to line up behind each other at the dinner or Holy Communion cue. Nowhere ever. No Sunday after lunch, hand-in-hand exercise walks in the park. It was customary to cue up while the sister opened the coveted cupboard where she dodged in and out from each girl's labeled shoebox. And hand out small tokens of sweets, depending what their parents had given them on their last visit or sent them in their care packages. If one's box was empty, there was no need to line-up. And if someone was punished, they were forbidden to stand in line for their snacks, even if all their goodies spoiled, oranges and exotic fruits. Some girls had such fine candies and foods. Pelegrine's box was pretty sparse usually, more like an open-air market after the season. Only once in a while her aunt, on a good day, gave her a load of expensive Bensdorp or Suchard pralines together with imported Tangerines bought from Meinl, where only the affluent could shop.

    The two culprits could not stand in line behind each other even on Saturdays, awaiting their turn to drop-down the apron wings for the nun to scrub their backs. The pupils showered collectively, twenty girls to a row, all clad in chaste aprons. After the fast back scrub, they disappeared, one by one, behind a curtained stall to wash their privates. Pelegrine's and Verena's eyes were the only objects no one could stop from connecting. Until halfway into the seventh grade.

Channel 26

    At Christmas, Pelegrine was allowed to visit her mother in the mountain village, a four-hour train ride away. There the young girl wallowed in the absence of rules. And so much that one January, Mom and girl gave-in to their instincts. Pelegrine did not go back to the boarding school in Vienna. She completed grades 7 and 8 where she started, in the public school for girls. Pelegrine had learned different subjects in Vienna than in the hometown school. She was behind in short hand and home economics. She found a tutor helping her write. Since she hated cooking, Pelegrine was assigned wood splitting, stove cleaning and shopping chores, instead. From this day, the sometime-aunt withdrew her helping hand for good. She had enough of Pelegrine's instability and Elli's "slovenliness, whining and slobbering motherliness. Let them rot," Tante Josefa declared and kept her word for thirty years till she died.

Pelegrine finished the eighth grade knowing a little English, math, German (largely incomprehensible grammar diagrams, no literature at all), geography, biology, drawing, short hand, cooking, knitting and history. Elementary, very elementary was her background, opening-up very little life, only third-rate trips. Really decent and intelligent people had clean, modern homes, real parents, no shame but options. These people went to school until eighteen. They then studied at a university. Pelegrine wanted to be like them, but did not know how, because she only felt the need, deep in her guts, not out loud in her brain. It would take Pelegrine thirty years to do what she had always wanted way back then, not be pushed aside, be educated, be a human being.

Channel 27

Night seems to connect memories for Pelegrine's story. Is it because she spent so many nights waiting and her subconscious is still full of these nights that it will take another lifetime to clear? Because it was such a night when she was four that she waited for her Mom to come home but instead she just stood transfixed glaring out the door. She sucked her thumb and did a few scuffles and never became aware that her bottom was naked because it was that way most of the time. The diapers either fell off or her Mom removed and hung them on the clothesline to dry, not to wash, but to dry. Brittle, rough and board-like, they went back on the raw and tender baby butt, only to get soaked again, to fall to the ground, at last. This experienced buttocks dropped more than diapers one night. A long tail dragged after the child, longer than a possum's, more like a slim bridal train twisted in a spiral. Shivers chill-shocked her as she tried to pull on the stretched elongation coming from her. It was slimy, soft and connected to her inside. She freaked to the toilet, screaming and jerking and tugging. Until the tapeworm snapped. It extended through all the rooms of the oppressing apartment, from bedroom to kitchen, to hall, to toilet.

Cod liver oil and lots of vomiting were Pelegrine's new encounters. They forced open her mouth with two people holding, to swallow a rancid and greasy liquid, only to throw it back up into the laps around her, all of it, including the carrot soup. They called that behavior bad and incorrigible. First she was bad for having a tapeworm and then she wouldn't eat the medicine.

What she did eat was fertilizer sprinkled in the side yards to make trees grow. Those green crystals looked inviting to the hungry kid. But that is how she learned that her elderly mother could really run, flying coat and hair, over fields and fences to the hospital. The nurses wrinkled their noses and refused to wash the shitty infant after it was saved with an enema. All that poison had to escape. But her Mom went into the bathroom and knelt by the tub, her rolled-up sleeves bared her arms deep into the dirty water, rinsing the brown body from its excrement. The hospital people were squeamish, but the mother didn't want to loose Pelegrine who had turned blue with poisonous convulsions.

Channel 28

Pelegrine doesn't always feel good about her memories. The story of her birth has been in her ears since she could hear. It is an incredible event. So incredible, that she can't stop remembering.

It was deep, deep winter, no trains, only a few with soldiers hanging from the handles, out the doors. No room for a pregnant women who HAD TO get on because there was no hospital, no midwife, no medicine man. The only town with facilities resembling a hospital was fifty miles away. But today her strength had to stretch over miles and uncountable hours and bitter cold winds falling on her baby in her big belly.

Good-natured soldiers took her into a squeeze, tightly knitting arms around to prevent her falling off the icy train steps, which only held her feet, not her body. War-weary soldier arms formed a collar around her wide waist cushioning her baby belly to reach the town that might deliver it alive.

The arrival was signaled by a sudden bombing alarm. Pelegrine's Mom jostled with the hordes and couldn't stop had she wanted. Masses of people piled on top of each other. Nobody looked-out for anybody but themselves. A pregnancy was not special under these conditions. After the first labor pains Elli collapsed into a pile.

"Please, somebody listen. I need help. My baby is coming."

It took many more pleas before two soldiers were ordered to take an ironing board and lay the woman on top. She scratched her nails into the sides praying not to fall off, as they were zigzagging for their lives through chaotic streets.

The baby team could make only very little headway. Every fifteen minutes the familiar "do-da-do-da" sirens blasted people into bomb shelters. The mother and her escorts were not that lucky. They had time only to hover inside arched doorways, huddled, pressed against massive oak doors of unknown houses, waiting for the all-clear signal to continue another leg of their journey. They never managed to get caught up by a people chain pushing into narrow shelters. To this day, Pelegrine's eyes and ears perk up when modern ambulances or whining fire engines rush through orderly city streets copying her Mama's siren imitation, reincarnating the gangrene sound of prenatal music.

The hospital, temporarily moved ten miles outside of town, refused to appear. The labor pains ignored the bombing raids. When they spotted a Franciscan infirmary, the soldiers pounded on the door and shouted to the nun who peeked through the door with this on her holy lips,

"Absolutely no births today. No doctor. No midwife. Go away."

"You must accept this case! We can not run another inch."
At this point, the Mom collapsed while another raid eliminated a response but pushed them and others fleeing on the streets past the nun into the building, tumbling down the steps into the protective basement. Already down there was a Russian gynecologist who spoke only Russian. He began to help with the birth

but ran away at every sign of bombing alarms. When the baby was half-out, he disappeared completely. Elli finished the birth herself with teeth and fingers vise-gripped around the doctor's torn-off coat tails. The straw in the gunnysacks with the flying debris were her only helpers.

In the next bombing gap, a surviving nun yanked-off her black shoulder cloth, wrapped the naked infant and rushed to a spigot amongst the coals and washed off the birth. Elli was terrified that the nun would permanently disappear with the barely born baby. She wanted to hold the frail bundle herself and not have a stranger vanish with her precious gift or blow up with it. Only in Elli's arms was the blue-eyed girl safe who smiled even when the grenade blasted through their basement window, sending mother and child on their private air trip from one cement corner into another.

They refused to die. After the raids subsided, hours later, they were dragged upstairs to the needle that would sew Elli on an operating table overshadowed by shattered windows, no anesthesia, no electricity, no heat, but plenty of stars. Dr. Sadursky stitched Elli in the silent company of snowflakes falling through the windows, melting on her Mama's belly, heralding Pelegrine's bitter cold, first December morning of her life.

The tiny child was placed in the nativity crib giving the Franciscan nuns a real Christmas substitute Baby Jesus for that year. They commemorated this unscheduled birth in their golden book of memories.

A week later when Elli commenced the return journey home to her parents, she could not find the train station. It was bombed away and it took the woman 19 days to carry her baby home to her family. Farmers took them in, offering tea and old bread. Nobody had much to share. And everybody was suffering.

Elli's father was standing at the gate when she arrived. His temples had grown snow white from not knowing if he had a daughter, a grandchild or neither.

Pelegrine has heard this story often. Her mother's pain never ceases to hurt her, always the same way.

Two years before Elli's death, she made a recording of her Mom speaking those memories on tape. And that is Pelegrine's single, most valued possession. The voice and the events stay frozen in time, forever real as if they were just happening, not a million years ago.

Channel 29

The 19 year-old fingers clutched the rail of the rocking ship. The storm was inside her stomach, at last. Gradually, the crowds disappeared and Pelegrine watched the lonesome plates sliding to catch the wooden rim of the dining room table, instead of falling with the rest of the passengers to the ground. Seasickness was a new one. A word comes to life. There were stretched-out groans and the squeaks of the rocking ship accompanied these symphonies. And when it hit Pelegrine, she, too, clung to the railing and watched her vomit fetch the wind and never hit the water, but scatter away sideways. What if she fell overboard with the slime? Would they have missed her? Perhaps, because then nobody could have received the telegram announced over the ship's public address. The people who were scared to invite her, Uncle Albert and Aunt Coco, did send a welcoming message from California to the Atlantic. But since she was meeting her fiancé, the pressure must have disappeared and they were freed to kindness. Pelegrine was thrilled. Now her own apprehension subsided of seeing her balding Tommy, the one she did not know if she loved, but had decided to join, in order to find out. He waited at the harbor and made the beginning smoother and less frightening. After all, what does New York look like to a scared head, having seen only dark hurtful holes?

A thick, mid-September sticky heat embraced Pelegrine and her boat. Tommy's eyes glowed and his shirt glistened with blue and British stripes. He took her receipts and helped find the suitcases, bike and skis. The hordes of people pressed and shuffled and the sounds were like in the radio, all mixed-up and unintelligible. The few English words she needed, Tommy understood. And it was a relief to sit in a car, a 1966 Ford Fairlane, a big and soft ride, all the way to Pittsburgh where he lived in a one-bedroom apartment, with hardly any kitchen stuff but a bathroom with a shower, a stereo for Barbara Streisand, whom Pelegrine couldn't stand. He had a place of his own. She slept on the narrow couch in the living room and Tommy kept his respectful bedroom and his manners. After all, she had just come to check it all out, not to get involved and stuck.

These feelings were in her unconscious and have cleared into words only much, much later. Her life and her actions have always been governed by an instinctual approach. Her guts always told her what to do, often in the heat of her emotions, unfortunately. Just because she also could make brilliant observations, quick and determined decisions, she sometimes became daring and handled most of her life's directions that way. Tommy was easy to control. He was soft, quiet and submissive. He respected Pelegrine's wish to wait for more than kisses. She was pretty experienced in warding people off. At an early age, old men had wanted to reach under her skirt or into her shorts.

Channel 30

When she was six, on weekend visits to her assumed Dad and his mean, chain-smoking, primitive wife, after he had left Pelegrine's Mom, she wandered around through the post war barracks and encountered the old shoe repair man who always smiled with a slimy, chewed-up cigar dangling from his wet mouth. His crooked finger relentlessly lured Pelegrine and his watery eyes beckoned with a halfway smile. Once she followed him and stood perfectly still while he dug his finger into her pants and into the middle of where she peed. She knew she should run away as always, but she lingered just a tiny bit because it actually did not feel THAT bad. But she wasn't supposed to like this feeling, and he wasn't supposed to do that. She pretended not to notice his intentions immediately and became engrossed in the assorted leather soles and ambos in the shape of a shoe. Pelegrine savored the promiscuous dig before she broke it off and, ran away fast to the chickens and squatted with them. Deep breaths and lower-lip-biting followed until she went back to her Dad and Mary to continue listening to the adored, snow-white sister talk. Zange looked just like Dad, black, curly hair, fiery, piercing eyes, exotic and attractive. Once Pelegrine asked how she herself could be described. A long silence and then someone said,

"You look Germanic."

Pelegrine wondered if that was good or bad or, at least, half as appealing as her sister's foreign, gipsy look. She asked what *Germanic* meant. They volunteered blue eyes, fine, yellow hair and fair. But it didn't make her feel good because nobody ever praised such features. She always got the feeling she was acceptable but nothing special. Even when she pressed her Dad to help her find aspects that would link her to him, they could only come-up with a similar fingernail shape. And Pelegrine clung to that fact and was convinced that she favored him a little, even though her sister was more his image, often nicknamed after fairy tale characters. Some called her cute little red riding hood or gorgeous snow white. At other times, Zange was singled-out in entertaining song parodies altered to fit only her. Pelegrine listened and observed. And later she remembered and spent years fitting old memories together so they would stop hurting.

Channel 31

And when Tommy, who obediently restrained his urges, took Pelegrine with him on his frequent trips, she saw what an American motel bed looked like, big enough for a family. There it was more difficult for Tommy to stop making advances. They were often curled like spoons. For the first time she felt the poking stick in her back. And she stiffened her body to get away from it. His kisses became more demanding and she had to insist more strongly that she wasn't ready for more. He had to wait, because she would do that when she was married which was very far off for her. Only she didn't know how far. And the poor guy agreed but wanted to hold her anyway. That she allowed.

And in his arms she remembered Kurt, the boy she left behind in Vienna, the boy she slid on woolen rags with to polish the parquet floor, and later shared a bathtub because his Mom was gone for the weekend. And his penis was just as long and sticking-up like Tommy's that she only felt but did not see. Kurt's she saw but pretended not to. And when she lay with him on her self-carpentered wobbly bed, she felt his erection also. Every flashlight reminded her of it. She was secretly wiping her private area in the sheets, at least a thousand times. She wondered why she had a jelly-like liquid secreting from her. And just in case he should get his hands there, she was making sure he would not realize her wet affliction. She did not know that she was lubricating in preparation for sex. She thought she had a vaginal problem but was too illiterate and shy to consult with anyone or go to the doctor. Because it happened rarely, and never having oozed like this before, she was sure it would pass. She kept herself dry and clean and Kurt away from her. Everything was confusing and stick-like and nobody there to explain anything.

Channel 32

Her mother's chin was exactly duplicated in her brother Albert's face. Uncle Albert had been shipwrecked and floated on a piece of wood onto Alaskan shores. Pelegrine met him for real when she was eleven. Until then he had been a legend, a myth that her mother dearly loved. He was the brother who smeared cocoa around his baby sister's lips while snitching her porridge. Elli's personal life history hardly ever affected Pelegrine, not until much later, especially after her death, like now.

She never actually knew her Mom, never had time to stop to breathe to relax to listen. Elli's parents were old when Pelegrine's grandmother, Pauline Kobliceck, daughter of a Czechoslovakian furniture manufacturer, was in the middle of her menopausal years, when her sexually hungry husband, school master, choir director, dramatist, painter, humorist and story teller, Franz Käfer, popped little Elli into her womb. There were already four older children, the youngest, Josefa, twelve; the boys, Albert, twenty-three, a machinist, talented, handsome, serving in the Austrian marines; Lothar, twenty, with big blue-eyes like Pelegrine, trolley driver and para-medic in the county hospital in Linz; Erbert, twenty-five, a privateer, gambler and ladies' man. The girl, Josefa, tall, ambitious, brilliant and articulate, did not know what to do with her baby sister, born so late to her mother going on fifty. When that girl baby was nine years old, she lost her mother and only protection. Three months later, Pelegrine's lusty grandfather re-married a rich woman from Linz, the textile merchant widow, Aula Anda. With her he frolicked in dead Mrs. Kobliceck's sturdy walnut bedroom set, hand-carved and crafted especially for her wedding in 1883. Elli's bed was on a canopy at the foot of the twin marriage beds. Pelegrine's Mom did not tell her this embarrassing piece of history till she was in her seventies. The old man and his new wife would make love with Elli in the room. She was afraid of these unknown noises. She only remembered the stepmother reminding the active man that the little girl might hear. But he assured her that she won't know what's going on and to stop interrupting. But old Elli remembered all too well. In her soft voice she indicated that she understood enough and felt ashamed, hurt and trapped. Pelegrine, too, felt a sting in her heart in anger toward these grandparents who had hurt her little Mom. She began to understand the beginnings of her mother's thorny life. Why men played such a devastating role, walking on her, hurting the children, but especially the mother. Elli had no role models either.

Channel 33

She began simply as Elli Maria Käfer. Pelegrine knows glimpses of her. Now that Elli has been dead for nine months, Pelegrine's memory is revisiting history from Elli's point of view. Pelegrine is digging her brain, trying to remember with and without pain, what her mother, her child, was like.

Elli was nineteen when her step mother, who was not fond of her, insisted that she go away from home, somewhere, anywhere, but away. Old Franz reluctantly gave-in to send Elli to a distant relative of Aula Anda, the college professor, Oliver Ernöi and his family in Budapest. The elegant family was supposed to teach her etiquette and proper behavior for a lady. Elli connected uneasily to the family. The wife was genteel and the husband something else. Their daughter, Wallica, a university student, rode horses with genuine puszta temperament. The hot Hungarian colors and the large, voluptuous city impressed Elli. Worldly Wallica was an experienced and well-versed city girl. Elli shared a room with the somewhat older Wallica. Wallica took Elli to balls and gala events with the dazzling Hungarian Hussar lieutenants. Their red uniforms elaborately decorated with imperial gold tassels stunned Elli. Elli's passion for dancing has been legendary. Electrified by the czardas and the energetic Hungarians, her blood began to boil. She danced feverishly with squadrons of elegant and charming men. Elli commented that Wallica was strangely dressed in a black smoking suit and having a masculine haircut. In contrast, Elli resembled an elf in pink lace, tossing her electric, brown curls. She had entered this capital city uninitiated, without a caution talk from anybody. Her Papa had never spoken to her of sex. Neither had the stepmother. Wallica, too, was dancing with fiery Hungarian temperament, sometimes even with Elli, making her feel strange. Elli thought they were a peculiar pair because it seemed as if a young gentleman was swirling her. Wallica also pressed her fondly and held her unusually tight. That same night, after the dance, Wallica slept in Elli's bed and seduced her. She was using the most refined and clever tricks on Elli who responded with all her might and passionate talents, which she had inherited from her beloved Papa.

    From that night on, they were inseparable. From time to time, Wallica took Elli to dances in an exclusive bar. But Elli later realized that time had been a trap, after all. The father, the old Professor Oliver, too, was after Elli's flesh. The aging lecher began a secret courtship. He betrayed his wife and arranged events one evening so that Elli and he were completely alone in the villa. He introduced her to Tokayer and kept pouring into her glass. For a very long time Elli resisted the virile energy of the old man. But the Tokayer in her head was taking its effect. The goat was stronger than the girl and, in the end, overpowered her. She was desperate. She saw how he slipped a balloon on his penis and commenced to torpedo her pelvis. After he had exhausted himself, she rolled the drunkard off her body, found his burst plastic and fled into the bathroom. Under tears and in great fear, she washed herself. After she returned, two empty Tokayer bottles were rolling on the carpet next to the snoring goat. Elli cleaned up, and slid into her room, falling into a dejected sleep. Wallica was out. When she came home, she crept into Elli's bed, hugging and caressing her. She noticed Elli's sadness and tears but thought it to be homesickness. Elli was afraid and did not dare to speak not even to Wallica. She often wondered later if she should have confided in Wallica. She just was not brave enough. Instead, she carefully avoided Oliver. Only once did he try to force himself brutally on her again. But his wife was coming and he dropped Elli and ran. Elli was horrified once again, especially since she could not speak with anybody--in her own language, even. The days were strained and long and slow. Elli pleaded to be taken home to her country when Wallica had holidays. They traveled by train to Elli's Austrian village. Wallica stayed through the summer where Elli continued to savor Wallica's lovemaking. Their nights were furious and savage until Wallica returned home. Wallica wanted Elli to go back with her. But Elli did not want to go to Budapest anymore. She had enough. She had received more than language lessons there.

Channel 34

Many months passed. Her sister, Josefa, got divorced in order to re-marry again, promptly. This time an older, outrageously wealthy baron, Carlos Üller. He was gaunt and bony, wore exquisite leather knickers while killing twelve-pointed stags on his private hunting domain. Josefa hooked him in the Leona Helmsley fashion. During their regular, all male, scat evening, one member was unable to come. They needed a fifth player. Josefa was quick to offer the cigar smoking gang her expertise. A woman, shortly after World War One, playing cards with men, respectable strongholds of society, was unheard of. Mr. Üller, however, intrigued with her guts, invited her to play and from then on sent his chauffeured limousine to fetch the outrageous woman, soon to become his wife.

Since Elli was only tolerated at home, with the permission of her new husband, Josefa suggested that Elli be their permanent houseguest in their posh country estate. Such an offer constituted one of Elli's many chances to escape into a better life.

Since she was known to suffer inordinately from homesickness, she did not go with her sister to a possibly promising future, particularly since she was afflicted with a perpetual secretion from her vagina after her trip to Hungary. She had never been ill. But Oliver had left his mark. She entered a new path of suffering.

She saw a doctor and received ichthyol suppositories to insert into her anus. With purple permanganic acid she was to rinse her genitals. But nothing was helping. Her agonies persisted. The situation continued for weeks going into months. Elli, finally, decided to visit her brother Lothar in Linz. He was alone because his wife had eloped with a secret boyfriend to Holland. Lothar asked Elli to keep house for him who was then working as a full-time nurse after retiring from driving trolleys all his life. He was employed at the state hospital on the dermatology ward run by Professor Schnopfhagen. At that point, Elli had continuous and throbbing pain in her lower abdomen. Her brother and she were fond of each other. Because she trusted him, she unfolded her secret. Lothar brought her to Dr. Schnopfhagen, a world-renowned expert. Her Pap smear showed sporadic appearance of gonococci. Hearing that, Elli wanted to take her life. But Lothar, her good brother, took pity on her because he loved her. They began an intensive treatment. Nobody, absolutely nobody, was to hear about this, especially not her father and step mother. Elli was staying with Lothar. That is all they were told. Back then, sophisticated medication was not available. Today they would have used Penicillin. Elli also learned that she had *chronic parametritis* and advanced *adnexitis*, serious infections in her uterus because of the delayed and long overdue treatment. She was ordered to take 30 tablets of Cibacol per day, followed by frequent uterus injections. The treatment continued until she heard, "pap smear after her menses." What followed were grueling weeks and three more pap smears with the crowning, "NEGATIVE!" She was well again and released from the hospital. Lothar, her savior, made it possible for Elli to conceive children. She was twenty-three years old.

Channel 35

Pelegrine has always taken over her mother's diaries. Franz, Pelegrine's grandfather, had labeled Elli's book the diary of a young woman *Tagebuch als junge Frau*. He was an artist who could do wonders with watercolors, pen and ink and lithographs. He illustrated Elli's leather-bound book, the size of a tape cassette. Pelegrine's mother recorded a first dance experience on December 31, 1927, twenty-three years before Pelegrine's birth. Her second entry remembers a meeting of the Imperial Athletic Club at the hotel "Linde." The next account shifts to more personal events. Her dancing pleasures came to a stop and the records indicate yearly gaps between her chronicles. Elli reported on the third page that she had an over bubbling, lively temperament and a tendency to suffer heartaches and grief, particularly after she lost her adored mother at age nine. Great happiness came to her a few years later in the form of her first true love. She called it an awakening from her childhood dreams. Sepi whom she married on April 28, 1935, consumed her whole thinking and controlled all her feelings. She was twenty-six. He was forty-one and a widower.

She was briefly happy. On April 26, 1937, Elli wrote that her beloved and adored brother Albert was going to visit her for the first time since he made a landfall in Alaska. He came with his wife, Coco, from Los Angeles, USA.

In the summer of 1941, Elli wrote that her sister Josefa had been cruel and abusive to her. In 1942, Pelegrine reads that her mother perceived Sepi's love wavering, as well as her trust toward him. In August 1942, brutal and harsh words from Sepi, expressing utter coldness accompanied by aggression, bordering on insanity. Later that year, Sepi's stomach ulcer was diagnosed which Elli recorded in Latin, something she loved to do. She had a passion for fancy terms and wrote that Sepi suffered from *Ulkus Ventrikuli*, which by January 1948 had turned into *Ulkus duodeni*. They drafted Sepi on September 10, 1943. Two years later, on May 15, 1945 he came home from the front with straight bones. Little Pelegrine was born December 18, 1944, in an air raid shelter underneath the Franciscan convent during a bombing raid at six thirty on an early, cold winter morning. Her second mother died September 21, 1945. Her father and her brother, Lothar, the following year. In 1947, her second daughter, Zange, was born. But her husband, Sepi Honigacker, had become a stranger. "I have been living like a housekeeper beside him." In 1948 he brutally beat her. In 1951, Honigacker married for the third time, a third woman called Mary. Elli's diary ends here.

Channel 36

When Pelegrine was twelve, she found her Elli's diary. She loved this brown leather book because it was her mother's, and, of course, because her Mutti gave her "everything," she could keep it. It thus became Pelegrine's book. She carefully chose the pages she wanted to fill with memories of her own to match her grandfather's delicate drawings who learned to draw in a castle.

He was the illegitimate son born in 1864 to a poor and hard-working cook, Franziska Käfer, employed by Count Parz at Wildberg Castle on the Bohemian border. Little Franz was destined to become a tailor but the Count, not officially acknowledging the smart, skinny boy as his offspring, nevertheless, fostered his talents and provided for his education—a privilege only available to the nobility back then. And that explains why Franz became such a learned and cultured man, an artist even who could draw and paint well, write poetry and original Arthur-Schnitzler-type dramas which he wrote so that his young Elli could perfom in them. Pelegrine remembers that the theater in her hometown often staged his plays. One such performance is well in her memory, "How Do I Get a Husband." Elli played the lead.

Anyway, Pelegrine chose drawings to match her feelings of the day and commemorated her conditions that way. When Pelegrine was thumbing through her mother's sporadic recollections of her brutal husband, she fused them with her own fragile memory of surly Sepi, the quiet, tall, handsome and dark, absent father from the mountains of Tirol.

Eventually, the question arose, whose book it actually was? Pelegrine never truly knew if it was really hers or really her mother's. She found a solution by simply saying it belonged to both, once to young Elli and then to young Pelegrine.

Channel 37

Periodic family get-togethers, invited obsessive discussions and gossip about the colorful past of the entire Käfer clan. Most vocal of all was boisterous and overbearing Tante Josefa. Lurid details were offered by devious Tante Anna, the wrinkly cousin of Franz Käfer, the woman that fell on the escalator steps with her legs pointing to the sky, showing the downtown Viennese high society her naked ass and red-haired crotch. She never wore any underwear. Pelegrine saw it with her own eleven-year-old eyes. She was the woman who favored Zange. Puffing on his cigar and listening to this circus with sweat pearls on his forehead was, of course, Mr. Sommer, the one Pelegrine forced herself to call "father" to please her mother. Pelegrine ignored much of what was said and listened half heartedly because she had heard most of it over and over and it was boring. But later, when she was remembering, she wished she had been more attentive. Certain episodes she never forgot.

Her handsome mother was traded like livestock so that Franz could have more room to fornicate his bawdy Aula. In the train, so goes the story,

Pelegrine's grandfather struck up a conversation with an older, distinguished looking gentleman. It turned out that he was not disinclined to marry an appealing woman and get all his debts, considerable gambling debts, paid off. A meeting was arranged where he courted Elli for the first and probably last time. She, of course, fell for his charms, his good looks, his tallness and the idea that she would marry the most desirable beau cruising in her village. Pelegrine also heard stories of his impotence, a word she did not understand till herself an adult. She also was told of his brutish bargaining position when trading for his young wife. She knew of his coldness and indifference toward vivacious Elli. Actually, Elli's reference to the beating in 1948 is nothing compared to Pelegrine's own memory of the same incident when she was still very young.

Pelegrine remembers that she begged her father to allow her to stand on top of his feet, hold on to his big hands and walk in tandem with him, let her lie beside him in his bed and tell her stories. He was reluctant and only gave in to such demands for a short while. During that remembered night, there was a screaming match between the parents. Pelegrine, no taller than a yardstick, clasped the leg of the big dining table with her cold toes, yelling, "Mommy, Mommy, Daddy, Daddy. Don't hit her anymore!" But powerful Dad smashed Mom's nose to pieces, regardless. Elli ran out the door, bleeding, weeping, with no coat but flying gypsy hair, to the hospital. Pelegrine stayed behind naked and shivering, drowning in tears for her abused mother. He rushed out the door, slamming it shut on his way to Mary, the waitress girlfriend with bundles under his arms as Pelegrine had seen him many times, carrying off the household monograms and silver spoons. "Why was he bringing this cheap, chain smoking, Dad-stealing-tramp our stuff?" went through Pelegrine's head as she recollected her mother's monologues while waiting for him to come home.

Later, Pelegrine went on weekend visitations to this man, she believed to be her father. Desperately looking for kinship, father and child had decided they had identical fingernails. But Zange was the lucky one because she was his spitting image.

Mary, his last wife, used every visit to indoctrinate the children with Elli's inadequacies as a wife, mother and human being. She supposedly never cooked right for Sepi, only served him cold and stale food, never cleaned and was a faulty wife. Pelegrine listened to years of humiliating details about her mother and never dared to defend her, maybe, out of fear that the few kind gestures like a warm meal, a clean table and a bath would vanish? When she returned home from such visits, Pelegrine was often aggressive toward Elli and chided her inadequacies. By the time Pelegrine went to bed on such nights, she had already regretted her attitude toward her mother. She knew they had told only partial truths because her Mom never did anything right in anybody's eyes. On such nights, Pelegrine also wet the bed, which infuriated Elli. She grabbed Pelegrine's head and smashed her nose down into the mattress, scolding her awful habit, which did not leave her even in boarding school where she was the laughing stock of the entire convent. There was so little Pelegrine had control over, especially her mother's decisions. Pelegrine could not really adequately protect her, except ask Elli to be more restrained and not marry so fast so often, especially those men that could care less about her two girls. The marriage to Sepi was dissolved after they had been together, in a manner of speaking, for fifteen years. Pelegrine was six years old, her sister four. But he had been betraying Elli since Pelegrine's birth.

Channel 38

And for eighteen years Pelegrine had believed that her weekend father was her real one, even though his mountain-headed, Alpine-thinking family never acknowledged the blonde, scrawny, blue-eyed child. They had conspicuously lavished their affection with presents and clothes upon Pelegrine's younger sister who did look like dark-eyed Sepi and was not just a fingernail copy. Pelegrine's sister was reluctantly sharing her possessions, contributing much sorrow to Pelegrine's already saddened life.

By twelve Pelegrine had suffered yearly throat infections. She decided that her tonsils should go as the doctor had suggested. One morning she packed her sister's cardboard doll suitcase. It had a latch and looked like a real suitcase, the size of a city telephone book. A large container back then. Pelegrine also lacked a proper hospital dress. Early that morning, she sneaked into her sister's closet, borrowed the pale blue cotton dress, two sizes too small for Pelegrine. That dress was a legitimate present from Zange's Tirolean relatives. Pelegrine squeezed into it, held her breath and could barely close the zipper. With sucked-in stomach, empty and scared, a paper suitcase full of nothing but a toothbrush, a piece of soap and a towel, she marched to the reception window to admit herself. The nurses commented on the pretty dress that they could hardly pull off Pelegrine. It was tight and had to be peeled like skinning a catfish. On the fourth day, her mother and sister came to the recovering patient who by that time could eat ice cream. Elli came with her usual kisses and baby talk. But the sister. She stood planted with an iron grimace and a sinister gaze. She demanded her dress and her doll case. But Pelegrine begged her to lower her voice so that the other patients wouldn't hear and be aware of Pelegrine's predicament. Good thing, the dress was not in the room because Zange would have taken it away and let Pelegrine walk home in her underwear. Pelegrine collected these memories but loved her sister anyway. Except.

  When they were seesawing on a makeshift swing straddling a board across a chopping block, Pelegrine mischievously bounced fat butterball, Zange, to the center. The precious baby sister pleaded for mercy. But Pelegrine was in control now. Nobody around to stop her and weren't there thousands of incidents to even out? What she did not really intend was to injure Zange's entire set of fingers. All ten, fat fingers caught between board and chopping block. And Zange held them out menacingly, bandaged in thick sausages, angrily swinging them before Pelegrine's eyes. Two sets of fingernails fell off after the bandages were removed. Nobody believed Pelegrine that her intentions were not as severe as the wounds. She only wanted to aggravate and scare the sister, not damage her like that. But then who ever listened to her anyway?

Pelegrine's childlike thinking was not taken into consideration also when as she was guarding the sister while they sat on the windowsill in their downstairs flat, six foot off the ground. They were eating cherries or, better, Pelegrine was. As she spat out the pits, she told Zange to reach and catch them. Zange obediently caught the cherrystones. But Pelegrine's spitting circles became larger and larger and Zange had to stretch further and further to catch the pits until she fell to the ground with the stones, screaming like hell. Pelegrine thought she never would see the end of that beating and prolonged house arrest. But she survived, just as did the sister the fall.

Channel 39

The problem with Elli was that she was perpetually searching for a husband, always looking in the wrong places, even when Sepi was a fighting foot soldier. Since the rightful men were gone, loving ones or not, soldiers were placed in vacant rooms in the homes of the waiting wives. Pelegrine's eighteen-year-old father took over Sepi's bed. He loved Elli.

Elli's prolonged absences, forever looking for a father and companion, are Pelegrine's most vivid memories of her mother and her youth. One night especially, when a courtier was calling for Elli through the broken windowpane. That darkness will never fade.

It was the ominously bearded forester from the mountain where Pelegrine and Zange had spent weeks curing their whooping coughs. He hollered for Elli and climbed through the window. The two sisters sat frozen and petrified on the bed, sucking their thumbs. He plopped down beside them, opened up his knapsack, pulled out ham and knife with a cutting board and started eating and grunting. Stamped on Pelegrine's mind are his volcanic red socks, burning eyes and greasy, black leather breeches. When Elli, finally, arrived she was indignant but quickly mollified. The girls were whisked off to another room. Blank goes the brain but not the pain. He did not marry the woman, but Mr. Panchina, a Rumanian refugee, looking for an Austrian wife, did. Pelegrine was eight.

Channel 40

Mr. Panchina lived in a barrack colony near Vienna. Elli packed up the girls and moved in with that man speaking only Hungarian with him. He did not speak a word of German. Pelegrine watched how they would close the door with a bent nail in the two-room shack. They didn't even have locks or keys. Behind that door she heard familiar noises, this time mixed in with Hungarian ejaculations. Nobody there spoke Pelegrine's language. She had to learn theirs. To this day chunks of the Magyar tongue have stayed with her, as she pleases friends with "Gösse nem seppe, Cese chokolo or Yona pot kiwano."

The couple was non-stop fucking for several months. Pelegrine missed many days of school but did learn another language, instead. Soon she was playing with the refugee children, their foreign toys, dried maze and Slavic songs. Elli ended up marrying that man, bleached her hair blond to make her look younger and was going to immigrate to the United States with him. Only with a wife and kids could he get political asylum, not otherwise.

Elli had merely turned the key to lock up her flat. Without further preparations, she planned to go abroad with her two children. She prepared as if she were merely visiting a nearby town and not crossing an ocean. Zange and Pelegrine were sitting on tied bundles of clothes, their feet not touching the ground while waiting for the airlift. They looked at the planes and waited for theirs, which would take them to cotton fields or coalmines in Virginia. "Virginia," Elli would roll that sound over her tongue and dream of a real life. But, as always, Tante Josefa, the influential, powerful savior aunt, arrived just in time before take-off. She dragged the forty-three-year old sister to the magistrate, bribed lawyers and a judge to annul the wedding of her imbecile sister whom she had declared mentally incompetent.

"You incorrigible fool," Josefa shouted publicly at Pelegrine's mother. "That foreign bastard only married you so that he could get to America. Once there, he would have dumped you as fast as a toilet tissue. And you, with your unblemished record of perfect failures, would have starved and disintegrated in the coal mines of Virginia where people have better things to do than look out for Elli Maria Käfer, alias Honigacker, alias Panchina."

The threesome went crestfallen back home, dragging their bundles, unlocking the apartment, going back to school, and making up lessons. Pelegrine had difficulties fitting her tongue back into German speech. The teachers, neighbors and friends thought she was faking. But she wasn't. Hungarian had become second nature by then. Nobody noticed her penchant for language.

Channel 41

Only two more marriages were in store for Pelegrine, the one at ten to Mr. Etzelsdorfer with a wart on his right eye. That time Pelegrine begged her mother not to marry him. They were happier without this intruder. For Pelegrine that would mean total freedom, no supervision and almost total control of her mother. She beseeched Elli to wait till Pelegrine was big enough to earn a living. Then she promised to take care of her mother, who only kissed her daughter, laughingly dismissing Pelegrine's heart-felt offer. Pelegrine wrote the promise into her diary because she meant every word of it. Elli, however, married catastrophe number three. Pelegrine overheard Tante Josefa saying the man could not have a proper erection and had to fuck Elli with a Knackwurst. Pelegrine was ashamed of her Mom and could not understand why she submitted to that. The aunt was surely not lying. But Pelegrine's own memories were in a quandary since they often lingered on the smelly fingers of her mother who was spending long stretches of time behind closed doors with prospective fathers who continued to disappear with Elli's good china. Pelegrine decided to hide the jewelry before it, too, would vanish. It was a smart move and came in handy later when they were hungry and destitute.

Channel 42

After she had divorced Mr. Etzelsdorfer, Elli met Mr. Sommer, husband number four and the last one to torture Pelegrine. He was the reason why Pelegrine could hardly wait to be eighteen and able to leave home legally. She had wanted to run away many times, pleading with Elli to give her the twenty dollars alimony from Joshi and let her live on her own. Elli tried to convince the teenage Pelegrine that she could not live on that. "I can live on rolls and milk. And on Wednesdays when we have street market with the farmers selling their vegetables and fruits, I will find stuff in the gutter," exclaimed Pelegrine to the astonished mother, who could only shake her head in disbelief and helplessness.

Channel 43

Pelegrine sat foot in the land of hope and stayed with Tommy and his Barbara Streisand records. Another British couple was inviting him and his fiancé, Pelegrine, to dinner. She did not own the proper dress. Tommy went shopping with Pelegrine and acted extremely knowledgeable in women's dresses. She yielded to his choice but wondered why it was so important to him that she bought the navy blue, conservative dress, appropriate for weddings and funerals. He insisted for the first time on something. And that on an issue of correctness! Tommy suddenly appeared prim and prudish. She registered the reaction but did not act upon it till later. The evening was as navy as the dress, bland and inoffensive. Whatever it was, Pelegrine felt uncomfortable and not at home with people who wore the right dress for the occasion, even for a casual dinner. Next day she wanted to cook Tommy the only thing she knew how, vegetable soup, which she had learned in her home economics class. But he did not own a large enough pot. She pedaled her bike to *Goodwill*, the second hand store she had known since she was eleven when Tante Josefa had sent huge, generous gift packages with loads of clothes everybody laughed at because they seemed like Marilyn Monroe--Hollywood replicas, looking ridiculous draped on bony, undernourished war-fed bodies.

She bought an aluminum pot, tied it to her luggage rack and bounced it back through strange and dark looking neighborhoods. "Why don't I see any more white faces and every single person is black, suddenly?" she wondered. Tommy was horrified and told her that she had just been through what they called the roughest, slum neighborhood, a concept that was certainly also new to her. That explains why she wasn't afraid. She only sensed that the area had a different feel from the one where Tommy lived. It took weeks before Pelegrine lost her shyness and opened her mouth in the store and stopped pointing to items and making people believe she was mute. The stay with Tommy expired by itself. She bought a Greyhound bus ticket to California to be with Uncle Albert who welcomed her as long as she was attached to somebody else and did not pose a threat to their cushy California life.

Channel 44

After three days and nights, her suitcases, bike and skis made contact with San Fernando Valley. Uncle Albert and Aunt Coco were happy to see her. They arrived in the Mercedes they had bought on their last Europe trip when Pelegrine was eighteen. They drove through desert hills and sunbathed stretches of dust and cactus, a landscape, Pelegrine had not encountered even on postcards.

Life there was great. Since she had nothing to do, only to perfect her English, Pelegrine suggested to become Albert's ground keeper girl, be in charge of watering the trees, painting the house, fixing broken slats, maintaining the home-made pool the size of a large living room. She did all that for one dollar per hour. That was splendid and it helped her save up a little money.

Albert was such a renegade himself, unorthodox and very similar to Pelegrine. He retired years ago as an engineering machinist from Lockheed

Aircraft, went into real estate and made his fortunes in the California desert. As far as Pelegrine's eyes could see on top of the Coyote hills, it was his land. Pelegrine inspected everything alongside her uncle, both in boots and shorts and ragged hair. Every day though they drove into the desert for a special reason.

When Coco's piercing eyes were out of sight, he stopped the Mercedes and slid over to let Pelegrine drive the automatic limousine. Since they were mostly on sand-blown desert roads where they never met another car, this drive was THE highlight of her days. The real purpose of the daily journeys was to feed his wild, stray dogs where Duchess, a big black desert species of an unknown combination, reigned as his beloved. Coco tolerated no more than the tiny terrier, Tippi. Albert who had wanted a wagonload of children had given up that wish because of his tubercular wife and her artificial hip. He had his dogs in the Mojave and Cindy, a mysterious lady friend. After feeding the dogs, Pelegrine slowed down and stopped by the halfway house "The Silver Dollar" for Albert to see Cindy, the waitress. Pelegrine had no idea what such meetings signified. Strangely, Mary and Honigacker flashed through her mind. She was told that this was one of their secrets just like driving the car and all was fine with Pelegrine, until her visitor's visa ran out, six months later. She renewed it in Los Angeles staying with Alfred and Rita, friends of her uncle's for twenty-five years. They were German just like Coco. Albert and Pelegrine entertained everybody with their funny European accents and similar Austrian temperaments. Alfred and Rita were in their middle fifties, twenty years younger than Albert and Coco. And thus began another major saga of Pelegrine's turbulent life.

Channel 45

Alfred and Rita had a town house in the posh section of Los Angeles. They drove a white Corvette with red leather seats, big enough for a family with mother, father and child, a dream of Pelegrine's since she took care of her own mother. All her life, she wished for caretakers. This L.A. couple was prematurely retired with some kind of disability because Alfred wore a bracelet indicating that he was a heart patient and Rita said that meant he could not bear excitement of any kind. That's why they had separate bedrooms. Pelegrine enjoyed the fun-loving pair. They went to parties, three, four times a week. They had gallons of friends with gallons of highballs. Pelegrine learned about swimming pools and personal refrigerators rendering perpetual ice cubes swimming in Bourbon and Seven-Up mingled with mindless chatter while she massaged the varicose veined legs of Alfred, she called "Daddy." She enjoyed sitting in "Mommy" Rita's lap on their trips to San Juan Capistrano or Tijuana or wherever. They were acting like her parents, and Pelegrine wallowed in that ecstatic fantasy. In the capital of whims and fantasies, they invented Disney World and cement for famous feet--why not make-believe California parents?

In time, Pelegrine was more and more reluctant to return to her uncle's isolated desert. Her aunt became a little jealous of this fast attraction to what were her best friends, but Pelegrine did not catch the politics of such a drift. She wanted to be with Mommy and Daddy exclusively. Especially after a certain starry event.

By November she was spending her first nights in Los Angeles under Mommy's and Daddy's banana trees. After highballing home one night, the question arose where should Pelegrine sleep. Till now she had slept on the narrow cot in the den. But that night, Daddy was dozing there and it was decided that Pelegrine should sleep in Mommy's big, more comfortable king size bed. "We should have thought of that sooner," was the general consensus.

Pelegrine massaged Daddy's legs as usual with a strapped-on vibrator on her hand, which tickled and made her fingers and whole arm feel numb and eerie afterward. She tucked him in and ushered him to sleep. Mommy fixed herself another highball. Pelegrine noted that the woman had a lot to drink that night. But then she always had a lot of everything because she was very popular, and enjoyed her status, especially with men. Pelegrine, too, had begun to adore her. Ever so subtly did she count among her disciples. She resembled

Rita Hayworth with that same expressive, sensuously red mouth, gleaming teeth, darting brown eyes and irresistible charm, accompanied by a raspy cigarette voice like Susanne Plechette, Zarah Leander or Sting.

Still in the car that night, Pelegrine snuggled on her lap, followed by hugs and a kiss on Rita's cheek. The old woman responded with every gesture tenfold, indicating whatever Pelegrine was doing was O.K. with her. The only hitch was, Pelegrine did not know what she was doing. She just acted on impulse, strong, very strong feelings and, loads of bravado. And with this thing called Whiskey, everything became easier. She relaxed into her loving and affectionate self. Pelegrine welcomed every bump in the car ride because it strapped her closer to Rita who showed no signs of resistance whatsoever. The heat of their bodies bonded in a 1964 Corvette on a hot California night.

Pelegrine continued her amorous embraces in bed and Rita passionately pressed herself against Pelegrine. Rita quivered responsively, turning into a flesh-eating, succulent flower. A candle like flashlight, Rita's vibrator, Pelegrine learned later, showered a seductive glow over the scene, accompanied by Mexican tunes, sizzling from the pink radio right above their heads. And during that foreplay, one kiss suddenly turned real, with tongue and hunger and all. The body language turned into volcanic fire. It wasn't Mommy anymore that Pelegrine was fondling, kissing and embracing. It was lovemaking to a woman. In a flash Pelegrine realized something she was wondering for years. All the dates that had brought her home, all the goodbye kisses she had endured counting the stars till the slobbering was over! She never knew why the evenings out with boys invariably had to end in a struggle. And why her stepfather had warned her never to get pregnant. If so, he would squish the baby to the wall like he did the little kittens. Back then Pelegrine wondered how one could get pregnant during such a cumbersome kissing orgy in the night after a date. Keeping the boys' hands off her body was easy. Getting the kissing over was an ordeal.

Anyway, this night that wouldn't end, four months before she should celebrate her twenty-first birthday in Las Vegas, she had no time looking at stars, no time wishing the kissing to end, no time for the night to close. It was the first encounter with her sexuality, which became clear to her in a flash, was not happening with a man, but with a woman. What did they call these people? She tried to remember, "queer, schwul, awful." Is that what she was now, too? Whatever the adjectives, she decided, she would accept them.

Rita and Pelegrine loved each other till the sun came up. Rita was insatiable and could not stop coming. She wanted more and more. Pelegrine was young, strong and willing to comply but the older woman was not old. Pelegrine worked till her wrists were hurting. When morning came, they slept and would not rise till early afternoon. Daddy was waiting with brunch and an itinerary for the day, the beach. Wonderful for catching up on sleep.

This heavenly period continued night after night. Pelegrine barely visited the desert and could not wait to go to bed every night. Rita felt the same. She, too, was perpetually ready to retire to bed. Pelegrine often whispered during the nights, "What about Daddy? I think I saw him go to the bathroom."

"Don't worry about him. He'll never get it. Come back and continue," Rita moaned.

Pelegrine kept an eye on the bathroom door and was not at ease until the shadow had passed back to his room. And then the night was theirs again. Pelegrine recalls Rita's unquenchable appetite for sex. Pelegrine's delicate piano fingers and refined hands weren't big enough to satisfy her. Not just one, but four fingers, including the thumb were often in operation. Rita's index finger was enough for Pelegrine. Rita had three orgasms to Pelegrine's one. When Pelegrine dropped in exhaustion, Rita used the vibrator-candle for additional thrills. Rita reached for the contraption one night, and Pelegrine helped her use it but did not want to try it herself. Too big and frightening and artificial. She only wanted to feel Rita, her skin, her touch, and her juices. She only desired to kiss those burning lips, eat that fat tongue and bury her head in those pillow-thighs, night after night, after night.

Channel 46

Time passed, nevertheless. After the visa was renewed once more, Pelegrine had to portion out her energies for keeping the day-time Mommy-Daddy routine intact, the nights explosive, and to arrange occasional desert visits to catch some needed rest and find strength for the long, arduous journey seeking legal sponsorship. Pelegrine knew that after the third renewal, she had to return to her country: to nothing--to no prospects. Uncle Albert and Aunt Coco had refused sponsorship on the grounds that they were too old for a young person like Pelegrine, the responsibilities too big, and they contended, that youth belonged to youth. They suggested that Pelegrine look into the possibilities of being a housemaid in a superstar family, then marry a son from such a household and stay in the US that way. But Pelegrine countered that her life in Europe was better than that. There, at least, she was a licensed druggist, a job that wasn't great but better than cleaning other people's garbage. The aunt was old-fashioned and figured that marriage was Pelegrine's best bet, as it was for all girls. But Pelegrine really wanted more out of life than just marriage. She had already passed up two opportunities that were headed that way. After all, she was twice promised to two men. But neither Kurt nor Tommy was alluring enough for marriage. Pelegrine wanted an education. That way she and not the husbands could call the shots. But that a girl should be so adamant to want to go to college was not readily accepted in California and especially not in 1965 Austria. Smart and enlightened parents, intelligent and caring relatives or a society that elected politicians to make that possible only enabled such a path. None of these Pelegrine could call her own.

Uncle Albert was a prominent Lyon's Club member and Mrs. Lynch, the local lumberyard owner's wife, was an active Woman Lyon. She invited Pelegrine to give a plea pitch to the club asking for the ladies' sponsorship to help her become a permanent resident. Pelegrine had difficulties speaking in front of a crowd of blue haired, well-to-do pillars of society. She gulped three highballs, clutched the podium and spoke vehemently of her desire to stay in

America and pursue college studies. Many members overwhelmingly endorsed her but not all of them. Some women had reservations and did not want to commit the organization to such a long-range undertaking. Rita and Alfred, too, did not want to take the risk. Consequently, obtaining residency became Pelegrine's private never-ending plight. The battle seemed hopeless.

On one particular evening, Pelegrine was to escort Daddy to his bed and tuck him in as usual. For some reason, he violated the rules, reached up and touched Pelegrine's breasts. She was shocked and calmed him,

"Don't think of such things. You know, you mustn't get excited. Your heart."

She covered him and turned out the light and went to Rita's arms. And there she whispered to Rita that she had made an important discovery, which she as his wife needed to know. Pelegrine told her that the husband was endangering his heart and that he was not as docile as everyone believed him to be. She made Rita swear not to mention a word but to watch him. Pelegrine trusted Rita's love and discretion without doubt. They made love as usual, the entire night.

Next morning, for the very first time, Rita was not in bed when Pelegrine awoke. She was sitting with Alfred at the fully prepared breakfast table and asked Pelegrine, politely and softly to sit and join them. Pelegrine sensed a difference. The conversation turned soon into an interrogation with Rita asking Pelegrine to repeat Alfred's alleged inclinations. Pelegrine gazed in disbelief at Rita, at Alfred and back at Rita.

"But you promised not to tell," Pelegrine muttered under tears.

"Yes, I know. But I had to confront Alfred. I couldn't help it,"
Rita responded in a never before heard matter-of-fact voice. Pelegrine had to act quickly and present her version. She looked straight into Alfred's eyes, and repeated verbatim what had happened. She wasn't accusatory, just scared and concerned about his heart.

"You touched me on my breasts, and you shouldn't have. They told me you are a heart patient and I thought I better tell your wife to look after you better."

What happened then was incredulous and has fundamentally disturbed Pelegrine to this day. Alfred, like Mr. Derwisch, denied everything. He made Pelegrine appear to be a stupid liar, a silly fool with fantasies. And Pelegrine's inordinately pronounced sense of justice, coupled with a passionate Käfer temper came into decisive play. She rose slowly from the table, starred at Rita, threw down her napkin and demanded that her uncle pick her up at once. She did not want to be in that treacherous house another minute. She packed her bags, and sat on the stoop till Uncle Albert came. Not a word was exchanged, and Pelegrine left her six months old heaven in utter silence and despair. She wondered whether there was another plot behind Rita's pretended love. Nothing was ever clarified but the story went to unfold itself bitterly anyway.

Channel 47

Life at the desert was never the same again. Pelegrine became despondent and silently grieved and questioned over and over why? Why Rita betrayed her?

"Why did she talk, when she promised she wouldn't? Why did Alfred deny the truth? I wasn't going to do anything to him. I thought Rita would seriously remind him of his risks. No more. Oh, people can be so cruel. And I meant no harm. It could so easily have been settled. What were everybody's motives for lying?"

Pelegrine was more concerned about his health than about the fact that he fingered her breasts. When she retreated in shock, she was sincerely concerned about his heart and wanted his interests curbed, interests she figured that would show up with other girls, too. And then he could die. That and only that was what she wanted to prevent. That was the only reason why she told Rita anything. Pelegrine never spoke to her uncle and aunt about the incident. Surprisingly, she was never pressed for reasons why she didn't want to go to the city anymore. The aging relatives accepted the explanations that her new interests were focused on staying in America and that she had to think of a way to manage that.

Pelegrine began reading local papers and spotted an ad asking for a companion to a ten-year old child paying with room and board plus five dollars a week. Pelegrine answered the ad. Mrs. Shriver's and her daughter, Claire's, needs ended her days in the desert. The ensuing months were good for Pelegrine. She gradually stopped thinking of Rita. She took care of Claire, did schoolwork with her after school, went roller-skating and baby sitting and warmed up TV. dinners before putting the child to bed. The mother came home at nine thirty after her job as a nurse for Universal Studios. In the morning Pelegrine was free to go to an adult high school, learn English, math, geography and American government, all in English. It was sheer torture because the language was slow and hard to know. Uncle Albert and Aunt Coco called periodically to see how she was doing and encouraged her return to Europe. But Pelegrine was not convinced that they knew how bitterly she fought her way to make something of herself. Coming to America to be a maid or a simple wife wasn't worth the costs.

The third time she asked for a visa renewal, she gave as a reason her desire to reside in America forever because she liked it and had a chance to make a life. But the stone-faced immigration officer found those reasons the wrong ones and denied her an extension. At other times when Pelegrine had simply asked or a visa extension because she was planning to return home, her tourist visa was quickly renewed. But the honesty of "I want to stay here forever because I like it here" brought her only a visa denial and a 30-day deportation order. No sleep that night. But next day, she went back, lined-up by a different window and repeated the untruthful reason for more time. And, voila--she received her third and last 6 months tourist visa extension.

Channel 48

Pelegrine began forming a fragile community with Mrs. Shriver and Claire. The mother also had a sixteen-year-old daughter, Kitty, who was living with foster parents. Both girls were from two different men. Mrs. Shriver reminded Pelegrine a little of her own mother with one big exception, the woman was taking care of her girls by having a job and not by re-marrying over and over. When Kitty came to visit, she disliked it that Pelegrine had taken over her room. But in spite of that initial dislike, Kitty befriended Pelegrine who was five years older but seemed more like her own age. Pelegrine had a 1951 Plymouth that she bought with her inheritance money from Mrs. Kobliceck, her real grandmother who had put the money in a trust fund in 1944. It was a lot of money back then, and Pelegrine wished it had been put into land or jewelry because by the time she was twenty-one, the enormous sum had been devalued by World War II to a mere 250 American dollars, just enough to buy the Plymouth and a year's insurance. Mrs. Shriver allowed Kitty to take a trip with Pelegrine to San Francisco. The woman trusted Pelegrine. But Kitty was something else.

Right above Santa Barbara, she wanted to pick-up hitchhikers. But Pelegrine didn't think it was such a good idea, especially since she felt somewhat responsible for the Janice Joplin looking teenager. In San Francisco they had no idea where to spend the night. They parked the car and went from bar to bar looking at the breathtaking sights, the barely dressed people, the dope addicts, the unconventional humans called transvestites. In the bathroom, Kitty and Pelegrine carried-on strategic conversations worrying out loud about their lodgings, hoping that somebody would help them with some sort of lodging. One woman took the bait, exited from her toilet and came up to the girls,

"Let me check with my husband. Our daughter is in Russia, and you poor things can sleep in her room."

That is how Pelegrine and Kitty ended up staying in Oakland for two weeks. During the day, Kitty taught Pelegrine how to panhandle, especially after the car had a radiator blowout right on the Oakland Bridge where stopping is suicidal. And no money bought no radiator. So they begged. Each took a different side of the street. The beggars walked up to nicely dressed gentlemen,

"Excuse me sir. You don't have any change you could spare?" Some men wanted more explanation and the storytellers elaborated,

"I just need a dime to call my Mom, or I need bus money, or I have no job and I am hungry."

One man even offered Pelegrine a dishwashing opportunity in his Fisherman's Wharf restaurant. But Pelegrine said that she wanted money, not a job. After about thirty minutes one of the two would scream across the street and holler,

"I have twenty bucks. Let's stop for lunch."

After the radiator was repaired, they liked the habit of hustling for money to buy good food. Kitty latched on to a guy and Pelegrine joined them to his hotel room where the adolescent introduced her twenty-one-year-old "baby sitter" to pot. Pelegrine smoked the stuff, but did not feel much. To experience a real high took several more tries.

After two weeks of begging, they drove back to L.A. slowly, taking their time, spending the night in sleeping bags at Big Sur, waking with dew drops on their eye lashes and pounding surf in their ears. The whole neighborhood block was glad to see Pelegrine back. So were Claire and the mother. But also glad were the Kimberly's living in the house right in front of Claire's.

They had an eighteen year-old son, Ronald, and a foster daughter, Dora. The brother and sister were really in love, much to the chagrin of Helen Kimberly, Ronald's mother. Dora, Ronald and Pelegrine enjoyed many nights in Ronald's Plymouth Fury convertible, riding up and down the Santa Monica coast, going bowling at night or playing tennis. The three were young, silly and carefree. When Pelegrine wanted a fourth visa renewal, the authorities finally refused and gave her thirty days to clear out of the country or risk deportation. "Now what?" Pelegrine brooded. There really wasn't much left she could do, actually nothing.

The whole neighborhood block was pondering and deliberating what could be done to keep Pelegrine in the USA. One woman begged her husband to hire Pelegrine as a UCLA chemistry lab technician. But Pelegrine was paralyzed with the thought of doing inorganic and organic chemistry, benzene rings, sulfuric acids, ketones and acetones in English. She could barely do them in her home language. No, that was not a solution. She still had so much to learn. Plus she could only get jobs that no US citizen could fill. Then she had a lightening bolt inspiration.

"If there were somebody who would marry her, not consume her, but only for the paper, divorce her after a safe while—that way she saw a possibility to reside in the United States and pursue a better life."

Thus she mused until she spoke it out loud to Helen Kimberly who quickly discussed it with her husband and Ronald. Since he was under age, she promptly signed his release. Two days later, the wedding party marched to the magistrate and afterwards to a Presbyterian church, with veil and all, Dora as the bridesmaid and the neighborhood kids as supporters. Pelegrine married Dora's boyfriend.

It remained forever perplexing to Pelegrine how total strangers did not bat an eye to help her while her blood relatives hymned and hawed to get out of aiding her. Her European relatives and the American uncle and aunt never fully believed the truthful facts surrounding this extraordinary marriage.

"But why would I lie?" said Pelegrine. "If he were my real husband, I would tell you. He is a nice fellow. But we are not sweethearts. We are friends including his girlfriend."

"Yeah, yeah, that's what they all say," were the smirky answers.
Pelegrine stopped talking about the subject and continued with her life. That was in the second September of her journey. She had planned to save up enough money to divorce Ronald immediately in the following year. Staying married that length of time would look legitimate she figured. But three months later in December, Dora's stomach began to swell. Ronald's baby had grown and they

needed to get married fast.

Off they went. The three friends raced in a pea-green Plymouth Fury convertible to El Paso, Texas, and on to Juarez, Mexico. They obtained an instant Mexican divorce. Three days later Pelegrine went again to the civil ceremony but this time as a bridesmaid to her ex-bridesmaid's and ex-husband's wedding with almost identical wedding guests with one exception--this time, the wedding was for real.

Helen Kimberly was sad. She had hoped in vain that Pelegrine would remain her daughter in law and that in time, Ronald would get over his infatuation with Dora, an affair Helen had never condoned. They did it all behind her back. Pelegrine was confident that their love would last because she had no intentions of ever remaining Ronald's wife, Helen wishing it or not. After all, she and Ronald had never been that way toward each other, and Pelegrine, still harboring her deep secret experience with Rita, was not sure what her sexual future was supposed to be. Pelegrine began dating boys like she did in the past. But it always turned out to be the same empty experiences with the same kisses under relentless stars. But what was she to do? With whom could she discuss any of this stuff? Since there was nobody, it was better that she just forgot that Rita ever happened.

Eventually she changed jobs. The babysitting-tutor existence did not provide enough freedom for her emerging independence. Mrs. Shriver and Claire wanted her around all the time, even on weekends. And the digging for old bottles in Death Valley, watching bullfights on TV with no actual trips to Mexico to see real ones, eventually bored Pelegrine enough to seek a change. She became a file clerk for Occidental Life Insurance, working from 5-10 in the evening, earning exactly one hundred dollars a month. Sixty-five went for the efficiency apartment on Rampart Boulevard, the rest for gas, food and nothing. Because the money wasn't enough, she invented a trick and started shoplifting after ten p.m. She put cold cuts, cheeses and chocolates into her basket-like purse. She felt no real guilt because of her poverty. Thieving from an impersonal corporate giant that was gutting people anyway, left Pelegrine totally without remorse. She could never steal from an individual person. She felt extreme compassion for other humans in pain. She also figured that other people had parents or relatives. But Pelegrine had only herself. That was her way of beating the system. And it worked. She never went overboard, and limited her night prowls strictly to food items.

Channel 49

School was progressing slowly. The subjects remained hard, especially English and American History. Cambria Adult High School was renamed to Mid City Occupational Training Center six months after Pelegrine had started. She kind of liked the old name better since the new one suggested training for specific skills and Pelegrine wanted a broad and liberal education, not a training that smacked of Austrian regimentation, molding people into traps. She wanted a real education like everybody else had, with a real beginning, progressing properly in a linear direction. She wanted to catch-up with the learned people and never be ignored again because of lack of education. A school with the name "high school" sounded like the right school.

Bill Folks was the principal of the school and Pelegrine promptly fell in love with him the same way she did with the priest in England and Father Fischberger in Austria when she was only fifteen, or the ski instructor at thirteen, or the older man she met while hitchhiking at seventeen. Pelegrine launched devastating crushes on all of them.

In her religious delirium as a young school girl, she went to church twice on Sundays, took communion over and over and had a girl friend watch to see if Fischberger's hands were shaking, because Pelegrine could have sworn that during the sermon he was looking constantly in her direction. She volunteered to be an actress in the annual passion play, which retold Christ's tortured life. The play was performed in church with the altar serving as a stage. Yet she never forgot that she was in the awesome cathedral and her voice echoed from the arches of the holy shrine where her beloved acting coach and catechism teacher helped her memorize endless religious lines. Pelegrine received private coaching for the play in his cloistered room in the abbey where he lived. The tiny, book-sized windows were wedged into massive walls. He had the windows partially cracked open and Pelegrine saw her happy self-mirrored in the glass. The priest was extraordinarily dramatic and had great acting talent in and out of the pulpit. Pelegrine just loved to be near him.

As the years passed, Pelegrine's mother kept him posted of her progress and after her experience in England, she accepted a job in a Tyrolean mountain village, near the Italian border. She was almost nineteen then. Mr. Fischberger had written to her that he was en route on a pilgrimage to see the pope in Rome. She met the father at the train station of a nearby village where his fast Rome Express could stop. Pelegrine noticed instantly that he was not wearing his white priest collar, usually always wrapped around his neck. She wondered instantly what that could mean. But she shrugged it off and played the debonair young lady having dinner with her once adored childhood infatuation. He had not really changed except Pelegrine did not have the same tingling excitement from four years ago. They chatted and exchanged pleasantries. He acted more like a date especially when he ordered the big bottle of wine which he drank with great gusto and speed.

Pelegrine's last train home to her village left at ten. At the station he insisted to accompany her all the way home and stay with her. The girl remembered her long gone feelings for that man. Had he asked her five years ago, she would never have hesitated. But now, now that he was serious, she was not. She urged him to go to his hotel because she only had one single bed. But that would be fine with him he pleaded. Pelegrine got scared because her feelings were dead and his, with all that wine, were alive and real. When the train came, she quickly hopped on and pushed him back, reminding him of his visit to the pope and what he would think if he saw him this way.

For Pelegrine it was a strange night. She could not sleep but marveled at the strange turns life took. She never saw Fischberger in her entire life again. A card from Rome reached her shortly thereafter, a thank you message with the deepest gratitude from a man who was doing penance in Rome on his knees. He thanked the girl for her fortitude and wisdom. Pelegrine knew she did not deserve this respect. It was easy to appear strong when one is not in love. Then it is easy to say "no." She sometimes thinks of him today and wonders what happens to people who are supposed to be celibate? Or what would it have been like had she yielded to him? Would the world of men have entered her life?

Channel 50

The experience with the other priest, the one in England was strictly platonic because it was happening only in the mind of Pelegrine--like so many of her loves and desires. She adored yet again a stranger. Again she went on confession binges after requesting a bilingual priest. She hurled her sins at him. In the past, she would scrutinize and carefully compose her consolidated items on her sin list. But now she dug out every possible infraction and split sins in two so she would have long enough sin lists. Because as long as she had sins, she could go there, keep confessing and be near him. She wanted time to stop still and regretted when she ran out of the Ten Commandments and could not invent any more new sins. Once they have been recited, the priest absolves the sinner and sends you on your way. Those days she must have been the cleanest soul in London, purging her soul of yet uncommitted sins. She was cleansing her subconscious and spent extended moments in a musky confession booth with her London fascination she could not see very well in the dim light. She could only feel him, smell him and sense him behind a ten-inch square window mesh that separated them. Because of this man, Pelegrine became once more a loyal churchgoer, confessor of invented sins and consumer of several communions in one day, which probably was one great big old sin by itself. But she always figured Jesus had a sense of humor. He was her buddy when she pretended he was sharing her narrow little bed in boarding school. He, of all people, had to know her agony and would forgive her, she knew.

At some point she dragged Anya along who had to sit in the front row for several Sundays, spying on his eyes and glances, similar to the adolescent Fischberger investigation, where another girlfriend had to scrutinize the Sunday priestly ritual, which Pelegrine was convinced, was influenced by her presence. In both cases, the verdict was negative. But Pelegrine was certain that she did not just *imagine* a fantasy in both priests' routines. The new observer, Anya, also did not agree with Pelegrine that he looked at her more or that his glances lingered on her longer than on anybody else. Pelegrine was certain he was, even if Anya was blind. Her distant idol with his gentle, brown and somber eyes were surely not able to give clearer signals because then he would have been in conflict with his vows. But Pelegrine insisted his glances have been meant for her. She accepted the hopelessness of the situation as long as she got a glimpse of him. She could feel a few moments of joy that way.

In her thirteenth winter, Pelegrine's ski instructor aroused the same hot passionate obsession in her. She singled him out because he was handsome with blue eyes in a tanned leathery face. Yet he was only responding to shapely women studs and totally ignored her schoolgirl crush. Yet, for Pelegrine her feelings were real, even though they remained consistently unrequited.

When she was almost eighteen, she felt that same infatuation again for a man named Wolfgang who offered a weekly car ride home after twelve-hour school days when she attended her professional training school, the days that never ended with trains arriving home at ten at night leaving her village in the pitch black dark of the morning. The once-a-week school day, a week's worth of instructions crammed into one single day, surrounded by five eight-hour workdays.

Some of those long rides home where shortened because he had a car. She still came home sooner than usual even after having a drink with him in the "Oasis," a tavern on the road. This smooth operator got her home by nine, instead of midnight. He was something else. He had graying temples and

Pelegrine tried to sound knowledgeable about world affairs. She spoke about John F. Kennedy who was in the news a lot. Pelegrine, like Tante Josefa, was fond of the handsome American President.

Wolfgang arranged his travels to be Pelegrine's chauffeur for many Thursdays. Pelegrine liked him, not passionately but with a growing and sustained affection until, one day she found out he was married. He had maintained he was single. Pelegrine did not want to get mixed up in older people's confusions. She reasoned that he was too old, anyway, more like a father. That could have never worked, she decided, and got over him. She cried only for one whole day.

Channel 51

With Bill Folks, the principal at MOTC, it did not matter that he, too, had graying sideburns. He aroused her feelings the same way these other older men had. Again, he did not know anything about the girl's crush. But something completely unexpected happened at that school which turned her head around rapidly, not only away from the principal but also from her mild engagement with an architect she had met at the sports car garage.

At that point Pelegrine had moved in with Zora, a Hungarian Zsa Zsa Gabor-looking blonde whom she discovered at her new night job as a Texaco telephone credit collector. Zora was recovering from a divorce and was living in a big house. She encouraged Pelegrine to share it with her, even agreeing to house Pelegrine's piano she was renting for 6 dollars a month. Pelegrine was looking for a piano teacher and Zora recommended Maxine, an ex-concert pianist and a real minister. Maxine was a trip.

She was enormous, tall and awesome, like a Rhino. Zora said that Maxine was gay and a real manly acting woman. Pelegrine had confided in Zora her one-time experience with Rita and also the fact that she did not know how to go about finding out more about that kind of life just in case she was meant to live that way. Since Pelegrine had trouble getting what she wanted, especially those crushes of her past, she never involved herself deeply with that which she could actually get. In those instances, she pulled back immediately when the action got serious. She attributed that perhaps to inexperience and an inclination toward a dual sexuality, an orientation of which she knew absolutely nothing. Zora thought maybe Maxine could help enlighten the confusion.

Maxine was a tough piano teacher all right. The dominating woman made her memorize Debussy and Bach and would not let her go till she played everything perfectly. But Maxine as a sexual person did not attract Pelegrine at all. She actually repelled her. Maxine started confiding in Pelegrine that she herself had the hots for one of her married students, a silly acting woman, Pelegrine thought. And ugly. But if that's what Maxine wanted, more power to her. It was wonderful that Maxine did not express interest in Pelegrine who wanted only piano lessons from her. It was also wonderful that Pelegrine met her first woman-oriented woman. But Pelegrine could not open up and talk about her troubles to Maxine because she appeared vulgar in her desire for the married woman.

One afternoon, a blonde, shorthaired, very butchy looking girl interrupted the lesson. She was introduced as Miro, Maxine's daughter. Wow. Lightening struck Pelegrine. That Miro was cute. And clever. She must have picked up the vibes, because before long, Pelegrine was visiting her and her girlfriend, Toby. They were friendly and a totally new kind of people Pelegrine had ever known. They always needed something from her, though. After Pelegrine's school day ended, they asked for a thousand car rides since they did not own wheels. What was strange and unexplained was that Pelegrine always had to stop at certain street corners, wait in the car, was urged not get out, wait and wait and, finally, drive them back home. In exchange they indulged Pelegrine with unusual presents. Sometimes they would deliver a dress, brand new, a skirt, bathing suit, a brief case or food. They never could say where they got the stuff. All they kept saying was for Pelegrine not to ask questions or to worry.

As time progressed, Pelegrine started getting attracted to Miro who was debonair and beautiful and bold. After dropping them off one night, Pelegrine stayed on the couch. Miro appeared in the middle of the night and made love to Pelegrine like nobody had ever before. That girl was experienced, knew how to move her hands and Pelegrine who had worked overtime with Rita, relished Miro's expertise. Miro teased Pelegrine's clitoris between two fingers squeezing gently while moving her body to the rhythm of the night. Pelegrine was anxious to return her pleasures. But Miro was strange. She did not want to be touched and caressed, at all. She was the only one that operated and "did" the partner. Pelegrine was absolutely aghast. In no movie or book had she ever heard of something like that. But she was much too infatuated with Miro to refuse her in spite of such a weird one-sided affair. Pelegrine would have let this go on. But Zora and the lice ended the one-way deal for Pelegrine.

Channel 52

Pelegrine was driving her second car at that point because she "lost" her Plymouth to the dope addicts. They had been after her to lend them the old Plymouth and eventually wanted to buy it from Pelegrine who had saved up six hundred dollars and bought a yellow 1959 MGA convertible. She loaned the Plymouth to Miro and Toby. They promised to pay as soon as they earned the money. Pelegrine wanted one hundred dollars.

After the night on their couch, Pelegrine's groin was itching for no explainable reason. She scratched and scratched and could have torn out every single hair because there was no relief. She also knew no one with whom could she discuss her affliction. An itchy groin. Who wanted to know? Nobody. For some reason the word "Filzläuse" from war movies came to her mind. She translated the word and learned that she was probably suffering from crab lice that thrived in genital temperatures. She was horrified and deeply shamed and had no idea what to do. The days became one long, endless agony until she could no longer endure the discomfort. She wrote a note to the pharmacist explaining that a neighbor of Mrs. So-and-so had crabs. She asked him to please give some medicine to the errand girl delivering this message. Pelegrine handed the pharmacist this handwritten paper and pretended she knew nothing of its content. It worked. The man presented her with a tube and written instructions. Pelegrine hurried home and instantly began her treatment.

Not only the lice but also another, most revealing and unforgettable scene took place in Miro's apartment that night. Pelegrine had only heard the word "dope" but had no grasp of what that actually was and what kind of people did that and the kind of lives they lived. Miro and Toby were heroine addicts. They simply tied their arms and injected heroine into their veins right in front of Pelegrine's eyes. They produced a candle, a spoon and tied a rubber belt around their biceps. It looked like they were getting ready for a blood pressure reading. Pelegrine just watched and absorbed every detail. She knew had they asked her if she was interested that she would scream NO. But they never asked. Toby started acting weird and it turned out that she almost overdosed. Pelegrine helped to get her in the shower and held her head under the gushing water. For Pelegrine it was a movie, a real-life movie. She was a little scared but didn't think she was in any danger herself. She knew that she would never do something like that, but watching was o.k.

Now she also remembered when driving Miro once, who had shown her the inside of her arm and asked if Pelegrine had not noticed those marks and blue bruises. Pelegrine said that she would not know what any mark signified other than an injury or some kind of birth defect. It never occurred to her to think otherwise. Miro shock her head in disbelief how anybody could be that stupid. But Pelegrine did not feel stupid since she had never been around a drug scene and knew that after this experience she never would again. It was no fun watching them withdraw from the real world. Plus the two girls became totally unreliable, never paid for the car, and were getting too demanding toward Pelegrine.

When she first moved in with Zora, Pelegrine even had affectionate feelings toward her. But Zora very quickly indicated that she only liked men and could not return feelings of that nature. Pelegrine accepted that. However. A few months later, after she had been intimate with Miro twice, she was more than startled when she found Miro and Zora screwing one night. She was hurt on more than one account. Miro, the expert lover, the one who did not allow reciprocal lovemaking, the heroine addict, the owner of crab lice, came and took everything there was to take. The car, Pelegrine and even Zora who said she did not like girls and whom Pelegrine had given up. And Zora, the bitch who said she only liked men, also betrayed Pelegrine.

Pelegrine moved out of Zora's house the next day and into an apartment in Hollywood. It was a cheap, two-room efficiency on Fernwood Drive, right behind Sunset Boulevard. After she had lived there for three months, the house manager's position became vacant and as she came home one day, Pelegrine met the new managers. Imagine her surprise when she saw the dope addicts, Miro and Toby having that job! It came as total shock to Pelegrine how these people found out where she lived and why they shadowed her like that? After all, they still owed her the car money. Pelegrine became very uncomfortable living in an environment that employed people like that. She finally realized that they never held real jobs. Their money was made in prostitution or stealing. They used the housemaster's position as a cover up for ways to earn money. Also at that time Pelegrine tried very hard to make it work with the handsome architect guy she had met at the garage that worked on her MG.

Channel 53

He drove a dark green Porsche, was eleven years older than Pelegrine and had a little gray in his hair. He was divorced, extremely attractive, and lived in a neat old house in the hills of L.A. Pelegrine spent many evenings there on his veranda, listening to his own jazz improvisations on the piano. He turned her on to this type of music. Through him she learned about Dave Brubeck,

Thelonius Monk and her favorite, Gil Evans. Gary was gentle and did not pressure Pelegrine. On Sundays they walked on the beach and he showed her the buildings he had designed and the ones he was working on. He began sharing his life with her. They cooked together, watched the moon and loved driving each other's sports cars. His was a lot faster, but hers was a beauty. Pelegrine felt pretty outclassed by this man. But she knew if she could hang around him long enough and learn from him, that maybe he would not notice that she was learning everything right under his nose. Pelegrine was still going to the adult high school and was about to graduate in the spring of 1967. She was twenty-two. During the winter term there she took a strong liking to her English teacher, Pontiac Wingo.

Channel 54

But the English teacher paid her no attention. Until Pelegrine was rocking in her chair, wild enough to fall over, and the woman had to throw Pelegrine out of the classroom. With shame and disappointment Pelegrine spent the rest of the hour on the steps outside the door. She did not want to miss what was said in her absence. The next day was awkward but not for long. Pelegrine tried a little harder to chat less with her friends. She only behaved that way to catch the teacher's interest. And it actually did work. Except. The kind of attention she got, was not what she had in mind. She really did not know what she was after, not even why she was climbing up the bathroom window to catch a glimpse of the teacher as she was leaving the building. Pelegrine wanted to know what car she was driving. She pranced into the parking lot, inspected the car, bent into the convertible to read her address attached in a plastic cover around the steering column. Pelegrine actually scared herself when she went that far. She decided to leave it at that. She took all the courses possible from this teacher whom Pelegrine respected, admired and adored. Pontiac Wingo was fierce and firm, but ever so eloquent with the English language. She was an orator and kept an audience spell bound with print-ready diction and poetry in her language. No matter what Pelegrine did, the teacher barely took notice of her, was kind in her words but did not go out of her way to encourage any interaction. Pelegrine felt extremely inferior to this person and would not have known what to talk about, anyway. Maybe that's why she avoided normal mingling, fearing a lack of discussion topics. Who knows? At any rate, Pelegrine's preoccupation with this teacher brought about a dwindling interest in Bill Folks who, they said, was queer. And Pelegrine wrote, all-knowingly, in her diary,

"Who needs that"?

Channel 55

Pelegrine graduated with honors and was accepted at Los Angeles City College with provisional remedial English instructions. All other courses she could take on a normal basis. Academic and intelligent English was Pelegrine's weakest spot. She had no problem talking or writing. But the elevated way of speaking, reading and drawing intelligent inferences were too difficult for her. Staying focused a long time on one topic was also difficult. Her syntax was awkward, sometimes even incomprehensible. She struggled with the language, history and sociology but had fun in her German class. Even though she wasn't learning the language per se, she was learning it from an educated perspective. She had no idea what present perfect and plusquamperfect, or imperative, accusative or genitive concepts were. If these abstractions could not trigger a reality she had experienced in her eleven grades of schooling, the translated terms today were useless. And when she did understand, finally, that dative signified the indirect object, it only reminded her that such knowledge never counted among her strength, even back then. Did not Elli help out many times when Pelegrine had an essay assignment? It was Elli who dictated the prose and Pelegrine fudged it up so that it wouldn't sound like her mother talking, because then the teacher and the whole class would know that she was too stupid to write her own essays. But the teacher seemed to know anyway, since she had to write corrections in class where Pelegrine had difficulties to produce matching versions. Pelegrine then decided to do her own mediocre stuff because replicating her mother's prose was impossible.

In distant California, her illiterate grammar caught up with Pelegrine. She studied her butt off with Mrs. Ulrich, a native German lady herself, who did not have much faith in Pelegrine. She thought the girl lacked what it needed and advised Pelegrine strongly against such a career after Pelegrine had meekly inquired if it were a good idea to study one's native language to the utmost polish and then teach German in America. Mrs. Ulrich told Pelegrine such a profession, even though it seemed easy to the undiscerning eye, required lots of dedication, preparation and the highest professional degree available. She doubted that Pelegrine would stick with it long enough to fulfill these conditions. And in some way, Pelegrine agreed with her. She was not sure she could produce high callipered sentences. It then seemed a superfluous pursuit. Since everything was so hard, Pelegrine classified her skills and decided to perfect those, which she already knew a little. But such an analysis put her right back to her native language again.

When she contemplated an eventual return to Europe, perfect English became a necessity also. And this subject seemed even more out of sync with struggling Pelegrine who could not get the fifty US Presidents right, the prohibition, the civil war or the Hopi Indians. Not to speak of Algebra, Trig, geometry and plain math. The long haul seemed endless. The dinners with Gary, the full time summer job at Preferred Creditors--nothing made things easier. The fears of the dope addicts in her apartment complex did not help either.

Channel 56

After her first good grades, she decided to write to Pontiac Reynaldo Wingo, the English teacher from the adult high school. Pelegrine wrote that she was doing well and that she wished they were acquainted better. She wanted to apologize for her bad classroom behavior and just connect with her. Within a week she had a reply, the most inspiring and eloquent letter she had ever, ever received. During her dinner with Gary, Pelegrine was reading to him what this wonderful teacher wrote. Even he thought she sounded terrific but wasn't nearly as interested in the details of that friendship as Pelegrine was. Pelegrine invited Pontiac Wingo for lunch and picked her up in the yellow MG in the school parking lot that she had eyed from the windows above, six months before.

Turbulent times were in store for the two women. After this initial rendezvous, they became inseparable. Pelegrine and Pontiac spent hours on the beaches, lying head to head till the morning sun interrupted them and they had to go home to sleep. Or Pontiac had to crawl into the window of the house where her husband, Tolstoy, was sleeping. The attraction between teacher and ex-student was motion unleashed and unstoppable. Both of them were swept away by an avalanche of love and affection. When Pontiac asked Pelegrine if something like this had ever happened to her before, the girl shyly nodded and commenced to tell the woeful memories of Rita. Otherwise, she conceded, Pontiac was the first real experience for her, too. They met for lunches at Pelegrine's apartment where Pontiac was fixing a salad once and asked for a big bowl. Pelegrine did not know they made bowls as big as she requested. She emptied the refrigerator vegetable drawer and produced a bowl. Both laughed at Pelegrine's inventiveness. Pontiac also asked for beer. Pelegrine had an old, partially drunk, corked bottle in the fridge and Pontiac screamed with laughter when she saw that. It had never occurred to her that somebody did not know that opened beer would not keep. Well, Pelegrine did not know. But she was learning fast, light years in a second. And Pontiac became a willing, masterful teacher, companion and lover. When they first exchanged kisses, Pontiac wondered how they would know what to do, since she had been married for seven years, but had never loved a woman. Should they go to the library and get books?

"Hell, no." Pelegrine wistfully smiled and heard herself speak like a hundred year old sage. "I'll be damned, if somebody has to tell me how to love. Pontiac, we just follow our feelings. The rest will happen by itself. Believe me."

And right she was. They were a remarkable couple, committed and loving. It was the first time for Pelegrine that she had a real beloved of her own. The two women safeguarded and nurtured their relationship. Pontiac was concerned about Pelegrine's safety when she heard about the dope addicts and she suggested one day, that Pelegrine move in with her and Tolstoy.

Channel 57

It was not unusual for Pontiac to have houseguests. Her household was an artistic one. Without exception, there were poetry readings, painters, potters or intellectuals floating about. Many spent the night after pontificating and drinking too much beer or wine. Tolstoy and Pelegrine found each other agreeable, except Pelegrine thought him to be a bit pompous and relying too much on Pontiac's expertise, for it was she who had to cut off her Yale studies to support him to get his masters degree. Both of them were poets. Only he was competing with her. She was the genius. When Pelegrine moved in, Pontiac was still sleeping with Tolstoy. But she spent part of every night with Pelegrine. Pontiac needed time to explain the situation and was unsure how to break the reality to him. He had wanted children but their efforts were in vain which deeply disappointed him. He also excelled as a businessman and needed a willing wife talking with the ladies in the parlor while the men carried-on men's talk in the brandy and cigar rooms. However, that is where Pontiac also preferred to be. She found the conversations with the pink ladies cumbersome and exhausting. Tolstoy disliked her preferences because he required a different wife. He needed Pontiac and especially loved her for nursing his epilepsy with injections and lots of mothering.

The *ménage a trois* survived several months in a seemingly idyllic routine. Until one graying morning, Pontiac had forgotten to return to her marital bed before daybreak and Tolstoy inadvertently discovered the two women together. Finally, the mystery was out. A big scene, fighting matches, a separation and eventually a divorce ensued. After those ordeals, the two where together for Pelegrine's ten happiest years of her life.

Channel 58

Pontiac mentored and nurtured Pelegrine in every way this human waif needed it. Pontiac was a writer, a poet and a most eloquent speaker, orator and thinker. Pelegrine had never known anybody like that before and after. She always contended that Pontiac should have been a stateswoman, a leader of a country or a college president. She was a master politician as much as she was a superior Shakespearean scholar. In Pontiac, Pelegrine found her private teacher, tutor, lover, mentor and mother, all in one. Pelegrine learned from Pontiac not only to value education but also developed the commitment to persevere to reach unimaginable intellectual heights. Pontiac instilled in the girl the intrinsic advantages of being a well-rounded humanist and abhor becoming a mere fact finder and research robot. Pontiac stressed that no matter what people strive for, they must address the education of their soul. She once replied to a student technocrat, "You have to be a man and human being first, before you become a dentist. You'll never be a good doctor if your humanity is undernourished." Words such as these stuck with Pelegrine and became her own guiding principles.

Channel 59

Pelegrine and Pontiac moved to the East Coast, where Pontiac was teaching English at a small liberal arts college. With stipends and scholarships, and selling Kentucky Fried Chicken when not cataloguing library books, Pelegrine paid for her undergraduate education. It was a slow and arduous journey. But in this southern college setting, with dedicated literature instructors and with Pontiac's tutelage, Pelegrine began her own intellectual bloom. She slowly excelled in all subjects and graduated in 1971 summa cum laude with a double major in German and English Language and Literature.

As a graduation present, Pelegrine and Pontiac went to Europe together. Pelegrine wanted to share her history and people with her mate. It was Pelegrine's first visit to Austria after six years. She began to understand what Thomas Wolff meant by the concept *you cannot go home again*. She was away too long and Uncle Albert's prophecy when she was a young child was fulfilled, "Don't ever leave your country. If you do, you will be sorry because you are a stranger in two worlds. You will never really be one of them at home. Never again. Always an admired visitor. Your language will deteriorate and you lose touch. And in America, too, you will always be a foreigner. Your speech will forever have this foreign tint. They'll never stop asking,

"Where are you from?"

For the first but not for the last time, Pelegrine began to feel the impact of these words.

Six years had taken their toll. People had developed. Cheap buildings were torn down and paved streets meandered where Pelegrine once played in the mines, puddles and rubble of an old, war-torn world. Only limited visits were possible from then on.

Channel 60

After Pontiac and Pelegrine had been together for seven years, Pelegrine went to Europe by herself. She needed to go alone. Having a foreign guest along during the first trip, sparked special tensions. She couldn't do everything she had wanted and remained primarily concerned with Pontiac's language problems which meant leaving much of her own needs unanswered. Pontiac was also strong in her attitude and Pelegrine found herself as a mediator between two cultures. Pontiac was not the yielder that Pelegrine was. Thus Pelegrine had a problem. She was torn between her own acquiescing nature and Pontiac's extremely strong and stubborn personality, which asserted itself even in translated transactions. And people did not really know who THAT woman was, anyway. She seemed to exert a lot of influence on Pelegrine they noted and was outspoken through her translator in her decisive rejections of their old-fashioned, chauvinistic Germanic patriarchy, prevalent in most of Pelegrine's visiting circles. And Pelegrine was not accustomed to take a stand and protest what she didn't like right at the moment. She tended to have a Charlie Chaplin "delayed reaction. " She reacted later, often in private after she was choked with overdue explosions. She then, finally, followed her drummer and answered her own needs. But only so much later.

This intense relationship with all its trimmings is best reported through Pontiac's diligent log she kept while her other half was away for an extended time. Pelegrine's letters are also included to shed light on the intense closeness of their relationship, how much they loved and depended (co-depended) on each other. Their correspondence will also illuminate their interactions with one another; possibly even prefigure the outcome of their life together? Perhaps? These chronicles will furthermore demonstrate their level of language mastery. Pelegrine could never match Pontiac. And so it goes.

Channel 61

    Pontiac's Home Log begins on June 23, 1974:

Arrived home from Augusta airport approximately the same time you are due to arrive in Atlanta. I decided to keep a daily log because I am prone to forgetfulness and thus may leave some "crucial" tidbit out. Turned on TV. and watched the end of Americas Cup Championship Golf. Jim Corbett won after a 4-way tie in what is called a "sudden death" play-off. (I'll explain if you like). <u>Sixty Minutes</u> *was not on because of the play-off. I watched "The Odd Couple." Excruciating. Ate dinner. The leftover potato pancake. I had one for dinner and put the other in my lunch for tomorrow. Then went out and watered the flowers and tomatoes. Sometime before 8 o'clock, I thought I heard a car door slam. So did Jim and the dogs. It was Koon and somebody in a pick-up truck. They came and got the left-over pipe (taking away your wedge on the pump shed.) I guess Koon is selling it for scrap metal. I found a short, thick board and put it against the plank that protects the lounge chairs. I hope it will stay securely.*

    The movie has begun. Diana Rigg plays a suffragette reporter. May be interesting. The heat has broken sufficiently for me to open the house and turn off the air conditioner. Everybody is in except you. It is now 8:40 p.m. and you are due into Philadelphia. I wish I were there to greet you. Augie came in a few minutes ago and went immediately to the bathroom window. Thank goodness, you obtained the stick to hold it up.

    You called, of course. And I could only marvel that you got off that damn wrong bus in time. Please, be at least couth to Jon. After all he traveled so far to see you. But <u>ah</u>*. I did not expect to hear your voice. And it shall stay warm in my ear until I hear it again. I do love you. (Being paged in an international airport is something that usually* <u>only</u> *happens in the movies! Also taking one's own bottle of bourbon to Europe is something that only hardened Southerners do!)*

Channel 62

On June 23, Pelegrine wrote a note to Pontiac to be opened after she had left.

My darling Pontiac!

I love you. It's so hard to write now when I am already missing you so! You call me the sentimental one--the Germanic mentality is famous for its romantic attachments--and I match your seemingly cool and composed affection, which, too, knows its soft spots. I just love you with smiles and tears, laughter and sorrow--any way I can show it! Don't you ever let me go away temporarily again. What a foolish pain. We don't have bad times--why invent them? Also, while I talked to the nuns, there was talk to come back safely, of course, for my job--but really, for you, precious! That is why I will not take chances--not get into Jan's car or compete with European assholes on the road. I will save myself for you. I am so glad you let me be sentimental and love me even in my Schmaltz. It is good to write to you again. This time I speak from my head and don't need to impress you with badly quoted sources. I speak to you the way I love you--impulsively, sentimentally, sweetly, REALLY, always! I won't even quote Zelda or Fitz. I don't need to anymore. Right!

You are my baby. I love you.   Pelegrine.

Channel 63

Pontiac writes on June 24:

I took the radio to the bedroom and listened till after eleven when I dropped off to sleep. <u>Everybody</u> but the fishes was in the bedroom! I held your pillow as I drifted off. It wasn't quite enough. Around 4 a.m. this morning, I woke up and imagined that about that time you'd be landing in Cologne. It is 5:30 in the afternoon here now, so I guess you are asleep at this moment.

Interesting. You are at the moment living life almost a day ahead of me. I am experiencing Monday, June 24 now, but you have done with that day and are into what is tomorrow for me. There must be some sweeping truth we can gain from that but I can't think what it might be.

I interviewed two men for the English instructor's job. One from Florida and one from Michigan. The one from Michigan seems more the technical college type--young, just out of grad school but with some experience from an open enrollment type of school. I'm sure he turned Sonny off because Markos (the kid's name) has longish hair, beard, etc. I gave him a higher rating than the Florida fellow though he seemed O.K. too. But the guy from Florida did pass on a bit of information--community colleges in Florida are feeling the money bite and tightening up. Seems they too are letting people go. He didn't say so, but I think he's been let go. I gave him a good rating. I think Sonny likes him best anyway.

The Pest Control man came today so the house stinks and I am suffocating with the odor. This morning wasn't so bad. I feed the animals, the fishes, and myself and got to work by 8:10! I missed our daily morning Rieber session. (Mr.Rieber was a character in the movie <u>Ship of Fools</u> and played by José Ferera. He was mostly difficult and a chronic faultfinder. Pelegrine got his nickname because sometime she behaved like Mr. Rieber. So any bickering between Pontiac and Pelegrine was labeled "Riebering.") Everybody asks if I am lonesome. I lie and say of course not! I will stop and watch the news. But you still interrupt. I find myself thinking of you in crucial moments.

After the news, I wrote cards to Kathy Hill and Will tonight. Decided not to spend money on a phone call.

Channel 64

Pelegrine writes on June 25 from Germany:

Dearest Pontiac!

I have had a B.M.! After five days! Shitting American food into a German john is exhilarating. Wouldn't you know, my sweet one, it is raining and my warm clothes are immediately unfolded with your and our sweet home smell in them. A three-hour trip from Cologne to Frankfurt took five hours. The train just sat and sat at one point of the journey. Seemed that the locomotive was exchanged. Anyway, picture this: I sit, squashed at the window with three Africans and a baby. No word of English or German. Across, two guest workers rattling in Turkish, eating giant, doughnut-looking bread things. I, hungry, hot and ill at ease, suffer in the stopped train. Suddenly, the baby next to me is breast-fed! I nearly faint. The train still isn't moving. After an eternity, train moves and baby vomits, partly on me. It was so "cozy." It was a nightmare.

In Frankfurt, my sister had waited for the wrong train--therefore missed me altogether. I find a wheeled cart thing and drive with its brakes on until somebody yells, "Push down on handle." Then the contraption moved. I had to hunt rental after rental agencies. If they had cars, they were Mercedes, only. The last place rented me an Opel Kadett. I am doing O.K. on the road. Plane didn't leave until two hours later because the stewardesses were late that put everybody in slight panic. I hardly talked to anyone on the plane or in Cologne. With my sister, it is the first time in nearly 64 hours that I speak in sentences with somebody again. I was terribly depressed and felt misplaced for quite a while after I landed. Now I'm gaining ground. Traveling alone can be shitty. When I get to Mutti, it will be all right. The German boys and girls look so strange. The boys' pants make them look like dancers--everything is so tight. They look gay in comparison to the American loose fitting macho style. The girls look more like in the U.S. But all, men and women, carry shopping bags forever and are always on the run to somewhere. It's all very strange. A real culture shock.

My baby, my soul. I love you and anxiously wait to hear from you. Your letter helped my spirits tremendously. You said the right things.
Your everything,
Your Pelegrine

Channel 65

    Pontiac writes on June 25:

I am going to stop watching "To Tell the Truth." For two days, I have been completely wrong. Those <u>you</u> would have voted for have been the <u>real</u> ones.

I've got 1/2 bushel of Kentucky Wonders from Sarah and I am busily engaged in preparing them. Tomorrow night, I'll can them. I need your help.

Later. I am still fixing those damn beans. But I did stop to fry two pieces of chicken breast for dinner--or rather I'll take one for lunch.

    Later. Well, Pelegrine, Kuch (a nickname coming from the German word Kuchen=cake. They loved to label each other endearing names characterizing their temperament and mental condition.) Last night I stopped everything because there was a pretty good TV. presentation on Mark Twain's home in Hartford, Connecticut. Today, I am canning what I prepared yesterday--we'll have nine pints of green beans--squirrels gathering nuts for winter--when you come home.

    I am also watching the third presentation of <u>Primal Man</u> on TV. tonight. It is excellent. It deals with Neanderthal and Cro-Magnon man. You would have profited from it. But they'll always re-run it.

    Sara is continuing with her protest. She has gone through Step One, which asked for re-instatement. The college president refused. Step Two is to ask for a conference and to inform them that she is going through grievance. The fellow at the state office is advising her at every step. He is even writing her letters--I don't have to.

    Tonight, I thawed some spaghetti sauce, put kidney beans into it and some herbs, so I am having chili tonight for supper. Shirley brought me a bag of squash, beets, and cucumbers. I'll cook some of it tomorrow. I might pickle the beets for you.

    Oh yes. Little tiny tomatoes on the bushes! I discovered them today. But I don't think the ones near the pump house will really make it. We'll see.

    What I am not saying is this is one hell of an empty house. I usually don't even bother to come home before 5:00. I do so much love and miss you.

Pontiac writes on June 27:
I have just received your first correspondence and have immediately written my first to you. I noticed the big Angelfish had died. He was alive this morning and this afternoon. Cause of death unknown. No sign of barb's having eaten away at him.

I am watching a Richard Burton bad movie on TV. Today in the newspaper, it was announced that Burton and Elizabeth Taylor had been granted a divorce. Augie just decided to come home. Wants dry food but I refuse. They have not eaten their regular meal this morning.

I came home today absolutely exhausted. I had two interviews with job prospects. My favorite is still that Markos fellow whom I doubt they will hire. Another one today--again from Florida, looks good, not so much as a teacher but possibly as an instructional materials man. Tomorrow, I have to meet with Sonny and give my recommendation--which does not mean it will be followed.

Kuch, your little card almost broke my heart. No Kaka, (baby talk for bowl movement) checking into a gloomy room and going alone to the Dome. And speaking to no one for so many hours! My Kuch! I would love to bring you close to me and hold your head, your burled head. I should not let you suffer these things. My baby.

I will stop now and experimentally freeze some squash.

Channel 66
Pelegrine writes on June 27:
My sunshine!

Beginning with this letter, I will write and save it till I have more of a letter. That way you'll get news stitched together like a quilt. Every night, I'll sit down and add my day.

Tonight it rains a good rain. I am lying in bed and shift from side to side so I can write. I rented a car, which cost me 100 dollars for four days. This horrendous rate includes 3.20 per day insurance. The car is rented through Friday. I intended to leave Friday. Yet!

Today, on the 27, Thursday morning, I got a letter from your brother, Keith. Zange and I immediately drove about 60 miles to find him in the barracks. He was thrilled. He was on his way to Worms to oversee ceremonies for the outgoing commander. Yet, when we descended, he changed his plans and spent lunch and the afternoon with us in an army cafe. Zange and I ate Bratwurst which Keith, sweet Keith, insisted to pay. He still needs to adjust so much--not only to being back in the service, but in Germany, the base, which really isn't a base but some point of operation. He also is adjusting to his new duties resulting from his degree and mostly to the feeling of guilt of his problems at home and denying his children a father. He wants to go out once while I am still here and we suggested Saturday. So I changed my plans and will leave on Monday morning, July 1. We will pick Keith up in Frankfurt and have a night on town. He will spend the night here at Zange's. Otherwise it would be too troublesome. Keith's car won't be here for three weeks. So what am I to do? Keep my rented car for another 100 dollars for the weekend, so two cars (Jan's and mine) can escort Keith around? Or shall I return the car as planned on Friday and for the weekend with Keith, travel in the Jan's car with me urging that Zange drive? I am in a shit fix. Why didn't you speculate on the probable improbability? I know I promised that I wouldn't get in a car that Jan drove after what we experienced with him, jerking us around on the backseat in 1971. I know we are retaliating in our own way. We just don't drive with maniacs like him. Period. But the truth is that I can't afford 200 dollars right smack for a car! Keith looks forward and I didn't have the heart to leave tomorrow, sorry. He also plans to come and visit me in Austria and I'll show him the wine places. Darling what shall I do? I don't want to break my promise to you. I could cry. I don't want to have to lie to you either. Since Keith will be in the car with me, your stipulation is actually altered. He'll provide safety and I will not have ridden with Jan. Keith

<u>and</u> I will have. Oh, please, let it be O.K.

I fixed tuna salad today and a Martini with cream cheese and Jalapeno Sauce. Everybody liked it.

I love and miss you. How are my baby animals? Please, write me. I need a letter from home. I put 50 kisses right here on this X. I'll start the travel-log-type letter next time. This one has to be mailed. I love you. Your, baby, always, Pelegrine.

Channel 67

Pontiac writes on June 28:

Kuchen,

This whole week I have read next to nothing. Not even <u>Time</u>, not even <u>Watergate</u> transcripts. If I don't read, I am empty in mind and know no satisfaction. It is, I am aware, a psychological thing. But I am quite disturbed about this peculiar result of your absence. Up till this point, there is no time in my memory that this one thing I have always done since I first learned how to was not uppermost to me--as important as eating and drinking. A thing of survival, even. I think my full living would stop if I did not read and learn.

You used to get so exasperated with me when I would read and not listen, or half-read and half-listen. I think it is as if the pole of my life has shifted. I have not shed a tear in your absence. I have held it in. But by taking care of appearances, other more important things are out of whack. I think I am in bad shape. I keep the radio on all night. I sit outside with a book in my hand and just marvel at the grass, the clouds in the sky, the trees. That's not bad. But then I come in and watch bad TV. programs while I eat. My own love. I must attempt to adjust. I wrote a letter to you.

Pontiac writes on June 30:

I am in the process of finishing my household chores. Yesterday I washed clothes and did the monthly shopping and picked up. Today I am finishing the house, packing and preparing for Eleanor and Margaret who will be here around six. They will spend the night. Eleanor and I will head south and Margaret back to Newton.

All in all, it has been a pretty bad week. And today I am despondent. I wish you were here, packing to leave with me. I will try to keep a diary for you in my little travel notebook and then pick up this when I return home. And when I come home, I expect to find a mailbox full of letters from you! I am beginning to exist simply from one mail delivery to the next. I have every line from you on the table next to my bed.

Channel 68

Pelegrine writes in July 1:

Darling Baby,

Today I left my sister. I am now on the train to my mother. I have packed very efficiently and have nothing on which to write. But I found this paper towel and let the railroad provide my stationery this time. Keith spent a marvelous weekend with us. We took him to a typically Frankfurt Apple wine pub and afterwards we danced till 3 a.m. at a discotheque. He requested, however, not to tell his family anything about this. I guess we can understand. He really doesn't even want to talk about his family. I wanted him to have pictures of his children on him, your nieces and nephew. But he fumbled around and found none. I wanted to show them off. Somehow he was uncomfortable about his personal life. Pontiac, it's really bothering him. Nevertheless, he really had a grand time and was a perfect gentleman. We could not have been with a nicer person. He finds it so ironic that he suddenly is touring places that you have seen. I felt a Reynaldo by my side, wherever we went. His eyes remind everybody of your eyes and it was so good for me to feel you near through him. Interestingly enough, this time Zange and Jan seemed a little more willing to be good hosts. Zange was sweet, as I expected. But Keith found even Jan nice. He'll look them up sometime when his German improves. He spent the night on the couch, showered, ate and was a refreshing American presence. You would be pleased.

A pro pos the car. I returned the rental on Friday costing me 78 dollars. This was less than I expected, yet enough. Keith and I took relatively short trips with Jan, which were just fine. I also bought a 200-dollar camera for 60 dollars. A great piece. Keith thinks so. So far I have 250 dollars left. I also purchased better suitcase rollers because mine really did a lot of sliding, not rolling. This set is like those semi shopping bag wheels and have a sturdier, more manageable design. They cost 16 dollars. They have a regular frame which collapses like an antenna. This train is shaky but it lets me tell you that I love you. After having been with my sister, time seems to pass quickly. Zange and I enjoyed so much being good to each other. The baby's behind shifted often and I know much about that busy body in her belly--enough to reassure me not to want any! She exercises and will have a natural birth. Anesthetic births are rare and expensive.

I wish so much you and I traveled the way I am doing it now. Independent and only experiencing the best of all sides because that's all I leave time for. I hope I'll find some mail at home from you, waiting for me at Mama's. You are my only one. I am precious and really very cautious for you, my darling. You are on my mind and in my conversations. I love thee. Your only one, Pelegrine.

Pelegrine writes on July 3:

My Beloved,

Thinking of your instructions, I ordered today a "Gipsy Schnitzel" with string beans and a mixed salad. A potato was unavailable. During my wallowing-in-all-the-meats-and-breads, I do manage to get some veggies. I can't stop looking and absorbing. Every second thought is YOU, though. "Pontiac would love this and that" is all I think and say.

My Mutti bought a tiny little refrigerator (her first in her lifetime!) that has a frozen compartment to make tiny ice cubes in a tray. The bourbon and water was too cold for her, but lovely for me. She even requested a beer warmer yesterday. Also, I am largely wearing my warmer clothes, for it has rained quite much. I love the moisture and only suffer from slight rheumatism in my right thumb. Mama has a resin salve, collected resin from pine trees, bee's wax, and butter--melted together on the stove. The butter is added so that it won't harden. As a matter of fact, I've just been treated and I am writing to you with a handkerchief wrapped around my thumb. I also am recovering from a sore throat and nasty cough. This climate just got to me.

I took Mama swimming to the indoor pool. This pool I had planned to build for her when I was dreaming of such things as a little girl. But now the city beat me to it. Good. I had a shower and a shave. I feel so clean.

I rented an Austin Mini 1000 car for one month till August. Was cheaper than the on-and-off deals. The price will be determined by the km's I drive. In any case, they put it on my Bankamericard. Therefore, I know you don't mind, for it enables much more enjoyment and allows me to appear the way you wanted: independent, somebody who gives a damn, somebody who can afford it (with credit cards).

Tante Josefa is said to look forward to seeing me. I intend to pay for the first meal we have together.

Other than that, I am enjoying my home quietly with little trips here and yonder. I must read *You Can't Go Home Again*. So many changes and when the people die, the place gradually transforms into someone else's home--not mine anymore. I hate that kind of change and if that's what progress means, I hate it, too. I still want to grow wild on an island with long fingernails and you.

I miss you. I don't have the words anymore to say how much. This separation is like an ulcer. Everything beautiful is saddened by your absence. Also, I must look strange and foreign. People look at me like a curiosity while being very deferential. So far, I have not visited anybody, only Mama. They all talk so much of you and "Pontiac" seems to be on more than one mind. I LOVE YOU. I am trying so hard to be judicious in my collection of junk. Only what I can fit in the suitcase!

I wonder why I haven't heard from you? Maybe it's because you couldn't find my Mutti's Austrian address in Fechelaponte. That suddenly dawned on me.

Please, write me!!! 1000 kisses. Hug my animals Lenya, Sibi, Augie, Jim and the two tanks and you, your only one, Pelegrine.

Channel 69

    Pontiac writes on July 6:

Drove all the way from Jacksonville, deposited Eleanor in Newton, and returned home tonight. Dogs had dug out but apparently today because I think Johnnie would have attempted to repair it. They were under the house. Jim met me in the yard. I'm waiting for Augie to return. Fish O.K. I left them some of their timed-release food.

    I am convinced that Eleanor is verging on the unstable. Reasoning was never a big plus for her but I swear she is more irrational than ever. And her memory reminds me of Aunt Lori's four years ago. And going to St. Augustine with Eleanor was no pleasure. She didn't want to see but two things--the fort and the old church. And Kathy and I let her have her way. When we got to the fort, she ran (I mean it) from one corner to the other; didn't stop to read a single sign nor really see the magnificent harbor of the first settlement in America but ran, ran, ran.

    Listen, you and I will return. They have reproduced a strict-of-the-original old town. And there's an old-fashioned apothecary shop that Eleanor didn't want to spend any time in because it was only about 100 years old and not worth her time. Shit. You and I--especially you--would love it. I need you to travel with.

    I got your one letter. The car dilemma you solved in the right way. I will tell you in a letter tomorrow. But I want--and need--more mail from you.

    Stamford just called and tried to get me to say I'd fly to N.Y.C. the Friday before you arrive, meet you in Philadelphia and then come back. I don't want to use the money.

    On second, more penetrating look, at the fishes, one of the two zebras has a crooked body, red gills, and is dying. May be suffering from malnutrition.

Maybe I didn't leave enough food. The others seem O.K. Augie March is home.

Channel 70

Pelegrine writes on July 6:
Babylein!

Finally received your so longed for letter on July 4. You can expect six days for each letter, my beloved. Write me more often, please. You don't know how I need your touch. Your letter nurtured me immensely. I love and miss you so much that I don't know how to tell you. Don't get along too well without me. Leave the house a mess so I can fuss with you.

Yet, I must tell you, it's really good to love you over this little bridge of time. It hurts but once more I am aware that I have " an only one." The days are beginning to shape up. I cycle and recreate what I can. The people are charming and quite a few ask for you, especially those that I did not think actually would.

Soon I shall descend upon Vienna. I am doing well with the money-- have 205 dollars, still. I am not a big spender. I let everybody treat me if they want to and they do. I do miss your loving care--somebody who tells me if the meat is spoiled. Ate some suspicious meat burgers. Thought I had forgotten their taste. Wretched a lot. Had first day of period, yet danced non-stop anyway. I am often enchanted despite the fact that I experience everything somewhat subdued. Now I am lying in my bed with soft rain falling and I am beginning to feel homesick for the US. The narrowness and the elbow -rubbing got to me on a hung-over day. Nobody's lot I would trade. I rather hustle the way you and I do because we love and have each other. These people here don't have time to love. They only do their duties.

I am still driving very carefully with bike or car. Mama is enjoying the occasional outings and Mr. Sommer is graciously giving her the freedom to go alone with me. He does not insist that we drag him everywhere with his limping foot. I will construct two bookshelves and do some minor repairs for Mama. My reputation seems to spread. I love being a handy girl. How is my home holding up?

You should know how I am writing this letter. I write, think about you, dream and wonder, start to weep and, finally, end up writing again. This has been a very "sentimental journey." I am saddened by too many departures. I am teaching Mutti the right words to "Donna gem the gentlemental Johnny." She can't remember, that she needs to say, "going to take a sentimental journey." I may have to leave her with her own version and stop trying to change hers. She was pretty surprised for a minute when I told her that those World War Two words of hers are only phonetic renditions and not the real thing. She acknowledged it but just as quickly forgot that fact again.

I miss you. Please, write more often. I have mixed feelings of sadness and joy now when I watch time pass. You are the one I love over the ocean. Hugs and embraces for my family. T.S. Eliot's "Hurry up, please, it's time!" is telling you that your "Kleinelein" (little one) Pelegrine is coming soon.

Channel 71

Pontiac writes on July 8:

Didn't mention it in the letter I mailed today because I wanted to check with the State Farm Insurance man first--which I did today. On the way home from Jacksonville, somehow a stone from the road flew up, hit the windshield and shattered a circle of approximately four inches in diameter. On the passenger side. At first, Eleanor and I thought it was a shot but no hole appeared in the windshield--just a shattered place and neither one of us was hurt. I called the agent. He said "no problem. Come down, fill out a form and a repairmen will come by the house and fix it." No charge to me--not even 50 dollars deductible. It seems to pay to have a good policy. Thus far, State Farm seems to be living up to its reputation.

I sort of hoped to have a letter from you today. Your last one was dated 6/28. You should have gotten to Fechelaponte last Monday.

I got a bushel of butterbeans for 8 dollars from Sara. They are selling in the store for 49 cents per pound. So a considerable saving. I will try to shell them tonight—what a job alone!—and then can them tomorrow. Too much to do in one night.

Everybody asks about you. I hope you are remembering to write a few cards every now and then. I still cannot grow accustomed to being without you. Right now I am frying one chicken breast for dinner. I'll slice some tomatoes and cucumbers, which Sara gave me, and eat dinner whenever the spirit moves me.

On the radio, "Spinning Wheel" is playing. I recall listening to that with you in the summer of 1969 when we were in Jamestown, NY, and its environs. I remember that crazy little apartment and you! All that is meaningful in my memory is significantly filled with you. I do love you so.

Pontiac writes on July 9:
I got two letters today from my Only One who by then is even more predominantly here with me! And here I sit at the table, having just come home, talking with you and having a cold beer--as we always did when I arrived home from work.

By now, you should have received at least two letters from me. Then another letter and a card, I estimate, by next Monday or Tuesday. I will mail you another Thursday or Friday. There is, according to the dates on the letters, at least a week's delay. But you seemed worried in your 7/3 letter. I mailed my first letter to you on 6/26! So far I have five letters, including the one you left for me, and a card. These comprise my most precious wealth.

If you were here, we would probably be Riebering (Mr. Rieber, remember him?) I got home a little after four--so tired. P.R. work for the State Board, which is meeting tomorrow. Visiting reporters, calling TV. stations and radios, taking care of last minute details and also trying to do some teaching. I called off my classes for tomorrow. The Board will be here all day!

The first thing I did was run the dishwasher when I got home--after reading my darling's so needed letters. Then I put on some butterbeans to cook.

I didn't finish shelling the damn things last night. Shelled about 1/2 bushel and today, I have a small blister on my thumb. It definitely needs a kiss from the Kuchen.

Then I sat down, popped a beer, poured it into my Zipfer Stein, and re-read my baby's precious words. She has been purchasing goodies. 250 dollars balance is not all that bad. Plus the twenty dollars, which she will receive next week!

Wrote my Only One a long letter. She has been gone too long but will return a month from today.

Pontiac writes a few days later:
I am not feeling well today. And so took sinus medicine and slept and read all day. Did not go to work. I lay on the couch almost all day. Needed my Only.

Channel 72
Pelegrine writes on July 12:
My Only One,

Now I am in Vienna. It is still raining. Ever since I've been here, I've had rain. Too much is too much. My throat is perpetually sore. You will have to cure it.

Tante Josefa is extremely kind and conciliatory. Much I have learned about the whole mess with Albert and Coco, Rita and Alfred Lange. Since I never spoke, and I mean never, it is interesting to see what stories the Lange's spread not only to my uncle, but to my European relatives, as well. Human beings are strange beasts, primitive and nasty apes. Why didn't anybody ever ask me? Don't I have a side, too? Tante Josefa and I are both convinced that the Lange's, Albert's and Coco's best friends, must have tried to eliminate me through any means as an heir to their wealth. Albert and Coco are unfortunately too old to stand up to confrontations. And they never wanted to sponsor me for fear of unwanted turbulence. I wonder what all of them were really protecting and where I posed a threat? I will never know the truth because I got cleverly eliminated. Tante Josefa is writing something to the effect that my side was never heard and that I may have been wronged. But I don't know how they will react and if it is even a good idea. Since they love their friends more than me, why would they want to hear anything negative about their precious buddies? They should have asked me some questions if they cared for me when all that happened back then with Alfred. But nobody wanted to know what I had to say, remember, Pontiac?

So far, I still have had only one letter from you. I hope when I return to Fechelaponte, hordes of your mail will have flooded into Mutti's letterbox. I miss you but love you no less. I take many pictures so I can show you where I thought of you.

I enjoy sleeping in my old Viennese bed in my aunt's house where I spent so much time as a child. I have millions of old memories crawling out of the walls here. At least they are still intact like the bullet holes from the air raids. They haven't been repaired and are constant, at least for me right now.

Now I have been interrupted and your <u>second</u> letter was delivered. Mama forwarded it express here to Vienna. The poor Angelfish. I am glad you, too, get along so badly without the other half. Your second letter took a long time to get here. It arrived at Mama's eleven days after you mailed it. The damn mail service! I have written about four or five letters to you, so far. They, too, seem to take their time. I own 188 dollars. I have very little occasion to spend money.

The pictures I took with me are as much for me as they are for others. I need to see my places with you. It soothes me. I am afraid, you will hear an accent when I return. My cousin Manfred has passed his high school exam except English and Latin. He has to be re-tested in January. I practice English with him and I can hear my horrible accent. You must drill me upon my return.

Tante Josefa is much impressed with my accomplishments and so may be others who are not envious. This trip, my darling, was very necessary. Everybody is getting old.

It's pouring again. Those Europeans may be drowning in so much rain. Everybody is pissed off at the miserable season. My luck. Tante Josefa supplied me with sweaters and I am wallowing in warmth. So far, my summer clothes have been superfluous. Yet everybody is duly impressed with my own creations on the sewing machine.

Only thirty days to Eureka. Wait and love me. Soon the aggravator, Rieber, will be back. I need you. I love you always when we are apart or near, your Only One, Pelegrine.

Channel 73

Pontiac writes on July 13:

I feel much better today but am still taking some sinus medicine. What we need, darling, is a good rain to keep the dust down and to break this heat wave we're having. I received a letter today from my sweetheart. That one event did more than all the medicine in the world for me. I am washing clothes but will wait until Sunday morning to clean house. I also made room in the freezer and then froze six pint freezer bags of lima beans and two of crowder peas. When we build our home, we shall buy a freezer. Freezing is so much less work than canning. I think of you while I am "squirreling" away food. I say to myself--it's for the sweetheart--and so the work, even the heat, is worth it, for I have a special one to do it for. And I imagine showing all this to you when you return again to your family. You are therefore here always with me.

I am having a Stein of cold beer now and cooling off a bit before I hang out a load of clothes. Unfortunately, no darling clothes to hang out! For the past week, the moisture has hung heavily in the air but rain has refused to fall. Thus the humidity has been killing. In your letters, you constantly write of the rain and the cool temperature--you are wearing warm clothes. Ah, I would love to put on jeans and a sweatshirt and be comfortably snug. I hope this evening will be cool enough to mow a little. At least the side yard. It was not quite so hot when I just went out and there is a bit of a breeze blowing. Each evening since I returned from Florida last Saturday has been much too hot and humid even to sit outside until way past dark. The front yard could use mowing but the side yard demands it! You would be such a Rieber in this heat, darling. But even that would be good! I wrote you a letter.

Pontiac writes on July 15:

Yesterday was a little cooler--overcast--and so I mowed the side yard where the grass was thickest. Today, it jumped back into the high 90's and I don't think I'll even go out. Already, it has been hectic.

The people came while I was at school and put in a new windshield. That meant I had to go have the Toyota re-inspected, for it is against the law to remove the inspection sticker from one windshield and put it on another. I held my breath about the back tires but apparently, no one noticed anything, so I got the new sticker and also gassed up. Then I went by the A+P to pick a few things and also to get your 20 dollars for the letter. All the cashier had to give me was a ten dollar and ten ones. So I said, "What the hell? I'll send the baby ten dollars now and thirty in the next letter." I just couldn't see sending that much bulk through the mail. Also I am confident you at least momentarily have enough money for now. I worry about you on the return trip from Fechelaponte to Köln. I hope you are thinking ahead. No need to fret so like a mother hen. You can take care of yourself. But then, probably not as carefully as I would take care of you.

We need a good rain, darling, to break this intensive heat. The sun shows itself to be, indeed, a ball of fire as it hovers just above the treetops. It is relentless. At least, I keep the birdbath filled so they can get some relief. And Oh--you speak of rainy days. I wish for a week of steady, soft rain.

By the calendar, I have 27 days to wait until your homecoming. You have been gone 22 days! That's longer than six weeks, which I originally thought! Six weeks would have been 42 days. Your trip was for seven weeks! Never again will I let you out of my sight for this long!

Pontiac writes on July 16:

> Pelegrine,

We have to have a serious talk. This is very important. And I would like for us to approach the problem as rationally as possible. Granted, it is a very emotional subject but both of us must attempt to think and discuss this thing through. I will raise the first question--"Why didn't I get a letter today?"

Which is not a head but a heart question. Ah...I had hoped for a letter. I read your letters to the girls and boys. They don't understand but they miss you anyway. If I don't hear from you every three days, I become unhappy and sullen. Today was the third day. I am unhappy and sullen. I grew exceedingly angry when I checked the mailbox and had no letter from you! Jesus. I wished we had agreed that you would call transcontinental. That is an irrational statement but it is nonetheless true.

This late afternoon we had a brief but violent thunderstorm. It did not last long enough to really break the heat wave but it cooled the evening a little. It has been almost unendurable.

Dorothy Mist just called. I will spend next Sunday with them, have my haircut, and socialize. They have your card and are thrilled. It is amazing all the people we don't even consider who have real affection for old hateful and want to see her again.

After all, I, too, am lucky. Old hateful loves MICH. Did you know that Jim no longer sleeps on the bed? Only Augie and I. It has been so since you left. I'm not lying. Augie though has been faithful--like Balthazar when I needed him in the old days.

Tonight after dinner, I went into the front yard to pick up pinecones so that I can mow tomorrow if it is cool enough. The girls went out also. And then coming down Dyches Street, I heard the little girl from the house beside the Texaco Quick Shop walking and calling her dachshund--GEORGE not Frank as I had thought. George just happened to be in the yard. I think this is the first place he visits on his rounds. And I pointed out George to the little girl--I guess about 10 or 11. And I said, leave your phone number and we'll call you when George visits. The little thing ran home, wrote out her name--Celeste--her dog's name and phone number, which I have posted, on the fridge. While I picked up pinecones, she stayed to chat, George in arms. It seems she knows our boxer Lenya well, having often visited her backyard. But not Sibelius, our border collie. Very interesting. We now know the runaway.

It soon got too dark to see pinecones. So I came in, got the flashlight and walked Celeste and George back home. Here parents aren't there tonight. So I told Celeste to go into the house, check it, and then come to the kitchen window and wave. She did. They should not leave such a little thing alone at night. But she confided, George is a good watchdog.

I told Celeste you were on vacation in Europe. She asked if I wasn't lonely. I said yes. Sometimes! Celeste said she wished she had more neighbors. I said yes, so wished I.

So if George strays again, I have Celeste's number and I will call so she can rescue him. And she promised to send Lenya home if she comes up to visit again.

Now I will go to bed and read. Perhaps tomorrow I will have a letter in the box when I arrive home. By the way, I went to vote this morning before I went to work. I'll be listening to the primary returns before I go to sleep tonight. I am reading <u>Elizabeth and Katherine</u> (of Russia).

Pontiac writes on July 17:
No letter today. I am furious! It is around 8 p.m. I am sitting on the front steps. This corner is as quiet as Saluda country. Traffic to the other houses has considerably slowed. Few if any cars pass. I have the portable radio out. A potato is in the oven. I have just finished cooking hamburger. And I am writing this on my lap! So...if the handwriting is unorthodox, know that it is because I do not have an appropriate thigh and knee.

Malcolm Mist came by for a couple of cool beers. We got very mellow and Malcolm talked and talked. Jesus, what is it about me that promises confession without penance?

The real reason that Malcolm and Dorothy left California is that Malcolm had a love affair with the hostess of the Brown Derby. But he confessed all to Dorothy. It took her several months to get over it, but she now doesn't seem to think about it and, as it was in the past, trusts him. And he says, it is like a weight was lifted from him. I'll tell you later but you must NEVER indicate that you know. He even went to a psychiatrist about it. It upset him so. I guess we all have these times. And now my time for confession. I love only you. Which is not all that much of a confession. You knew it anyway.

The rain has cooled things marvelously. Luckily, the constant water has made the ground too soggy to mow. And so I can sit out here and enjoy the cool without thinking I should be mowing.

Kuch, I need to get letters from you *often*. Don't forget me in your Austria. Wrote a letter to you today

Pontiac writes on July 19:

Finally, a letter today. You waited five days between letters! But then on July 12, you had only received my second letter! What would be amusing--if I were not an emotional participant in the whole thing-- is that you and I both "wait" for mail and become so disconcerted when it does not arrive upon the schedule we have mentally set. (I bet you thought I wasn't writing regularly!)

I have fussed around the house for two days. Actually, to me a letter a day would not be enough! I am lonely for old Hateful! I have become so accustomed to that old Nag that I do not know how to live without her. And when I don't hear as often as I think due me, I say--O.K. she's too caught up and isn't writing as regularly as she should! Ach...!

You speak of rain! I long for cooling rain. But isn't that the way it works? When we were in Europe together, the same thing happened. But oh, my darling, you are hardly ever sick. And I am not there to examine the throat, make you gargle, give you tea and toddies. No one, but me, can look after you properly. You are so very precious, like a newly found jewel--and all this after seven years this July 28 when you first visited Cambria to see me. (After you had graduated but came back for me!)

Kuch. We figured out long before this that the Lange's were after Albert's money! Well. You have made it without that money and never--even before me--asked for a dime. The irony is that the male Lange died before he could get his hands on it. She will probably hang around but it will become dust in her mouth, too. I know you think I am an idealist but ill-gotten gain takes its own toll on a human being. Thank goodness, Tante Josefa seems now to be hearing both sides. Maybe your not seeing her during that first trip was a good thing. And your coming independently on the second one revealed to her that you did not particularly need anybody's help and your visit to her was prompted by love not need. That, in itself, will draw respect. And rightly so. You have struggled and you made it! A hell of a far cry from being a housemaid that the Käfer's wanted you to become. I know *I* am proud of you! You took opportunity by the forelock and made it yours! Funny thing, Albert did not recognize that the Langes wanted his money. You wanted love. I guess, in the final analysis, love is harder to give than money. Because love implies a one-to-one commitment. But sometimes people get love and money confused.

Pontiac writes on July 20:
Well, Fleanna, (another nickname) this Saturday has been a hard-working day. The lonely squirrel has been storing food for it and its mate for the winter!

The day got off to a good and easy start. I slept until ten. I slept on the couch because the heat last night was so bad. I fed myself, animals, and fishes and then started washing clothes. Then I began "picking up the house" which I finished. I got some tomatoes from Sara and I knew I had to can them this afternoon. Around noon, Vincent came by and gave us 1/2 bushel of Crowder peas! He stayed to have a drink and chat a bit. Left within an hour. Incidentally, he was so proud to have a card from you. You have made so many people happy through such a simple thing.

Now a little after six, I have shelled one-half a bushel of peas, frozen eight bags for the baby and prepared a canner of tomatoes. I still have some tomatoes to do tomorrow afternoon when I return from Malcolm and Dorothy's house.

But oh--I can imagine the Kuch coming home and getting excited over the things I have canned and put in the freezer. And I say--well, it's for the darling and me! So I don't mind being tired. (I never got around to vacuuming! I am "wading" in sand and dog hair!)

I am still high from the letter I received yesterday! I feel so close to you right now. I am waiting for Dan Rather's "Saturday News" to come on.

Pontiac writes on July 21:
One month ago today my baby flew away from the home that is silent and bleak without her. I returned late from Malcolm and Dorothy's, straightened up the kitchen, emptied the dishwasher, took the trash out and fed the fish.

It rained very hard today and so has cooled things considerably. If it rains again tonight, then the heat wave may be broken. Tonight I will sleep in my bed for the first time in two nights. I have been sleeping in the air conditioning. But I won't even need the attic fan tonight.

I also visited with Sarah and Vincent. Everybody speaks of you and wants to see you immediately upon your return. But I'll keep you here alone with me for weeks and shall refuse to share you with anyone!

I think somebody is getting ready to move in next door. When I returned home today, people were over mowing the lawn. I don't know how many are moving in but I have seen four people. A man, two women, and a teenaged boy. From here, they look what your mother calls the proletariat. But who can tell. I bet, though, we won't have "unseen" neighbors again! Ah well. They'll probably move in just as you return. Too bad we couldn't have shared this lucky privacy. But let's hope for the best. The dentist tomorrow!

Channel 74

Pelegrine writes on July 23:

My Baby,

I have been in Vienna for over two weeks and find it impossible to leave. Soon I'll move on. I, therefore, cannot answer any more of your letters. I miss you. All major theaters and opera are closed and I saw "The Merry Widow" as an unplanned performance in a small theater. Tante Josefa is traveling with me to see Mutti. In Salzburg we'll probably get to see some of the better stuff during the festival weeks. Tante Josefa is pleasant and indulgent. The only money I have spent lately is on gas and minor incidentals. She gave me a platinum (!) ring with nine diamonds and one pearl.

I am enjoying my visits and often miss much sleep. Yet, my waste line is growing. All my clothes are tight. You must put me on a diet when I return. Please.

I have acquired from Tante Josefa two handsome field glasses covered with leather and metal embellishments. These genteel looking glasses will help us see our birdies better. My English is alarmingly deteriorating and my German is indulged by a splendidly cathartic splurge. Eleanor shall be pleased with my accent--that hussy! I am soaking up every single impression--every dirt, every smell and sound--they are all engraved in my mind. You, darling, can't imagine what a wrenching experience this is. Momentary illuminations of past memories occur haphazardly and I cling to them for survival. I miss you and my home while I collide with an old home, which was mine only for brief periods. My, my, what a convergence an emigrated immigrant is entitled to. I drink cow-warm milk and smell, golden old shit. I am having a private orgy of the mind. You will relive it with me, shortly.

I am doing many people's minor repairs. Will you have plenty of work for me to binge on? You are my strong current, always present. Thank you for letting me have this! I love you, Missy! Your Kleinelein, your Goldkind, your Überalles, your Hateful, your Rieber, your Kuchen, your breath of life. Many Bussis. Talk to Augie, Jim, Lenya, Sibi and the fish for me. They are good animals. My little family, I'll be home soon!

Channel 75

Pontiac July 25:

I have been remiss in writing this journal. Monday I didn't come home. Tuesday, I came home but went directly to Sara and Vincent's. Wednesday, I wrote a letter to my darling.

BUT! No letter from her for almost a whole week! Last Friday was the last time I received a letter. Mein Gott! Old tough me. I can't be happy seven days without some words from my Only.

The Judicial Committee is debating on TV. whether to recommend impeachment of Nixon. They will. Then the House of Representatives will be voting on impeachment. If they so vote, then the Senate will try Nixon and either find him innocent or guilty. I am presently glued to the TV. It is like being involved in the continuum of history. I wish you were here beside me.

I am also canning tomatoes tonight. Ach. You will be happy about the freezer and the jars of food.

Well, the house next door is inhabited. A family with apparently teenagers, too. Ah well. Back to keeping the curtains drawn.

I have worked quite hard this week, particularly on PR and committee meetings. Then coming home and getting to bed early, reading, playing the radio until drop-off time. Also after a long drought, it has rained every day since Saturday. I'll have to mow again. And by this weekend, we'll have the first tomato off our bushes. I need to do some more tying.

I also need to clean house! Mein Gott! Eleanor arrives tomorrow for the weekend. That's the trouble. People have not left me alone recently. But I have accepted almost all invitations so as to help to combat loneliness without my Kuch.

My only real worry is Augie. He left this morning before breakfast and has not returned. Too soon to get upset though. But recently, he has been sticking fairly close to home. I'll call again later.

Archie was in a wreck yesterday. He had a blowout on the front tire and turned his truck over twice. Had to have several stitches on the side of his head and has hurt his back rather badly. I'll call tonight to find out about him. Those damn bad tires.

It seems the Greek dictatorship has fallen in all the chaos over Cyprus. I'm still not sure exactly what has happened but at least, I'm happy that those damn tyrants may be out. But I can't quite figure out first causes yet. I am too cynical, I guess.

10 p.m. Augie has just strolled unconcernedly home!

Pontiac July 26:

No letter! One week has passed! Jesus, how one does measure time in terms of a beloved. It was July in 1967 when we first came together. And this July, seven years later, we are apart and oh--the hurt of it.

On TV the Judiciary Committee is debating impeachment. I am glued to the set. I rant and rail my convictions. Only Lenya and Sibelius look up even. The boys are too placid to care! I wish the darling were here. She would at least ask questions. She would help me curse. Oh--she would really rail against Nixon. She is such a companion.

Eleanor is due any minute. I have prepared a pork roast, fresh lima beans, salad and rice. I will take this pad which ordinarily lies on the table to the bedroom so perhaps I can sneak a line or two later. Twice, it was almost seen. Once by Malcolm and once by Margaret. The truth is, I have this pad and have clipped all your letters together beside the pad. I use your letters as if you were talking to me and this pad to talk to you. In addition I have taken to speaking aloud to you--others would call it talking to myself--as I go about the daily business of living. I say--well, darling, nothing on TV so let's stretch out and read. I say--Kuchen, it has cooled off and so let us go sit on the front steps until the mosquitoes drive us in. I say-----and so it goes. So it goes that I love you when you are here and when you are temporarily out of sight--for you are here immer, über alles.

     Pontiac July 27:

The Judiciary Committee voted to impeach Nixon! Now the whole house must also vote. Then to the trial in the Senate. Eleanor and I got home at nine tonight and have been excited all day. Dare and hope, darling, that the crooked son-of-a-bitch will get what he deserves? I need you to help share my exuberance!

     I am in bed. Eleanor is in your study. I need you to feel as I drift toward sleep. I am thinking now of a piece of metal sculpture I saw at the Craft Fair in Greenwood that I would want for our home. I can't afford it but I got the man's name and address--Hartsville--and after we build, we go down there with money in our pockets and get something for our home.

     Susan's little get-together was fun but not too much. You will like the location of her house. Most of the people she had were rather ordinary. Only one couple seemed fun. I love you.

Channel 76
     Pelegrine July 27:
Dearest One,

     Today I returned to Mutti after a two-week stay in Vienna. I couldn't tear myself away from that marvelous place. The time spent there was divine. I soaked up so much Viennese shit, music, people, corner stones, air, etc. I could burst with my intake. Unfortunately, upon my return to Mutti, I did receive four (4!) letters from you with altogether 65 dollars (to my delight!). Oh, darling, up to this point I have had only two letters--now four at one time. It was like reading a chronicle. Mutti had numbered all the letters to ease the flow of reading. By the way, I mentioned my name change to Kimberly for simplicity's sake. She took it nicely and rather nonchalantly. Sorry, to have kept you hanging as to my whereabouts. You will understand, my baby, since your mail to me seems to have been fouled-up besides waiting here, I had no idea what you needed to know most. Since my letters to you seem slow, that makes our actual communication choppy. I also live a very excitable life right now and it is often difficult to sit down and quietly remember to tell the right details. I will do so most perfectly when I hold you in my arms again. I most likely leave Fechelaponte on August 3. So after you read this letter, maybe write no more. I'll spend the rest of the time with Zange and perhaps her baby. Tante Josefa drove with me to console Mutti after I am gone. I have some surprises for you, which I'd rather not tell you about, or else I'll have no Christmas in August for you.

    Your letters are soul food for me, too. They caress me and breathe of you. I need you! I'll call you immediately from Philly. Thank God you take such good care of our finances. You are quite capable, you know. But you do need me, I keep telling you. You, too, are absolutely indispensable. I need somebody to nag. I've been on too much impeccable behavior for the past few weeks and I need a good fight.

    I have so much to tell you that I could bubble over. You know, baby, I, too, find it difficult to picture you in your present state. What time and distance does--it blurs the memory and makes one of its own. I see you, real, and nothing but you. Yet, a fog creeps in on the visions and dilutes the clearness I am trying to capture. Damn events! Can you "hear" my accent in my letters? I can as I formulate my sentences. Maybe you write an express answer to this letter to Zange, provided you get this one by August 1. You must allow for nearly six to seven days to reach me with an answer. On August 9, I'll leave Frankfurt and spend the next night in Köln again. Then to you in a hurry. I love you and I am glad, so glad, to come home. Viele, viele Bussi, your Kleinelein, Pelegrine.

Channel 77

    Pontiac July 28:

*The failure of the light
is signet
for the last of a certain moment
called day.*

*What are you then
but a moment of certitude
in continuing eons we call time?*

*Break down the structure of eternity.
Call the designated partitions
Epochs
Eras
Epics.
See the scope of sensitive existence.*

*And still
I would flit the periods away
for that tiny point
when you flourished
and so loved me.*

    Pontiac July 29:

Tonight I am not necessarily rational. I have lived from letter to letter from you! I have lived a seemingly usual life, having gone to work every morning, returned in the late afternoon to do a few chores, read a little, then gone to bed to wake up in the morning for more of the same--which is not fullsome without having the one that I do all these things for--you.

    I have conversed and had contact with others who seem to value me for one reason or the other. And during these weeks, I have accepted invitations I would ordinarily evade and accept only if pinned down. I have told no lies about being busy--as you and I would often do in order not to have to do things.

Yet these appointments and make-do activities have been largely because there was nothing really to do except sit home and lick the wounds of loneliness. Still, all these things have not really counted. Because I looked to the mailbox. And for 11 days there was nothing in the mailbox. I attributed that to the slowness of the American Postal Service. The letter I received today indicated otherwise. You had not written in 11 days!

I should understand that you are caught up in what you are doing and have not had time. I should understand that being away from Fechelaponte and my letters, you are perhaps waiting to reply rather than to tell. But I must confess that I am not rational on this point. Therefore, your letter today was both a relief and an enraging proposition. If you were here, we would be having one hell of a fight. Your letter preceding this was dated July 12. This letter today was dated July 23. Jesus Christ.

I understand that I am being totally selfish. But if I did not think that our love was what I needed and wanted, then I don't think I would be quite as dependent. Love is essentially selfish. It propels two who need each other together. And requires constant tending, as does fire. It will choke on its own smoke if fresh fuel or air is not allowed. And my fire is burning brightly as is yours, my darling. But oh, sweet love, eleven days' silence could be wet wood that chokes and brings tears to the eyes. But the fire has been well laid and will not smother. Thus we remain constant in our companionable spark, in the full knowledge that even the most moist log can be brought to flame upon the live coals which have been properly laid.

I wish I could have heard the "Merry Widow." I wish I could go to the festival in Salzburg. I do wish I could have more than a page and a half from you.

Today, before I went to Columbia, I drove by the post office and mailed the last letter (on this occasion) I will send to you.

All goes onward and outward and little changes. I suppose by now the rain in Austria has stopped. I suppose you are doing something or other now. All was fine until you couldn't find time to write. Until when you finally got around to it, you couldn't really fill two sides of a piece of paper. That realization has certainly put me in my place.

Pontiac July 31:

Well, Eleanor left here Monday morning with an assignment. She filled it and returned yesterday around five with the completion of chapter two and the first segment of chapter three. We had worked all afternoon Sunday on her dissertation. Yesterday, we worked from 7 p.m. to nearly 12 and then we got up at 5 this morning. She stayed today to type up the changes until I went to work and left around 5:30 this afternoon. Thank God, really.

I think Eleanor 24 hours a day could really get too much. I love Eleanor; she has that quality. Still, I am convinced Eleanor is not all that rational. Since this summer, I am beginning to understand her children's exasperation!

Little Rodney and I have been doing our chess lessons. We had one this afternoon. Afterwards, we go down to the canteen and have a Pepsi. He is a very serious student. At nine years old, he knows the meaning of symbol; he knows fairly complicated relationships. You'd be fascinated.

Ravenel won the Democratic primary for governor. The Judiciary Committee has voted to impeach Nixon. And I still unalterably love you.

Everyone asks of you and for you.

On September 4-5, I must attend a statewide college conference in Greenville. But before that, on the Labor Day weekend, perhaps the two of us alone can go off somewhere together. Perhaps to the beach. You'd get Labor Day off. So we could arrange to go.

Ah, Kuch, the summer days' inferno hot hastens to fall. Fairly free days have almost passed. What have we here but sweet August days that bid your coming soon.

Channel 78

    Pelegrine August 1:

Babylein,

    I got your last letter with the last 20 dollars today. All the money has come in. Baby, I am a little worried that you are displeased with me. I wrote as much as I could and hoped you would understand the turbulent times I'd be experiencing. Please, be kind! I love you and am with you at all times, no matter how often or little I write.

    Today, Mama, Herr Sommer, Tante Josefa and I drove to Bad Reichenhall, a grandiose, natural salt spa in the Bavarian Alps. Did much gargling and breathing in the good air for my sore throat which I have had since I stepped on European soil. The Southern sun will cure it soon. And my darling will kiss my throat to wellness.

    Tomorrow I'll spend the day with my old school friend, Schwert Kati. We will sunbathe and dive into our Attersee Lake childhood.

    Everybody is getting sad and old. I really dread to think that some people I may never see again since my visits are so far apart. Papa is old and weak. Mary just had a breast removed and is losing weight fast, which is a bad sign. Her cancer may not have been arrested. My mother and Herr Sommer are also wobbling along. I wonder for how much longer? I built Mutti a bookshelf and fixed odds and ends--and this with a man in the house! I also toasted to you, my darling, with the "Old Grand Dad" I had left. I mixed it with orange juice and my own personal ice cubes. I can't get into my bathing suit. A diet is overdue--but what the hell, not until I'll get home. You will, please, help me? I beg you.

    Don't do too much in the house. Your little aggravator will be in your arms shortly. You better get an extra oxygen supply, for I intend to suffocate and smother you with kisses. Please, don't let an absence of letters hurt you. Remember, I am enjoying myself without forgetting us. As a matter of fact, I thought I was pretty good with writing. You were good, too. You seemed only a slow starter. Your letters, at the beginning, did not come fast enough. We may both be suffering a certain neuroses and tend to emotional exaggeration; neither one of us can be pleased but with each other. We are a good couple though and deserve each other. I love you. Please, be patient with me. I am your joy. You are my sunshine and strength. Soon, honey! Your Pelegrine.

Channel 79

    Pontiac August 1:

In drought--
even the valleys shade themselves
from unrelenting sun.
They cry Rain
from throats gone dry
and rasped with dust.

You call yourself
the child of the sun
Goldkind
who spreads precious rays
upon the looted treasury
of some bankrupt heart.

Yet I of Southern persuasion
who have known summer's store of heat--
sweat provoking--
season of sun spells--
call you the nourishing rain
that enables the laborer to breathe.

    Pontiac August 2:

It is now verisimilitude green
since the storm
when the little black dog whined
at my feet.

The clock was struck
and the red second hand moves
more slowly--
untrustworthy.

The voices of the children
rise like intelligence
above the emerald calm.
I cannot count the cadences
of the charm
they lay upon the evening.
They accumulate next door.
I peer from a window…for a glimpse.

Pontiac August 4:

This Sunday--a week from the day you are to return--has been a rainy one and thus a cool and quiet day. Augie March woke me up around eight this morning--such a willful creature. I put the coffee on, fed the menagerie and then went out for the papers and Sunday goodies for breakfast. I read until around ten and then in the cool before the rain, I worked in the yard. I picked around twenty tomatoes today and four yesterday. They will still be ripening when you return but many of the bushes are beginning to die. We will, I think, have enough to have a couple of "green-tomato breakfasts."

This afternoon I have done the bills. I put 200 dollars in the savings account. I examined our running tally on the savings account and there's one figure I can't understand--or an amount that possibly was not subtracted. At any rate, we may have over 700 in savings as of this month. When my raise finally comes through, we should be able to save more. I paid 50 dollars to Master charge but did get 25 dollars from the bank on Master charge--that was to cover the last 20 dollars I mailed you near the end of the month. But--notwithstanding--it's coming down and should be completely paid off before Christmas. That will be one more debt paid off and more for our savings--and our home! And of course, you will be getting a raise in September--so we are doing quite well with our little schoolteacher pay.

You are today in Hattersheim. I am happy that you and Zange are hitting it off. Perhaps they learned a bit of a lesson from your last time. Wouldn't it be exciting if the baby were born while you are there? Of course, you would go into panic! I wonder what you'd do if you had to drive Zange to the hospital?

Tonight, I will fry a flounder and then take the extra piece--the one my darling would have eaten had she been here--for lunch tomorrow. Tomorrow night, I go to Sarah and Vincent's for dinner. Friday night, I went over to Margaret's. We cooked steaks. But I was home by ten-thirty--in the bed reading! My! What a dull life.

It is a good, quiet, steady rain today. I wish we could cuddle together in bed. For once, it is cool. No need for air conditioning. We could roll and play games. But then next Sunday, you will be home to me. And ah. Then it shall be a perfect Sunday.

Pontiac writes on August 5:
A letter from you reached me in four days! And the Kuch was upset because I had been upset. I do, intellectually, understand that sometimes you could not write. You have been very good and have written many letters filled with the love I need. But, my only light, I cannot be reasonable. I can be reasonable just about everything but you! I am unreasonable about you my darling. A letter a day may have been enough but I doubt it, for I love you unreasonably much.

I worry about your throat. A sore throat that lasts for weeks is serious. I wish you had gone to a doctor. If you still have it when you get home, I will insist that you go.

This week, my darling, will be the longest week. It will drag by with crippled feet. I leave now to go to Sarah and Vincent's for dinner. Next Monday night, I will make dinner "für die Fleanna!"

Pontiac writes on August 6:
It is still five days until the light of the life returns home where she has belonged since eons before even the sun was created? It is indelible upon the spans of time that at this slight instance we call the 20th century, in a flicker of moment in

that instance, two people would so converge upon each other--those two people are we.

I have you now in the trying days of my country. And you are right; I am a patriot--a lover of these United States--a believer, even a worshiper of the ideals of this country. That is why I become so upset when these ideals are threatened--and they are usually threatened by stupid, selfish people within our own country. Yet, we have managed for a period of nearly 200 years to keep the ideals at least in consideration. In spite of this nation's brief history, we are the world's oldest continuing democracy. And this impeachment mess is a good symbol of why we may endure. There are still some things we will not permit if they go contrary to these ideals.

I wish, in a way, you had been here during this impeachment summer. Even Republicans have been turned back to patriotism--not lip-service LOVE-US-OR-LEAVE-US stupidity.

One last laugh. Only Strom Thurmond seems to be touting the Nixon line.

You will be with me to rejoice in the FALL of a man who sought to turn around the constitutional freedoms of Americans. And a supreme court packed with the men he nominated to it--found him wanting. What irony!

There are rumors that he might resign. I hope not. The constitutional process calls for impeachment proceedings. We need now for that process to be carried through. If Nixon has any respect for this country left, he will not resign but will let impeachment take its course.

You are probably bored by the above. But except for long distance phone calls, I've had no one to talk to. If you were here, it would be different. All Nixonites at the college are either silent or have--increasingly lately--renounced him.

Yet it is no pleasure to me that such a low-life character inhabited our highest office and now he's getting his due. It is a disgrace that the American people elected a man of Nixon's ilk to the highest office in the land! Had they bothered to find out, they could have seen in the first time when Nixon ran against Jerry Voorhis in California for the House of Representatives that Nixon was a man who played filthy--not dirty--politics.

I am back to being a bore, am I not Kuch?

I go back to the fact that I have five days after this one when I shall see you. I need to hold you quietly in my arms, to put our heads together in nodding warmth, to feel your cheeks in my lap, and to wander off to sleep.

I called Lilly and Jed tonight regarding sizes for Jed's birthday. He now needs size 8. We will fix a box together when you return home. We must get him an Evil Knievel motorcycle toy. Lilly said long pants--including blue jeans--were desperately needed for school. Jed will be six on August 22. He also needs winter pajamas.

Pontiac August 7:

Only three more days until the day of your return. You today are probably saying--only three more days left before I leave--and that's natural so we won't discuss it at all. You won't believe that the bloom is still upon the zebra plant--though not quite as glorious as it was a couple of weeks ago. The bloom will remain upon the plant until you return.

There is much for you to do here. Lenya the bitch has regularly been digging out. I have been shoveling--which I finally stopped--and stacking wood into the dugouts. We-you--must lay better cement. Almost every day I have shifted wood.

Rodney came over for his second chess lesson today. Archie butted in. And it took Archie 1 1/2 hours to defeat Rodney. Then Archie insisted that I play him. I beat Archie in 45 minutes. Archie wants us to play more and that's good because, actually, I am still in the learning stage--as you are. I am going to take our traveling chess set to school tomorrow.

Friday, I must go to Sonny's for dinner. I said no for last Friday and I couldn't say no two weeks in a row.

Amelia wants us for dinner when you are back. I said you may have plans--Jon might be here--but I'm afraid I must go. Drats! I would prefer that we could spend the rest of the summer just knooching. (Hugging and squeezing)

Yes, indeed, we must work on your syntax. Your sentence structure, however, has not suffered all that much. Your verbs have declined. (I hate such a pun!)

Ah, my Only, my spirits lift upon a daily level as your coming draws near. Old self-sufficient I have for the first time in my life discovered that the I, the ego, is not all that is necessary. Old self-sufficient I have finally comprehended that another one is more than just desirable for a fully lived life.

The both of us shall go on an iron diet together. My little vain one requires it for her psychological well-being and I certainly need it for my physical well-being. I pledge it

Ah--I want you here sooner than Sunday, Kuchen. I want you here now.

Pontiac August 8:

Nixon has resigned. But not admitting that he did anything wrong but that he had lost his support in the Congress. I am/was opposed to resignation. Impeachment should have gone its course. I'm going back to TV. However, even in this period of tension, the primary thing in my mind is that in two days' time, I will hold you in my arms. And--as you accuse me-- that's a whole hell of a lot. I put you before my country! Yes, I do. But that doesn't change me a whole lot. It's that I LOVE YOU.

Pontiac August 9:

Tomorrow, you will be leaving for Köln. Then Sunday you will be flying back to me. Tonight and tomorrow nights will be the last lonely nights for me. Sunday, I will await all day your call to me.

I just returned home tonight from dinner at Sonny's. Actually, I enjoyed chatting with Mary Bess. But all in all, it was a very boring dinner and evening.

Gerald Ford became 38th president of the United States. He said all the right things in his acceptance speech. But though probably very honest, he is <u>so</u> conservative and I'm afraid not too intelligent.

Nixon cried on TV. today in a televised farewell speech to White House employees. He was maudlin--evoking memories of his mother and father. He seemed to dwell on death. Read a long quote from Theodore Roosevelt about the death of TR's first wife, talked about his two older brothers' death, etc. That was the peculiar part of the thing.

I hope the worst is over so this country can get back on course; maybe the Congress will even clean itself up a bit--who knows? At school, we spent most of the day watching the momentous events on TV. So we didn't do much work at school but nevertheless, the day was somehow exhausting!

Bad news! It has rained every day this week and the forecast is rain for the weekend. Wouldn't it be awful if you arrived home for rain? Ah, but sweet one, rain with you is better than sunshine alone. I want rolling days with you! I want all days with you.

Pontiac August 10

It is around 11 a.m. It must be around four or five where you are. I envision you on that terrible train ride! I hope you are having better luck this trip--and at least do not get vomited upon.

Jon just called. Eleanor--damn her--had suggested that Jon meet you at the airport in Philadelphia and that you ride down with him. I tactfully replied that 1.) I did not know when you would arrive and 2.) that you would be awfully tired and 3.) that you had to take a train from Frankfurt to Köln, then the plane here and that you could get home in four hours from Philadelphia as against twelve by car. So it would be better for you if you got home and rested a little. He then is driving down from Newark tomorrow and will stop in Newton. You will call him when you reach home.

Kuch. There is no avoiding having him next week. He is a sweet fellow so we'll have to make do! And he has saved part of his vacation for this trip. He does not understand the special thing between us. So we'll have to do our very best to be hospitable to him.

I am in the midst of cleaning house and washing clothes. We have a few hours of sunshine today. I hope I can get the clothes dry before the "daily rain." Actually, the house is not spic'n span but only a little "straightened." I know you shall find many faults. But--darling--you know how bad a housekeeper I am!

Around 7:40 p.m.

I do not believe it! Eleanor Mann just called me tonight and asked if I could look over eleven pages Monday afternoon! Now she sees our relationship as similar but better than her and her children's. She has said so--in so many words--time and again. And I guess she assumes that I'm really not interested in getting with you and finding out what you've been doing--hearing your stories. (She doesn't even suspect that I have to hold you close and feel thy warmth). I'm convinced that essentially Margaret is right. She has not paid good attention to her children.

At any rate, I said No. I said that I wanted to spend some time with you-- give you a chance to talk about your trip, "in other words, Eleanor," I said, "she'll want attention because she will be excited." Anyway, she said that Jon was driving down tomorrow. I told her that you would call him.

She's coming to Ashton to interview for a part-time job in a special government sponsored program, which just started this summer. I'll tell you all about it. If she doesn't mess up the interview, then I'm 99% sure she'll get the job. I told her she could drop by the house to see you. I couldn't very well say you can't, since she'll be in Ashton anyway. Shit. I have had an exasperating time with Eleanor this summer! She does not think!

Ken is already back--with 35 dollars in his pocket. Eleanor said the reason she suggested that Jon drive you home was that she thought you might be like Ken and have overspent yourself. I cruelly said to Eleanor that I can't think of any two people more unlike.

But none of this shall spoil my darling's homecoming. I will not allow it. I want my darling to myself for at least a day! Oh--sweetheart. Tomorrow will be the loveliest day of the year!

I just had a transcontinental phone call from my crazy darling during which time she told me not to talk. Or at least I think it was my baby--some little girl with a thick accent! We shall have to do vocal exercises!

But oh--this Sunday will be so long! It will help though, sweetheart that thy beautiful voice rings in my ear. It is not nearly ten a.m. in the morning and thus I must wait ten more hours before I once again hear my Only's voice. This will be the hardest day of waiting.

8:25 p.m.

This has been the longest day of my life, and it stretches interminably into evening. Night begins to fall. It has been a very green day--no rain but humid, a little sun in late afternoon when the dogs and I sat on the front steps and tried to while away the hours until at least you called. It was/is the last lonely day. Its tenacious fingers reaching into night.

Milton said that those who wait also serve but I say such is servitude and not compatible with freedom. What must I do then? Ah, I can only wait with the stone of the minutes upon me. I sit by the window and watch the daylight blend into dusk and the dusk into night and listen for the blaring ring of the phone and hope it will be you I answer to!

What could have gone wrong? I ask myself. Perhaps trouble at customs--I never know what you will try--perhaps no flight tonight to Newton. Perhaps anything. Delay in flight. Bad weather. Anything.

It grows darker outside. I wait. Night is now upon us--the dogs that noticed my nervousness wait close by. Jim sleeps. Augie still paroles. [End of log]

Channel 80

This is the end of Pontiac's agonizing wait. Her beloved Pelegrine could not get on a flight to Newton that night. They had overbooked and put her up in a hotel. She nearly had a nervous breakdown at the airport, knowing that her precious Pontiac was waiting at the airport. She could not reach her by phone. They paged her at the airport. Then, alas, the sad news that they won't be together till the next day--and so put an end to their strenuous first separation of more than six weeks.

Twenty years later, Pelegrine still does not fail to acknowledge with deepest gratitude and affection her intellectual debt to this uniquely brilliant woman. This lady made learning a lifetime pursuit for Pelegrine. This woman presented Pelegrine with no shortcuts. This woman placed the rungs higher and higher. This woman did for Pelegrine what most parents do for their children. This woman was Pelegrine's Socrates, her key to a thoughtful life, a life lived deliberately.

And as she is proof-reading this first bound copy for one LAST time, Pelegrine is still crying for her Pontiac, for her wings, thirty years later.

A 1967 diary entry reveals:

Living in my darling's household. It is with Pontiac Reynaldo Wingo, once my English teacher. For the first time I feel the absolute joy of loving somebody and being loved in return. Tolstoy, her husband is an elegant poet. But Pontiac is the better one.

I asked Pontiac for a definition of the word "ruthless." This is what I got for an answer:

*Ruth being after all Ruthless
Among the wheat where hungry
They searched for careless shreds,
The two resigned their mouths
To absent bread but bound
Their souls in ruthless love.*

*Thus Ruth forgot old gods
And Naomi denied
Her liberal understanding.
She would not send the girl
away.*

Pelegrine, it is ruthless of me to neglect my paper grading, for if I were a compassionate teacher, I would feel my students' need--even that some are apprehensive of possible grades--and hurriedly get their exercises to them. Yet pitilessly, I spend time on not-so-good poems to explain at least one possible interpretation of a single word.

Truly, Pelegrine had a live-in mate, tutor and loving lover, all in one person. She had somebody who took her under her wing and taught her practically everything. Everything from manners, the love of language, Shakespeare, Chaucer, Milton and Emily Dickinson. She taught her to savor the lives of those who love poetry, music and art. Pelegrine soaked it up and to this day is relishing and building upon experiences that began with the advent of a woman called Wingo.

Channel 81

They lived six years in the house where the dogs were digging out of the pen, where Pontiac wrote her diligent "Home Log," where the heat was rarely broken with spells of rain. In 1976, two years after the European separation, Pelegrine writes again in her diary:

Every other July, so it seems, I am writing in my diary. Zange was here. I still weep and wail. It's all over too soon. Her son, little Lok,i is two now, a sweet and rather dear child. Jan is ordinary and stiff like an ironing board. I feel sorry for him. I wish for Zange that he were nice and expressed feelings for other people. 4 1/2 weeks were long but good. My temperamental nature, not allowing me to live too close, too long next to people, let alone three differently loved people, survived all right. I am so happy I live here in this country. I have grown accustomed to my only family even though they aggravate me. But the European pettiness always comes through when I am around them for a while. It never fails. They are different. My sister, Zange, is pliable and adapts easily like my mother. I wish she could live somewhere in this country and could be my relative to visit on holidays. That way we could keep a family, our family alive. Her in-laws, will, however, triumph in not only making Zange a German, but Loki a Lutheran. Zange must not be ashamed of the background of our mother.

Pontiac and I are having a difficult time. She seems far away and often mad at things, I don't see or don't know I'm doing. Why can't she understand what it means to be tied up 24 hours with two guests and baby demands? Now that they are gone, it is peaceful and normal again. And I really do love Pontiac. She has stopped writing poetry nor writes on her I, Huckleberry novel. She says she's lost her genius. Bullshit! She's lost her inspiration and desire. Only she can make it work. My pleading is useless. I see her reluctance as a failure and it hurts me. But I don't know what to do about it. Except beg her not to abandon her gift. I agonize and try not to despair. Maybe her spark will come back. I hope and pray.

Loki was 88 cm (43 inches) in July 1976. He is my godson and I love him. I hope Jan's personality doesn't rub off on the boy. Jan acts possessive, and my sister is so weak.

Channel 82

Pelegrine's diary entries are sporadic--often a year apart. Her life with Pontiac was peaceful and harmonious. But signs of discomfort where noticeable. And since they lived an extremely closeted life, and everybody believed the myth of aunt and niece. Eventually even Pelegrine herself got so used to being in her own act. She WAS the real niece. They never cultivated gay friends, bought helpful books or discussed their hidden hurts and fears. Pelegrine had needed the comforting shroud of Pontiac posing as her aunt. It, probably, was Pelegrine's internalized homophobia, learned after being rejected by Rita, Uncle Albert and Aunt Coco and much, much later, as will be seen, by Tante Josefa, too. But never by her Mutti or Zange.

Pelegrine was convinced that their private lives were nobody's business and enjoyed the small benefits from the imaginary family creation--the aunt/niece facade. The tiny college town indulged them, so did the faculty friends and students. Creating such an illusion made every bit of life livable especially in the South. Pontiac never wanted the disguise, but agreed to Pelegrine's pleading. They devised a marvelous wartime love story, made Pelegrine's father an American instead of the real German soldier. He became Pontiac's oldest brother and they baptized him Malcolm. By weaving together as much of her real and truthful past with the equally unclear and mysterious history of an unknown father, Pelegrine delivered an astoundingly convincing portrait of her World War II, American GI father. Thus, the aunt and niece lived a compatible, productive life, condoned by society. Harmony would best describe their togetherness that lasted a decade and was never to be found for Pelegrine anywhere again.

Channel 83

After Pelegrine's successful graduation, she decided to pursue a Master of Arts degree, which she completed in one year. At that time, Pontiac's job as a college professor came to an end, and both had to go job hunting. Pontiac accepted a job at a Technological Institute as a technical writing teacher and college public relations liaison. Her superb command of the English language always landed her top-level positions. Pontiac was not very happy to leave the liberal arts setting, but the job market was tight and English teachers a-dime-a-dozen. Pelegrine was willing to accept a high school teaching position because that way both women had jobs in the same town. Her pay was ridiculously little. 6000 dollars per year in 1972 was a joke. Thank God, Wingo earned three times that. Since they were never competitive with each other, they were not bothered by this monetary discrepancy. Pelegrine's foreign language skills were not needed in the same towns that looked for Pontiac's English talents.

Pontiac and Pelegrine had a perfect understanding from the very beginning. Pontiac helped Pelegrine finish school. The part time jobs and student loans were not enough to cover all expenses. Thus, after completing her final degree, Pelegrine was grateful and not fighting for career status. Being able to live together outweighed all other options.

In her nearly ten years of teaching high school English (!) and foreign languages to American teenagers, Pelegrine became a little legend to students, parents, administrators and state agencies. She was tough, fair and loyal. People, who met her, admired her energy and never-ending supply of creativity. At home she was the all-around handy-girl, fixed and broke things while learning how to fix them. She made bookshelves, attended a car mechanic course. All that at a time when seeing a girl under a hood made men say,

" My, my, that boy has a fanny like a girl!"

"That's because, I **am** a girl," Pelegrine snatched back, and came out from under the hood smiling into their dumbfounded faces.

"And I don't mind. Do you?"

The smudgy faces laughed and turned red under their grease. And in good humor, the American boys accepted this girl's tinkering with cars. Women's movements and girl power, were unknown then. Especially in this deep, forsaken rural hole.

The MG was later replaced with a TR4. Pelegrine owned that car for over twenty years. She cared for it like she always does, like a good caretaker. She wrote a poem about her treasure:

TR4 Freedom 1964

The triumph is so simple
so straight
forward
so this-is-the-way-I-come
so without adornment
so without springs that save
the bouncing butt from screaming so
But
You always know what's wrong
there is no much-to-do-about-nothing
it is always about something
clearly known and clearly fixed
with clearly unavailable parts
But
Then there is always somebody
ingeniously copying an obsolescence
But
When the snow comes through the crack in the soft top
When the rains hit you gently on the knees
When the winds caress your stiff neck in the 30's
When the bumps remind you of the stiff suspension
extra harsh because of age and no longer
the original reason
When the smell of gasoline lingers in your fancy robes
with a sometime smudge on the white
Then
The sun in your hair playing with the wind
Racing to the engine's dual purring
Over highways with Michael's "I'm Bad" bouncing in your head
Then

You engrave the moments behind a heart
Breathing slightly faster
Without notice
While ecstasy
creeps under the skin
every time
and continues
during the predictable but RARE quirks of your
straight-to-the-bone original ride.

Channel 84

By being also an administrator, Pontiac Wingo was squeezed into an 8-5 work grind. She was on a ten-month contract, had two weeks off every year. Her off time was always during exactly the weeks that Pelegrine had to work. Pontiac came home with the general 5 o'clock working world. Such a time frame posed sneaky problems. Pelegrine returned home from her work around three in the afternoon. This actually wasn't so bad. But the summers. They posed long stretches of finding things to do by herself. She enrolled in summer enrichment classes and persuaded a local motel owner to let her sit and swim by his pool, making drivers think the motel was occupied. She talked him into it that this was a good sign for a business, not to speak of the free attraction she offered, since bikinis looked good on her. Sitting by the pool became a regular daily summer ritual for years to come. Her day started like this. First classes. Then swimming, reading, sleeping, smoking a joint, talking to guests, going home when Pontiac was due. Pelegrine looked tanned, healthy and happy.

However, so much freedom and time by herself, laid the foundation for another event. Pelegrine suddenly developed a devastating crush on her summer school English teacher. She was surprised why something like this could happen when she was happily betrothed. But once she allowed herself on that roller coaster, reasoning by herself did no good. And whom else could she have consulted? Nobody.

This feeling had been forgotten and the last time she felt it, it was for

Pontiac Wingo. Now another English teacher caught her fancy. She behaved silly and childlike and wrote poetry, cheaply disguising her true emotions for that woman. Pelegrine had the nerve to read these poems to Pontiac and let her suggest improvements. And on one such reading, Pontiac suddenly looked up and straight into Pelegrine's eyes, "Who is this in the *Story of The Green Pearls and the Black Buttons?*"

A Story

*People
strung
into necklace
not yielding a chain.*

*A sun painting sun flakes
melting queues
into myriads of heat.*

*Pearls in green
ascend the ashes
looking for silk
and a pattern to linger.*

*After black buttons
chased embers
velvet embroidered void.*

*The carnival of confusion
swallowed the pearls.*

Why do I have to expire?

And Pelegrine admitted that hers were the pearls, and the teacher's black eyes were the buttons. She had never lied to Pontiac and was relieved that this partial charade was getting exposed. Pontiac said nothing. After a long and empty silence, her voice shook,

"You better not enroll in another course with her."

But that was exactly what Pelegrine had planned. But now she sheepishly cancelled Part II of a course she didn't need in the first place.

She was upset and disturbed that her infatuation had come this far. But she hated more the fact that her heart had become unfaithful to Pontiac. She was deeply remorseful, could not explain why she was susceptible to falling for somebody other than Pontiac. She promised Pontiac not to take another course and drop the matter. She never laid eyes on the lady again. In no way did the teacher ever know what was going on during her lessons in English composition with one of her more lively pupils whose papers she couldn't believe were original, a fact that angered Pelegrine because it demonstrated the English education teacher's limitations.

She had requested "sources" for original ideas. Pelegrine was fascinated by Orson Well's radio play "The War of the Worlds." She developed a theory how this work could be used for lessons teaching critical listening. Of course, she turned-in all her academic investigations not without Pontiac's blessings. So, anybody, who dared to question a logical conclusion or a metaphor, had to deal, in effect with two authors. When this unworthy English teacher started questioning Pelegrine's imaginative ideas, Pelegrine knew deep inside she was dealing with a fool. And knowing this, made her pursue the dull teacher even more. It seemed when she encountered an object that probably was too stupid to resist, Pelegrine became a hunter and had to conquer this object at almost any price. But Pontiac stopped that enterprise in time. The case and the chase were closed and never discussed again. Afterwards, Pelegrine engulfed herself in even more swimming, trying hard to forget her failed conquest:

Invalidation

Another hot day at the sun
Burned away some little
Of the nagging timber
Eroding slightly
At the bottom of the
Swimming pool.

I rise as a water log
But do not drown
Merely turn a thousand turns
In the rock bed of the
Blue
Deceiving calm.

Channel 86

And so the days passed into fall, winter, summer and spring. Year after year. At age 30 Pelegrine took up playing tennis seriously. With tennis teacher and all. She bartered for the lessons. The man wanted to be a minister and needed to learn German. She was actually gifted in tennis but soon realized that she should have started playing a lot earlier in her life. Back in Fechelaponte where she could only bike up to the fence, staying seated while grabbing the mesh with her fingers to balance herself. Until she was beckoned by the wealthy tennis playing crowd to be their ball girl.

She was born too soon. And tennis was not to happen for her until she was in a world were it wasn't birth and breeding that decided whether she was quick, lithe and gifted to swing a racquet, smashing fuzzy balls. But altogether, tennis was yet another activity that separated Pontiac and Pelegrine. These were times they could have been together. Late afternoons, when it became cool enough to play. Early Sunday mornings. Evenings. Pontiac quite clearly expressed her displeasure with Pelegrine. This obsession with tennis seemed to her, incessant and obsessive. They also had occasional disagreements about the hour chosen for a match. Pelegrine didn't like it that Pontiac was so fussy, especially since it was her 12-month job that separated them more than anything. The girl went ahead most of the time with her plans but did cancel several tennis dates. She did not want her tennis to interfere with her marriage too much.

Channel 87

All during their time in California and at the first college job in the South, Pontiac and Pelegrine would go camping a lot. Pelegrine learned about tents, charcoal fires, outdoor cooking and roughing it from Pontiac. These together times were fun and most constructive to their relationship. It wasn't until the later years that they spent more and more time apart with Pontiac coming home beat and tired every day from her draining job, inviting bourbon and water to her nightly rendezvous.

It absolutely drove Pelegrine up the wall, when she smelled Pontiac's alcohol breath while she watched her aspirations decline, her poetry vanish, her novel lie dormant and her mental activities focus exclusively on political issues. In the end, it didn't matter that they had been saving for years and years enough money to buy ten acres of farmland and were building a two-story 2400 square feet, angular, contemporary house.

Something must have happened over these years with no explanatory talk between them. When a new situation approached their relationship, especially when new and not mutually acceptable people came close to them, such encounters were often forbidden and underlying causes ignored, as was the case with the English teacher infatuation. Without role models, neither of the two women was knowledgeable and enlightened enough back then in the late seventies to avoid dealing with what causes a human being to go astray and to fall prey to illicit attractions. They only had each other and were fragile to the outside world and knew only to continue to live their tightly constructed partnership and bonded commitment. In retrospect, the English teacher episode was a first sign of discontent, which neither of them dealt with.

Not long after this incident, Pelegrine experienced some restlessness as far as her job was concerned. It did not make her too happy if she had to do this for the rest of her life. Consequently, she casually gathered information that would lead to a more advanced academic degree. She remembers cutting out an ad for two universities, one on the west coast and one on the east. She tucked the advertisement in a corner on her bulletin board for some day in the future, maybe. At that moment it seemed too much, too unrealistic and, of course, too costly. They were still saving money for their house like crazy, not having any vacations together, not enjoying emotional renewals or seeking couples therapy. Only work, books, bourbon for Pontiac, sleep and work again for both.

Channel 88

They had one couple friend, Nora and Archie Woodruff. He worked as a drafting teacher at a nearby institute. The wife was an insurance appraiser. The foursome was compatible in age and some interests like eating dinners on Thanksgiving or Christmas or Fridays. Going on a coon hunt with Archie was something else. He shot the fury creature and let it drop it at Pelegrine's feet. He was a heavy drinker and became a perfect drinking and discussion buddy for Pontiac. Pelegrine could not keep up with them. She tried, but very quickly got sick on a regular basis. She rarely enjoyed a buzz. Drinking for her usually meant falling asleep or vomiting. After she learned to drink slowly and small amounts at a time, she still never really enjoyed alcohol. Something in her system kept rejecting alcoholic beverages beyond dinner or social cocktails. If Pelegrine did not heed the signals of her body, she invariably paid with sickness.

Pontiac and Archie shared bourbons and politics. They rambled into late weekend hours and Pontiac enjoyed reducing Archie's illiteracy and his abundance of one-sided, red-necked information. Smart and well-read Pontiac would eloquently set him straight, teach him what he should have known and if the discussions got loud and boisterous, there was always Pelegrine who would vehemently defend Pontiac's position, even though Pelegrine's grounds were not solid like Pontiac's. But she felt that she had to save Pontiac's bulging veins on her temples and send some of the loud arguers, especially Archie, on his way, tuck Pontiac in and call it a night.

Channel 89

In spite of their many differences, the foursome developed a strange but strong friendship. It was the redneck side that flourished with the Woodruffs. With them Pontiac and Pelegrine could play monopoly, go out dancing and simply socialize a little with the world. With them Pelegrine could turn over the monopoly card table when everybody ganged-up and insisted that she did not have a hotel on Baltimore, and she was sure, she did. She was high and crazy and indulged by the group. She behaved sometimes like an infant. Especially when she made a bet with Archie that she could hold her liquor in a drinking race with what he called "boiler makers." A shot of whiskey was chased with beer or a whiskey glass was dropped inside a filled beer mug and all of it was gulped quickly. They were on number six, when Pelegrine had barely finished saying that she was fine and her head had fallen on her chest, and her body on the ground in her own living room floor.

Actually Pelegrine's behavior could be best described as temperamental and impetuous. Primarily when she felt misunderstood, misjudged or wronged by people. She had an explosive temper when she experienced injustice toward her or someone near to her. She voiced her passionate convictions and tried her utmost to convince the bad listeners that they were either unfair, narrow-minded or ill informed. Periodically, that which she perceived to be her extreme sense of fairness was challenged. And Pelegrine was infuriated when humans did not exercise democracy and justice toward everybody. To this day she is plagued with a crusader-like spirit for weaker, softer people. She wants to help underdogs and people being crushed by lack of real empathy and callous indifference. Someone once called her a Marxist. And she had to laugh. Pelegrine could care less for defined political views. She is she, no matter when and where she lives. Labels exist outside of her. And she exists outside of labels.

Don't label me. I hate labels. They confine and limit expectations. They prejudice thought into only one channel. As soon as people put labels on me, they want to tell me they know how I think. Let me be me, regardless of movements and symbols attached to the way I happen to be. I am the way I am with and without a tag. I am independent. I am a survivor. I would be that way if I were a mother to a child or a wife to a man. I would be the same, magnetic, adventurous and curious daredevil with her very own prescription.

She continues to have to guard herself and not explode too easily when injustice and self-serving complacency toward the less fortunate is practiced and tolerated. But there, in the company of her friends, Pelegrine let go of herself easily. Since they loved her, they put up with such behavior. Even if Pelegrine had a good and valid point to make, her ways to communicate her feelings were not always toned down with civil restraint. Her convictions often became hot, emotional outcries for, what seemed, centuries of silence, let lose in one burst of energy. This unexpected avalanche frequently deflated her impact because she usually did not select her audience with caution, nor did she weigh her plot or her agenda. Oppression and powerlessness angered her. Any person not caring for such matters found themselves in her firing line quickly. Thus issues dealing with personal space, choices, freedoms, empathy, humility, sincerity, leadership and philosophical insights could release Pelegrine's trigger.

At any rate, back then, her tiny family of friends indulged her tirades. Did they do her any favors? When did Pelegrine stop to grow up and why? Why could she never learn the techniques of proper discourse?

Channel 90

Archie bought a lot next to Pelegrine's and Pontiac's and eventually built his house there, too. He wanted to be close to them.

At the end of every week, he came to visit Pontiac and Pelegrine for his regular Friday unwinding drink. On one such evening, he opened up quite a bit. He revealed that he had marital problems. His sex life with Nora was zero. He had married her right out of high school and prevented her from becoming a nun. During that session he also confessed that he had a strong attraction to Pelegrine. The women's eyes quickly brushed each other. And they were very somberly taking turns to explain why he could not have such feelings. Pelegrine told him outright that she wasn't interested in him as a man. She only felt brother-like love for him. Another reason was his being a married man. And Nora was both their close friend. They told him to get those ideas about Pelegrine out of his thick head and to start working to communicate with his wife and maybe improve his love making techniques. Pelegrine and Pontiac asked him some pretty forward questions. They wondered whether he did enough foreplay, stroking and kissing and was able to wait and not rush into penetration. He just glared and couldn't believe that one needed to wait and refrain from humping. He only delayed that if "the wife," as he liked to call her, insisted that he just lay his penis between her tightly squeezed thighs. He would then just rub himself into an ejaculation.

Both listeners disliked his logic, but since Nora was not present, they did not know what to say about that, but did speculate that perhaps her vagina was too small or he was just not ever getting her "ready" to accept him. He admitted that he was a pre-ejaculator, which made matters worse. Pontiac and Pelegrine were no sex experts, on the contrary, they told him to get Nora more excited and for him to read books on different arousal techniques. The wise ladies even suggested for the couple to go to marriage and sex counseling. If only someone had questioned these two women's knowledge base and checked out their own love life! If only.

He came one day and showed off his see-through, black laced bikini underwear for men. Pelegrine had to laugh and told him she could never be turned on by something as stupid as that. She found such cheap tricks disgusting and thought that Nora probably did, too. Then the subject of sex was dropped for a long time, especially since Archie had admitted romantic feelings for Pelegrine. He could hardly control his emotions and seemed to become agitated whenever they were talking about sex in general. So they stopped talking about intimacies and continued their friendship with outdoor activities, horses and camping trips.

They grew vegetables, bought a horse together, which Pelegrine rode wildly through the woods every day like in the movies. She didn't know why horseback riding came so easy to her. It was another sport she taught herself. They fished in the nearby Saluda River and had great fish fries. They went on a long camping trip near the Cherokee Reservation in North Carolina. Pontiac and Pelegrine slept in their hammocks gazing at the stars. Nora and Archie were alone in their six-man tent.

The friendship with Archie and Nora filled only a small void in Pelegrine's life. Several "earthquakes" erupted in 1978 that were to change a lot of lives.

Channel 91

Archie had drawn the plans for Pelegrine's and Pontiac's house and Pelegrine took these blue prints often to her school. During lunch, her colleagues marveled at the nice home Pelegrine and her aunt were going to have. One teacher, in particular, showed a great deal of interest, Werra Weiß. She was bony, tall and an artist. When Pelegrine first started working there, she distinctly remembered seeing the lady in the hall and registering that she had that ambivalent androgynous, possibly latent gay look about her. She did not know why she thought that of her, maybe because she had large, capable and very attractive hands. For Pelegrine hands have always been important windows giving clues about a person's hidden persona. She immediately starts studying people's hands intently when first meeting someone. She guesses in split seconds what lives they have shaped or have shaped them. By analyzing the form, strength and gestures of hands, she very nearly always perceives a person's character. She likes useful, strong and practical hands, especially in women. When the veins were slightly protruding, the fingers intelligent and long, and the grip tight and solid, it was the spinal cord, the psyche, the brain, and the heart that spoke to her through a person's hands. Hands are the eyes that can't disguise the real self.

Pelegrine realized that her theory was challenged when she heard that Werra had three boys and a husband. Werra was friendly and had politely asked Pelegrine if she wanted to join her and a group of students at her beach cottage and be a kind of chaperone. Pelegrine declined but wondered why the woman had chosen to ask her.

Nearly six years had passed before Pelegrine spoke to Werra again with more than an office hello and good-by. Werra taught her art courses in a separate building and worked only convenient, part time morning hours. It was easy not to meet. And after all, the woman had a family. She did not need a pseudo-single woman friend.

But by the time Pelegrine was drawing plans for her house in the woods, Werra's husband had died of a cancerous liver--a by-product of his plutonium production job, a chemist, at age 48. Two of her sons were grown except twelve-year-old Pinocchio. She had drafting experience and was eagerly analyzing Pelegrine's house plans. And as Christmas 1977 approached, Werra invited Pelegrine to spend some time at the beach cottage with her. Pelegrine, thrilled, asked shyly if her aunt could come along, too.

"Of course, why not?"

Pelegrine noticed a strange, new feeling. She wished that she could have gone alone without Pontiac. She did not spend much time thinking about this inclination, but comfortably repressed it, dutifully making sure that her aunt was invited also.

Channel 92

It was fun at the beach house. They partied, ate dinner and Pontiac, unfortunately, got into the bourbon too deeply too fast. She passed out early in the evening. They put her to sleep and Pelegrine and Werra continued the party. Pelegrine had brought along some pot and introduced Werra to it. They were laughing and giggling, jumping around like school girls, and could not stop throwing little objects at each. Wherever they landed, the person who threw it had to come over and also remove it. They used rolled-up pieces of tissue paper or small pieces of driftwood. Since the women were extremely high, it was funny as hell, to throw them into each other's hair, sweaters and necklines, always in a new place to surprise the other one. That added to the excitement. And brought about such results!

This game allowed them body contact by pretending they were looking for the token. Clever inventions people come up with when they are in heat. As the evening progressed into night, they ended up lying on the couch, gradually becoming aware of each other. Pelegrine placed a quick kiss on Werra's neck who lay still like a log. Pelegrine wasn't sure why she didn't move. It could mean only two things: disgust or surprise, disguised as a delayed desire for more. All she heard was Werra's strained voice telling her that she had never done anything like that. Such powerful feelings were new. They were overwhelming. But they were welcome.

Now the chase was on. The hunt and the conquest Pelegrine enjoyed beyond description. She remembers many such junctures when her interest was sparked in somebody and she instantly had put herself in high gear with a desperation that knew no limits. These moments count as her most intense and highest and craziest. If her success rate had been more negative, perhaps, she would have learned to curtail these addictions for people who expressed an interest in her and whom she, too, found attractive. With the advent of Werra, however, a significant pattern of what kind of woman, what kind of situation with its attached hopelessness that triggered Pelegrine's interest, began to emerge.

Pelegrine was feverishly attracted to so called "straight" women. She experienced these brand-new connections with the same depth of anxiety as she did when she loved Rita, the first real woman love in her life. It seemed as if the strong taboo and out of reach status of a "normal" woman represented Pelegrine's ultimate excitement. These women were worthy "subjects" truly deserving her attention. Whenever she encountered an openly gay woman, she did not experience the same, lasting degree of contentment and exhilaration. They very often did not interest her at all.

When an attractive and capable straight woman was attentive to Pelegrine, however slight, it was very likely for Pelegrine' feelings to reach an epidemic level of obsession. She found herself in her personal whirlpool of emotions she called love.

But it wasn't that she was just a "head hunter." No. On the contrary. The whole experience centered on affection, attention, love and loyalty. It was a question of time, until one of the areas failed. Then the inevitable drama of doom entered the scene. But with Werra, Pelegrine had invited a pivotal shift in her life. She couldn't have known it at the time when they were exchanging paper curls on the couch before they kissed each other's necks.

Channel 93

At one point during the fateful night, Werra asked whether Pontiac would mind should she wake up and discover them. Pelegrine sighed deeply but avoided facing what she was about to enter.

"Oh, my aunt doesn't know about my inclinations. We'll have to keep it from her."

She doesn't know why exactly she lied. Probably because she was not ready to face reality. It was the most convenient and shortsighted answer for the moment. And the signs of lying began to show in the morning. Pelegrine wished intently that Pontiac were away and treated her unkindly. The tension became thick and Pelegrine wanted to go home that day even though they had planned to stay there longer. The arduous path of hiding the truth lay ahead. Fog and confusion followed.

Channel 94

Pelegrine was pre-occupied with Werra, her neck and her lips. And it wasn't until two days later that Pontiac suspected what was going on. And again, she asked Pelegrine point blank if she had feelings for that woman. And Pelegrine said yes. Shortly after this discussion the doorbell rang and Werra appeared with a New Year's Azalea in full bloom. Pontiac was disgusted and demanded that Pelegrine throw her out. But, of course, she couldn't. She arranged a meeting with Werra and told her the truth of her relationship with her "aunt."

She asked her to keep this information private, especially not to tell anybody at work. It also became clear that neither Pelegrine nor Werra were inclined to stop continuing what they had begun. The first kiss wanted company.

Channel 95

Pelegrine told Pontiac she would try to forget Werra knowing that she probably could not. For whatever reason, she never considered the real consequences of her actions. Perhaps, she was unable to visualize any of them. Her relationship with Pontiac was unstable but it was too early to see a path. She certainly did not want to face anything at that point. It pained her to put Pontiac through this but it became bearable by just following her heart and not her head.

At first, Pelegrine was not aware that she clumsily changed her patterns. She explored the town on her bike at times and in weather, which she had never done before. But that was the only way she could visit Werra for a few hours before her son would come home from school and interrupt. For quite a while, they didn't have time to do more than look at each other and dream of the rest.

Pelegrine had asked Werra not to call at her house out of consideration for Pontiac. But strangely, Werra refused to honor this request, not even on the day that Pelegrine had engineered a skiing trip with the ski club. She persuaded Werra hurriedly to join although she had never skied in her life. On that trip Pelegrine was hoping to be in a room with Werra, alone, finally, two weeks after their first kiss. Werra picked up Pelegrine at four in the morning. Instead of waiting in the car, she insisted to use their bathroom. Pontiac found that tacky. And silly Pelegrine defended Werra.

"Well, why couldn't she use our bathroom? You are so possessive."

"And I didn't even know the bitch skied and you didn't tell me that you were going on a ski trip with her."

Werra's piss-stop made them fight. And it was no surprise, that Pontiac decided to move out temporarily, stay with Eleanor, until Pelegrine got this madness out of her system, she said.

Channel 96

Yes. A most passionate encounter between Werra and Pelegrine was to follow. They could not get enough of each other. However. Pangs of guilt and sadness were gnawing at Pelegrine also. She was both extremely happy and deeply sad. Pontiac had moved out and after three days, Pelegrine went to see her, snuggled up and cuddled and asked her to come home. She did not like the fact that it was she who imposed such pain on Pontiac. At the same time, she had no one to talk and did not know what to do and did not want to stop her passion for Werra either.

Pontiac returned home. But Pelegrine continued her affair more discretely. It meandered into the month of January--the month they were ground breaking and erecting their house. They continued through the months of choosing wallpaper, parquet tiles and bathroom fixtures. Why in the hell did she continue to build a house with Pontiac <u>and</u> a romance with Werra? What kind of chicken shit was she?

Pontiac's and Pelegrine's house should not have been built.
But haven't lots of books already been written about foolishness like that? Who reads those and who learns from them? Who?

Channel 97

Werra and Archie helped move Pelegrine and Pontiac in June when the house was brand-spanking new and ready, waiting for healthy, happy people. Archie eyed Werra and asked Pelegrine who that good-looking woman was. "Nobody for you," Pelegrine replied. It was really shabby of Pelegrine to allow Werra's help in the move.

But Werra was also very clever. She did not think she would be in the way. And Pelegrine was too stupid to see through such a warped attitude. Again she also agreed with Pontiac's side that considered Werra to be a cruel bitch that knew full well that she was wrecking a marriage. Pontiac blamed Werra more than Pelegrine especially since she was 14 years older than Pelegrine and should have had the decency that Pontiac forgave Pelegrine for not having.

Channel 98

Werra was very similar to Rita, in complexion, character and temperament. She was beguiling and gentle and way too cunning and shrewd for Pelegrine. The affair with Werra was intense, hot and passionate and came with a huge price tag. After the settled, sometimes restricting but essentially stable relationship with Pontiac, another love-starved elderly woman, a widow this time, swept Pelegrine off her feet. It was a woman who would let Pelegrine in the window at four in the morning, who would come and throw pebbles at Pelegrine's window so she would crank up her 200 cc silver Vespa scooter and follow her love bird home. Pelegrine's diary reveals:

That which began December 26, 1977 and is, as of today, February 11, 1978, still going on, is an impetuous or is it tempestuous love affair with Werra

Weiß. I did not really get Pontiac inspired to write again, but her novel is finished. And I'm in love with Werra. I also love Pontiac. I love her with a quiet, settled, permanent emotion. The other one is hot, passionate and foolish. Werra is weak. She goes out with others, too. She seems starved for affection and touch. But since I am such a toucher, hugger and kisser, qualities that I have inherited from my mother, I can easily oblige. Sadly though, so can others for her. And she succumbs easily. I don't know what will happen to me, to Pontiac and our house. I live on the edge and want to get my bearings back again and fit Werra into my life. She needs to fit me into hers also. She wants a partner, but not me. A man. I am what I am. Susceptible to affection and irrational passion. This is my downfall.

Two months later in April, Pelegrine writes:

My involvement is stronger than ever. Pontiac and I are going our separate ways. We both find lovers outside the home now. I strayed first by falling in love with Werra. She and I want to be together constantly but don't know how to go about changing our lives. We are dreaming of togetherness. We have no models and don't know how to structure a second life. It might work. One day. I'll always love Pontiac. But we lost our romance. Right now I am in a pool, sunk in feelings, stirring elaborately but without direction. Her eyes burn when they look at me. Her body quivers with mine. We tremble when we look at each other--my heart reaches out for her--I want her continuously. She is delicately tender, affectionate, loving and strategically shy. Maybe we will marry?

Pelegrine volunteers in June:

On Saturday, June 10, Pontiac and I moved into our new house. Fantastic place. Spacious and airy. Move tiring. Furniture from Austria, Mama's hand carved walnut bedroom set with mirror, pendulum clock, side tables and princely beds arrived two days ago. I still love Werra. Pontiac still suffers from the separation. Werra and I don't know what's going to happen to us. We forever get turned-on to each other when we hold, touch, breathe, whisper and blow at each other. Her skin is like silk stuffed with cotton clouds. Her lips are soft as if I bite into a honeydew melon. Her breasts are like molten gold, slightly solidifying after frequent touch. They get sore from loving. Her fingers caress my places and mine seek her moist warmth. She excites me to no end, like nobody ever did. Maybe she will be crazier about me if I sleep with men? I would, if I knew she especially liked that--not so much for my sake but for her pleasure.

On another day, she writes,

I am all alone in the house. Werra is at a convention and Pontiac at the beach. Pontiac is still angry with me and possessively attempts to gut me. I am going to be the most mature person I have ever been in my life. I will learn, at whatever price, what it really means to avert blows. I will, for once, not react. It is so difficult and I feel constantly as if a sheet is pulled out from under me. I know Pontiac is hurt. I also know it is a tremendous presumption to continue to stay in a broken-up household. Our finances must be taken care of--then I am going--I don't know where though. I do know that I love Werra. But since there really is no future for us, I must gradually get ready to leave from here. I have to find other directions. Necessity is the mother... All things can be weathered. I hate it that my choices are so limited. Every choice is cruel to somebody.

Channel 99

Werra never could make up her mind whether she wanted to be with Pelegrine or men. Pelegrine wanted faithfulness and the feeling that Werra really wanted to spend her life with her. Pontiac, in her desperation began experimenting with other lovers and eventually subscribed to the "Wishing Well," a mail-order partnership program. Pelegrine still lived in the new house sporadically and guarded Pontiac from the "wrong" nibbles. She continued posing as her protective niece and actually helped Pontiac remove some of the less desirable leeches that came and had moved in with her.

In the summer of 1978, Pelegrine's mother came and Pontiac drove with Pelegrine to pick her up in New York. En route a truck hit them and they had to rent an emergency car to narrowly rescue the mother who was simply standing in the middle of the international arrival hall at JFK, waiting for Pelegrine as if it were the Fechelaponte railroad station.

Pontiac was still hoping that they would find each other again and repair their relationship. But it didn't look like it. Especially with no input. By itself it could only go one way.

Elli's visit was shared between Pontiac and Werra, both of whom were very fond of the little 69 year-old woman, good-hearted and easy-going as always. She didn't ask Pelegrine any questions and seemed to just accept that suddenly there were two women in her life. But that things weren't right was surely apparent to her also. Yet nobody talked about it. Avoiding confrontations seems to be the easiest way to enter another era of wrong.

Channel 100

Pelegrine finally moved out of her house In the spring of 1979 into a cottage, rented cheaply from her school. It was a retreat cabin located in the middle of a bamboo forest. Pelegrine moved only essentials, the washing machine, her old furniture and cooking utensils. At first, she called Pontiac every night. It was difficult and unbearable to be without her. Pontiac was kind and helpful. Pelegrine was still experiencing problems with Werra and still didn't know what to do.

Werra indicated that she did not want to live with Pelegrine and that she still needed men every now and then. Pelegrine just could not get used to Werra's unfaithfulness and her lack of commitment. Especially since Pelegrine had put her whole life on the line and Werra nothing.

Thus began their period of arguing, alternating with a period of making up, breaking and making-up. A seesaw. And every time, they were separated,

Werra would sneak up with tempting presents, clothes, fancy gadgets, anything to lure Pelegrine back. This tactic worked for a long time. Pelegrine's materialism was satisfied because Werra had quite a bit of money and let Pelegrine feel the power of it. When they were eating out, Werra knew just which tabs to pick and which to split. She was the master engineer of Pelegrine's emotional life. Pelegrine enjoyed this material privilege especially after the austere years of belt tightening with Pontiac. It is very likely that Pelegrine was lured into Werra's arms through her material goods, her fun beach house, her car that always started and even had air conditioning, her sensuality and, above all, her enticing tactics. The older woman knew she broke Pelegrine's heart every time she went out dancing with elderly gentleman who wanted to marry her. Why Pelegrine put up with that is unclear.

Channel 101

Werra eventually developed orgasmic problems. Pelegrine confides:
She must not want to be homosexual. Now she can't come anymore. She will cry and whimper, `I can't help it. I'm just not that way. Good knows. I tried. '
I had to tell her, that this thing one ought not <u>have to</u> try at all. This one does by choice and because it pleases. I angrily vow never to `bother' her or stay entangled with her anymore. Werra even went so far as to suggest that we could make love until we reached our limits. Then she could go out and get her supreme pleasure and orgasms elsewhere with a penis. I told her she was crazy to subject herself and me to such a triangle. I'll be damned. If she lived that way with her beloved husband and cheated on him that way, no wonder they had marriage problems. I will not go for something like that. I will never be a jilted female. I am capable of loving properly and being properly loved. Werra has grown weary of my touch, my way of making love, my everything. She asked whether I am seeing others. What a thought! This suggestion alone split me into a thousand pieces. Recently she also told me that she did love me deeply but maybe not as much as I did, but a lot, nevertheless. Now what am I supposed to

feel after that? Does that make me look like a shit ass or not? A fool without a brain? A blind bat without a head? Or just a human being refusing to think rationally? I told her that as long as she means as much to me, I could not easily or willingly go out and seek others. I decided that we had to stop. We parted. I moved my few things. I am away from her home. I took her pictures down and cried my heart and soul out for her and my stupidity not to have acted sooner. I aged overnight. I am a wounded animal. This is the deepest pain I have ever felt. I don't want to taste and feel and touch such a hell again as long as I live. Or am I in for the biggie yet? God, please, don't punish me again.

Channel 102

Pelegrine was helpless. Her temporary resolutions were hopeless. Two days later they were back together:

My baby returned while I was still asleep. She parked the car on the main road, fearing I would refuse her. I couldn't. I was hurting too much. We talked and decided we will try to live together in the future. My career goals must be steadied. Back packing through Europe mostly on foot and by rail keeping spending at a minimum, might help point the way toward our future. Living with me does intrigue her she says. I must let her have men occasionally, an open marriage to a degree. I can have her 99%. I love her so. I don't know what I will do. I want to care for her when she is old. She is all I have. Why does she want me?

Channel 103

In the summer of 1979 Werra and Pelegrine went on a 60-day backpacking trip through Ireland, England Germany and Austria. It was a good journey, on the one hand, and a journey that mirrored their reality, on the other. Only they did not consult the mirror.

They had the best of times together, and the worst. It was exhilarating to sleep on bathroom floors at railroad stations when all other beds were full, hiding the cumbersome pack under bushes in the cemetery while sitting in laundromats huddled in rubber rain pelerines while washing and drying their clothes for the hikes of the road. Werra's flirtations with fellows interrupted their temporary bliss, which Pelegrine knew one day would permanently overshadow their differences. But until then, she drifted with her emotional tides, continuing their relationship with clock-like predictable ups and downs.

Channel 104

On a better note, Werra insisted that Pelegrine have her first gynecological check-up. It was hard to get the stubborn old girl to go. She was mortified but Werra made the appointment and paid for it:

I have never been to a gynecologist. Only worked for one. Wow! What a doctor. She is somewhat like Stendal of Vienna, firm and rough but admirable. She had her finger all the way up inside me, almost coming out my throat before I knew what was happening. Everything went so quickly. The Pap smear taking hurt a little. She decided I had a cervical irritation and wondered why I hadn't noticed an increased discharge. I always accepted that to be a woman's normal "affliction." I now have a vaginal cream to squirt into myself. I don't like to do that. I still love Werra. Her 14-year-old son is a bit spoiled and driving the household crazy. She and I had differences over child raising. I come off invariably too strict, too European, too ancient, too different and too harsh. I am told things aren't done this way here. Bullshit. All the homes with intact families and healthy kid relationships, use quite a bit of that old country ethic. She is right about one thing. I do over-react and magnify situations. She settles me, teaches me to tone myself down. I am a propeller without a plane, a compass with an unscrewed needle, a butterfly without a flower.

Some days they separated, and then got back together only to part again. Their relationship was like a turbo engine, always racing, sometimes following and then going against their current, driven by fears, indecisions and lack of a consistent plan. Pelegrine basically suffered from not getting Werra's total commitment. She was used to a proper pledge and investment of one's self just as she had known with Pontiac. She did not know, free people could be weak and cowardly and only take what they want for the moment, and not aim for a bonded partnership. Pelegrine felt caught in Werra's web and she struggled, in vain, to free herself from it. This involvement became a pattern for her future life. But she had now way of knowing that.

Channel 105

From time to time she visited Pontiac and discussed her unhappy relationship with her who remained her friend, in spite of the careless treatment Pelegrine had offered her. But Pontiac was wise and kept telling the stubborn and eternal child that Werra was no good and not the right woman for Pelegrine. Pontiac found her selfish, cruel and unstable. Pontiac pointed out that Pelegrine needed only to consider the way Werra havocked their lives. But Pelegrine insisted that she herself had as much to do with that and excused Werra who, interestingly, had a strangely distant relationship to her sons whose favors she also "bought" with things. But Pelegrine saw what she wanted to see. No more. Her diary entries were going in circles just like her brain. These entries remain a testimony of her short-circuited early tactics involving emotional relationships:

I really fucked up my life as far as my connection with Werra is concerned. I am going to D. to study for an advanced and final degree. Maybe then I will be free of her. She is dating a widower called Elton. Four men have asked to marry her since I have been in her life. Tell me, am I dumb, a sucker or what? I have got what I asked for. I wouldn't listen to reason. My God, why did I get hooked to something like that? I feel miserable and dejected. I was stupid by spending intimate time with middle-class bastards. People who believe everything they see, hear or smell are not what I need. Hilton Head friends of Werra's who think there is nothing more corrupt than the Democratic Party! They are all suck artists and male chauvinists to boot. To hell with all of them. I want to be a Huckleberry anyway. Screw the world.

Channel 106

Before she left the cottage to study in the North, Archie suddenly appeared because Pontiac had revealed her true relationship and breakup with Pelegrine to him and Nora. Pelegrine was furious because she thought she should have been consulted prior to divulging their sexual engagement to anybody. But then, in light of Pontiac's plight, it was forgivable. What was interesting was the fact that Archie had shown an interest in Werra and suggested a three-way sexual encounter. Pelegrine asked Werra what she thought. The woman was not disinclined. Pelegrine was bewildered. First of all, she had never been with a man at all. Second, why do this when she really loved Werra? Yet, there was something alluring in it. She did not know what though.

Pelegrine engineered Archie's appearance at the beach house one night. The three had smoked pot. When Archie and Werra were dancing and becoming sensuously close, Pelegrine stared at Werra and couldn't believe that she could go through with it. At that moment, Pelegrine felt hurt and disgusted. She sulked and pouted and wanted to end the party. Pelegrine threw Archie out. She was nauseated with him, too, and wondered why she had ever agreed to this fiasco.

Pelegrine was depressed the next day and didn't want to be close to Werra anymore. She was wondering what to do with her life again. Everything was suddenly even more complicated and confused. Archie would appear frequently at the cottage and repeatedly proposed sex with Pelegrine. He came so often, that it reached the point where she thought it might be a good opportunity to find out more about men. After all, she was "free," not counting her shambled liaison with Pontiac and her decayed one with Werra.

And, furthermore, she wanted to know if she had a large enough capacity for what Lisa Diamond calls sexual fluidity that allowed her to respond erotically to both a woman and a man. Many of the women in Diamond's research study had similar types of fluctuating sexual directions. Sometimes it was heterosexual women falling in love with women, and sometimes it was actually lesbian women falling in love with men! So, Pelegrine wanted to know if she belonged to this fluid spectrum of attractions moving inside a range of possibilities and not just between two extremities, where you are either one or the other.

In fact, she had often wondered what exactly her sexual orientation was. Now that Archie presented an experimental opportunity which did not appall Pelegrine, she was even more interested in the definition of bisexuality.

The experts think that traditional bisexuality involves individuals who tend to have more consistent patterns of attraction to both genders. But Pelegrine's experiences sound more similar to a phenomenon that has been described as "being attracted to the person, not the gender." In other words, someone might have a generally stable pattern of attractions for men or for women, but they might also have the capacity to respond strongly to someone on an emotional and intellectual and interpersonal basis--that sort of general psychological bond can, in these cases, "spill over" into eroticism. Often times, when this happens, Pelegrine is not necessarily even paying attention to the other person's gender. She is simply drawn to that person as a person. In many ways, this seems like an entirely different form of sexual orientation. In other words, some people are attracted to the opposite sex, some people are attracted to the same sex, and some people have the capacity to respond to folks regardless of their sex. However, some bisexually-identified individuals WOULD call that sort of experience "bisexual." The truth is that there is no single definition of bisexuality, and it is a topic (and a definition) that is hotly debated among sexuality researchers as well as bisexually-identified individuals themselves.

But to Pelegrine, her experimentation with Archie was not supposed to prove any of that. For her it was only important to see if she could get aroused and enjoy it. She had always known, that attraction came first and gender second.

Channel 107

Pelegrine felt safe with Archie since he did everything she demanded. He was a lusty and over-sexed bull. The minute he looked at Pelegrine he announced his hard on to which she replied nonchalantly,

"Well, that's too bad for you. You should restrain yourself a little."

As she was speaking he would come. Her voice and her whole body excited the man beyond control. When they were intimate, she dictated every move, held his penis, marveled at its beauty and tried to teach him to hold his sperm by pinching the skin at the tip slightly. She had read about this trick somewhere. When he tried to enter her, she was squeamish and said for him to be slow and careful and under no circumstances ejaculate on her, not to mention inside. He always pulled away just in time to the awaiting towel. But every time he squirted into the towel, it was the point where Pelegrine was getting aroused and had an interest in the act and wanted him to stay with her and continue making love. But once he had squished his shit into the towel, he rushed up and was not at all inclined to continue his otherwise never-ending interest in sex. That's when she realized sexual intimacy without love is just awful. She could not understand how someone who professed such virility had to wait before being able to go on again. But then what did she know about male sexuality, virility and the age of a person? Zero.

His staying power apparently was quickly spent. And if he knew only to hammer away at anything beneath him, he was surely not a good lover. Pelegrine, however, made an important discovery. She became aware that sex with a man was not out of the question for her. But it had to be somebody whom she was attracted to and could emotionally connect and not someone whose hair on his shoulders repulsed her and who was only interested in the back-and-forth, pounding motion, and even that for not very long. She found out what she needed to know. She was a sexually ambivalent woman. She had always suspected that emotionally she was quickly drawn to women and sexually she could enjoy both. But that sex with a man could work and even be fun, she never had an opportunity before to find out so safely. It pleased her.

Channel 108

Between Werra and Archie, Pelegrine needed a new life. She dug out her old brochures on continuing her education. And in the fall of 1980 she entered a prestigious university as a doctoral student in European Studies. She left them all behind, kept up a phone relationship with Werra who visited Pelegrine from time to time. But the distance and the fact that Werra was not right for Pelegrine to begin with, took its toll. She stayed entangled with Werra for over two years. When Pontiac was approaching foreclosure because she and her unemployed, clingy new lover could not keep up the payments, Pelegrine asked Werra to become co-signer of the mortgage. Pelegrine's student status was to her disadvantage at that moment and she needed financial backing. Werra, needless to say, hesitated and left Pelegrine no choice but to beg Pontiac to put the house on the market.

But something must have happened to the brain of once brilliant Pontiac. Maybe the new woman, Shanty, a mouse-like creature, ill advised her. Pontiac did not want the house sold properly. She was willing to sign it over to Pelegrine, but that wasn't good enough for the bank. And so the vicious cycle began and the house ended up being GIVEN AWAY TO THE BANK FOR NOTHING. The bank and a realtor took over the mortgage responsibilities and released Pontiac and Pelegrine of their obligations. The realtor eventually sold the house with the 15 thousand dollar profit that Pontiac and Pelegrine would have made.

Pelegrine was in utter despair over Pontiac's foolishness and Werra's selfishness. She realized that she was completely on her own again with not a human soul to lean on. She fiercely pursued her studies, which represented her only ticket out. Pontiac's irrationality and Werra's cold-blooded passivity were everlasting gifts and events that had bitter repercussions eventually. How many chances does a human being get, building such a nest egg and cashing-in later when old and interest payments have surrendered to equity and retirement is nothing to be afraid of? Everything Pontiac and Pelegrine had suffered for: love, land, house, decency and trust, disappeared that day and Werra stood watching it go.

Channel 109

At the university, far away, Pelegrine had her hands full. She was in the midst of much younger classmates, but they liked her maturity and her experience coupled with her helpfulness. Pelegrine was 36 then. Rosemarie Sand, her poetry professor, 42. The woman spoke Pelegrine's mother tongue and had an unhappy marriage and was attractive and kind and responsive and answered Pelegrine's poetry and kissed her but did not allow herself to be touched. But she did caress and fondle Pelegrine.

Such was the contact that produced 365 epic pages of a prose poem lamenting unrequited love and the torment inflicted by a new problem: a sexually repressed woman who had an a-sexual relationship with an absent husband who stayed married because the wife was paying for mortgage and frills while she was hoping to win back her man. On top of that, Rosemarie had feelings for Pelegrine that were chased by guilt because of her unresolved marriage predicament, hanging in limbo for eleven years. Pelegrine believed her each time, each Christmas, Thanksgiving and summer when she would disappear and promise to make a clean break. Pelegrine was supposed to be patient and wait just a little bit longer. Her and waiting on women! In order to soothe her suffering, she wrote day and night to Rosemarie. A Viennese feminist publisher expressed an interest in the unbelievable intensity and abundance of emotions splashed on hundreds of pages and agreed to publish her document, her own bequest and proof of this agonizing courtship that lay buried in a novel that lasted two years.

Channel 110

Pelegrine:

I am once again imprisoned in the chestnut desert of soft and wet earth beneath me. Restlessness suffocates me. Pain and life are one. And you don't know it although you see and hear me and are nice to me and perhaps even like me. I live in a window with no house. I don't know what I should do with myself. I bear one poem and melt into the next one. I stumble in a non-stop, poetic fever. I am mercury outside its case. I am the rhythm of all instruments. I run between air. I hear my thoughts as I sing the sorrow of my pain. Where is the hand that will catch my fall?

Channel 111
> Rosemarie:

I have a few questions about the poems. I liked them. But what can I say? I am almost afraid to spoil something--to ruin it. Affection and enthusiasm become temporary so easily--they tend to dwindle so fast. Perhaps, you have time this weekend for a little literary chat? Explicate your poems? Maybe you even would like to have dinner with me? I would really like that.

Channel 112
> Rosemarie:

Busybody is probably not the right word. You shouldn't call me that. Sounds a bit like peddling too many wares or meddling in other people's affairs and that I don't do. It is not my nature. But at the moment, I am in a position where all the duties, which I have accepted, leave me very little room to move, to be flexible. Thank you for the soup. I was really pleased, but, as you may suppose, also a little embarrassed, because I don't quite know if I deserve such kindness and good will. Distance and coolness are a kind of protection, no doubt. I am really looking forward to Saturday. I am so eager to talk and think with you, to be with you and to analyze, `dissect' your verses if you wish--as far as one is allowed and permitted. Please, don't be angry or disappointed.

Channel 113
> Pelegrine was exhilarated and motivated to quickly like the woman even more especially since she encouraged her by responding that way. The women wrote back and forth. Pelegrine had a daily literary rendezvous with this intelligent professor woman. Rosemarie was always well inclined towards her. But she was

the woman with no time.

Pelegrine:

I became a cloud under your water gazing at your pleading eyes that were saying 'don't smother me.' But they were also not un-smothering mine.

Channel 114

The very first private and very personal meeting between Pelegrine and Rosemarie was indefinitely postponed until a distant date when Rosemarie invited her to go visit her personal hiking spot deep in the forest. There they roasted chicken in a wire basket, dangling from an improvised plumbing pipe. There they shared the loft of a hiking shelter lean-to.

Pelegrine:

I am afraid of a meeting, afraid of what I will discover, while I am expectantly hoping for it all to happen in the first granted, yearned-for evening. I am afraid of me. I am feverish and anxious when somebody beckons me when I should actually calm down, be patient and not bend in both directions, for her and for me. Can you help me, tame me, lame me but not maim me? I am harmless but, ah, ever so responsive to the slightest suggestion.

Today is like Christmas. Can one be worn out from too much joy?

Channel 115

Pelegrine prepared lots of questions and brought them along to the nervously anticipated first meeting alone with a lady she most deeply adored. She had given Rosemarie those questions ahead of time and hoped for answers on their camping trip in the woods. Pelegrine was asking because she was also curious whether Rosemarie was aware what kind of love this attraction could procure.

Channel 116

Pelegrine received written answers from Rosemarie even before they went on the camping trip.

Rosemarie:

Now I sit in bed and write a kind of response to you instead of correcting papers. I find that very easy because I like to fantasize and dream. My answers will correspond to each one of your questions:

1. Do you have any idea what this is all about?
Yes, I have. But we'll talk about it better when we are sitting before a nice fire in the woods, yes?

2. Do you have questions for me, too?
Yes.

3. Should I withdraw my attention and be more reserved?
No, I never contemplated that.

4. Do you find my feelings pushy and annoying?
I have the deepest respect for genuine emotions.

5. Do you have a preference of how I should act toward you?
Tender, quiet and cautious so that neither of us gets hurt.

6. Do you have fears of what this could lead to?
Disappointment and pain. But that is not easy because we don't know ourselves very well. At least I don't.

7. Do you feel the way I do?
I don't know. Yes and no.

8. Are you aware that you are affecting me deeply?
I did not know.

9. Why can I not do little favors for you?
I don't easily let people help me. It depresses me. I'd rather help. That makes me happy.

10. Do you wish I should stop or continue to be passionate about you?

I don't want to encourage nor discourage you. Neither one would be right. Either it is in you or not. Whatever that may be.

Channel 117

Thus the special day arrived and Pelegrine and Rosemarie traveled far to be private and alone. They rode in the tiny TR4. It was small like a matchbox. Steel wire cables blocked the road they needed. In no time the small, topless car coasted quietly underneath the lifted cable. They were gliding through valleys of golden foliage. Her husband had once discovered the lean-to and Pelegrine was the first and only person to be told of this secret hideaway. It was a public A-frame shelter holding simple provisions for lost hikers. Rosemarie climbed the ladder and made one big bed for the night. Pelegrine's heartbeat quickened instantly. In the meantime, she prepared the fire, laid out the reading materials, the questions and answers and poured Chablis. Their cheeks were glowing soon and the charged atmosphere became thicker and heavier yet. Rosemarie never clearly answered anything. She gave evasive double-talk responses from which Pelegrine gleaned what she wanted to hear. Therefore, she assumed Rosemarie was interested in her but only afraid to act on it. She would help her with that she thought.

Channel 118

The moon was their chilly companion, as they were lying atop the loft intensely aware of each other's warmth and rhythm. Pelegrine shifted and slightly bent over Rosemarie's ghost-like face and inhaled her breath. They were both panting heavily in unison until Pelegrine placed a kiss on Rosemarie's neck. "Always these necks," rushed through Pelegrine's head. Rosemarie did not move away. She responded tenderly and allowed the progression to the mouth. But Pelegrine was actively restraining herself and remained in the kissing mode. Of course, she had been waiting ardently for this moment, but she really cared for this lady and did not want to be like men and go for the "kill" on the first night. She remained respectful and polite laboring with cumbersomely contained passion. She thought there would be other times offering a natural progression into further stages. They fell asleep in each other's arms and in the morning Rosemarie got up first, busily moving and running about making breakfast.

Channel 119

Pelegrine climbed down the ladder, sleep in her eyes and lint clinging to her hair. The first apprehensive glances after a first night are usually anticipated with some trepidation. But Rosemarie smiled and Pelegrine was relieved that everything was still the same, a day later. Only Rosemarie was in a rush to get back home. Such haste would become Rosemarie's trademark. She never stayed anywhere very long. Shortly after arriving, she always wanted to run farther or back, where she came from. She always was on the run, run, run. Such conduct meant a lot of adjusting not only for Pelegrine but also for their few common friends. But for the time being, Pelegrine was more than willing to oblige from that day on. A little encouragement went a long way for her. And with Rosemarie's reassuring ambivalence, who could tell where they would end up?

Channel 120

Pelegrine's poems became a vital outlet for her dissatisfaction with Rosemarie's perpetual pull and release, but more from her never going further than touching Pelegrine. She never allowed Pelegrine to reciprocate lovemaking.

It is a miracle that she got anything accomplished in her studies, at all. She had to do double over time because being in love like that and pursuing a higher degree required extraordinary energies and endurance. She would rush home to her apartment, which she shared with Peter, a young, poor lawyer, quiet, acquiescing but a little weird. He had a yellow note pad under his bed where he scribbled his nightly pornographic phantasies. While checking through his things, the "landlady" Pelegrine couldn't believe her eyes. She read how he was "holding his big cock, throbbing and ready to be sucked...." Well, it did not bother her, as long as he could separate what was on the pad and what was expected of him when the rent was due at 666 Bassett Street.

Pelegrine hurriedly performed her assignments, fast and furious so that she could get back to either her aching poetry or her one-sided girlfriend.

Channel 121

Pelegrine:

Now I know what brings me peace. I could study only in bits and pieces. My head always skidded. Always to you. The same place. But today on a Sunday I went there in person. And suddenly all was well. I could be me again! I gorged myself on you, on the sun, even on interruptions, on the homework, the wasps, the cat liver, the hopeless search for ribbons, the slippery car drive, the moments, ah, the moments where eyes rested upon eyes. I could totally dissolve in you. When I am near you, I find peace.

Channel 122

Meeting

My eyes went down only to
rise swiftly with yours
long enough to linger before
parting.

Channel 123

Red Whispers

*Is it outrageous
if I kiss flowers in October
on the floor?
I was forced
to lie down with them
because I am
paralyzed by desperation
seeking escape.
Seven red witnesses delicately
testify.*

Channel 124

And Rosemarie did for the first time what she would do forever--LEAVE. Always suddenly. And especially when time became available for togetherness like Thanksgiving, Christmas, and summers. For those occasions, Pelegrine speedily prepared oodles of notes, poems and questions to give to Rosemarie on her journey so she would think of her and bring back some needed answers, clear ones, not wishy-washy-maybe-ones.

Channel 125

Pelegrine:

You say you don't want to <u>en</u>- and you don't want to <u>dis</u>courage me. O.K. Does that mean, I can let my feelings run freely and act the way I see fit, regardless whether you respond to my currents or not? Do you have the courage to tell me to stop? How do I fit into your emotional jigsaw puzzle? Am I the only one active and you persistently passive? What does your response mean? Are you waiting? What do you feel? How do I fit into your life? Is there room for me?

Channel 126

When Rosemarie was away, Pelegrine wrote and wrote and wrote, twenty-four hours a day. She only stopped to eat and sleep and do her school work in record time, only to get back and continue making plans, resolutions and facing cancellations.

Pelegrine:

I will try to behave more quietly and not set the hall on fire acting like a hurricane. I will leave the steering to you. You have moderation and surely are more capable to tame your tempests. I will walk and sleepwalk like puppets with mechanical souls. Maybe it is easier not to act and sit on my feelings, just holding the door shut. No wind disturbance. Everything stays the same and becomes bearable. I must silence my rage. I will dive into my work, which I am usually in love with when it's not people. It is constant and doesn't go away. Once, let me lose myself and twirl in heaven with you. What an awful realization that I have to join Goethe's Werther pains. I hate reading <u>and</u> re-living him simultaneously. Because of you, and only you, I understand his agony and even his death. So, literature really makes sense only if we have been there. Otherwise we only understand abstractly. Wow!

Channel 127

I feel like an attachment appended to you
the unnecessary chore amidst thousands
the fifth wheel and the spare
the one course that exceeds the limit
the intruder into your turbulence and confusion of a daily circus you call day
the rain that doesn't cease to hammer hailstones on a tattered tent
    I am the lasso circling to rope you, the beggar,
asking to be left alone but holding me at bay
the cork sitting down in your neck when your sign says
occupied but available
the lawn mower running for you while you scream
stop and go
the window shutters slamming into your storm windows.
    I am superfluous,
The ornament serving no purpose… Right?

Channel 128

Death Lives

Death is lively
Because death is alive
Yesterday they leaped
Today they weep, the limbs, body, soul and hair of me
Because you left again
You took away stroking, holding, loving, folding me.
I was warm but now I am cold.
I am freezing in October.
I am hungry in the sunshine grown cold.

Are you sad because you did not have time for us?
Or do only I miss it so?
        I know I have swamped you with the subjunctive of two people.
Maybe I smothered and robbed your breath and knocked us over before we had a chance to dance?

Channel 129

    Pelegrine's troubles flowed relentlessly. Her reports swelled into a black hole, a black sea.

Mirror: 200 Years Old

You were my bookmark while reading 'Werther'
Your telephone number glistens in my head and Schiller declares

    `*That which one flees is inside oneself--*
What one looks for, is eternally outside.'

Do we flee from our feelings or seek to confirm only to destroy that which doesn't meet our expectations? Do you have any idea at all what it is like to read 'Werther' while living through an identical hell?

You, literature professor, what do you know?

Channel 130

The Roof Is No Terrace

Today, Sunday
a week later exactly as it was then—

so sunny, so blue, so new.

But now I sit here with me not there with thee
where once I sunbathed in you.

Today anything yellow burns my skin
Red doesn't melt my cold heart
My heavy eyes freeze without you

Channel 131

  This evening you were absolutely great! I just realized how beautiful you are. Your sight struck deep inside my soul. You were cheerful and happy and stayed in one place for a little while. My insides were racing and could barely stop. I could not take my eyes away from you. Your tender body transfixed me. Your smooth skin glowed softer than your silky blue, skin-tight suit. Your hips were narrow and made me tremble. My wall has crumbled. Your naked feet lay in my hands. You let me warm them and not the opened oven door of the kitchen stove.

Channel 132

  Now you have walked on my floor and sanctified the threshold of my home. You have eaten with me and your lips have blessed my cup. Your eyes charmed my things. Did you want to find me? You like me enough to let me help you, the one that can't easily accept. There are also eager other helpers adoring you. How come you let me?

Channel 133

Dark Rendezvous

I don't dare say what I really feel. But I am not silent either. This night I passed along your street shortly before midnight so I could catch a glimpse of you. But, heaven you caught me till two in the morning. I could not say adieu in the growling car. A spell held you and me. I wanted to touch you and love you. In spite of your swollen work, you are eating with me till morning hours and let us drink from each other. I take passion baths and soak up ecstasy and frenzied love.

Channel 134

During this delirious affair, Pelegrine did not stop to chronicle her life:
I am a doctoral student at this fine university. The first snow flurries with cold wind were icing up my head today. I love every minute here. I love the force that lets me be so fortunate. I enjoy learning as if I were a straying dog eating knowledge after long bouts of hunger. I miss Werra and Pontiac. Werra will visit. She is lonely but I don't know what will happen to us. I still care for her. But I am living my life now. I hope I don't let her stop me from continuing my growth including the one going on outside my studies. Somehow she has eel-like qualities that always come around when I have freed myself of her. Then she tries to catch me and wants to be with me. I wonder if she wants me as a part-time love, turned-on and off like a radio?

Channel 135

Werra and I are finally where we belong. Separate. I told her about my new feelings which I re-learned after she had hurt me so often. I told her I loved Rosemarie Sand, a professor of mine. This attraction is similar to when I met Pontiac, yet wiser. So it seems. She is cautious, married and interested in me. She is also driving me crazy. I have written over 100 pages of poetry to her and I am really in love. I don't want her to do me like Werra though--me giving her so much of me and she so carefully unfolding and holding back herself. I want her. She is genuine and a truer person than Werra, for sure. She is also Austrian and I can love her in that language. I love her voice, her speech, her body, her timidity, and her gentleness. I want the gods to give her to me. I want a life with her.

Channel 136

I am insane and desperate. I love this woman. She cannot return the feeling. She is good, kind and absolutely divine but forever withdrawn into herself. She will not share her soul with me. I think I am wrong again. Every time it really, really mattered to me--not an infatuation that ended in dust--no, really a potential lifetime partner, it always was unavailable for me. Why? Werra still tugs at me. But Rosemarie has me. I am afraid of myself. I don't want to give her up. She says her long-distance marriage is hell. But she is convinced she can't give me what I need. Rather than disappoint me, she suggests I go for others. Yet, she doesn't want me to turn away my affection, yet, yet, yet. Damn! What a replay! I must need to be shot. I am not fit to live. The right people don't want me.

Channel 137

She called me to join her. We drove to repair her typewriter, pick up my bike, and have coffee. Forever I ask the same questions. Rosemarie, if I must turn away from you as you wish, how does that work? Help me. Which will hurt you the most and the least? Should I:

1. Become cold, reserved, preoccupied, trying to forget?
2. Be nice, your friend but not intimate?
3. Be intimate with others instead of you?

And you answered that number one would hurt you and number two and three also. But you don't know why. You said that you would have no right to feel hurt in number three but you can also not say that it wouldn't bother you. **I think I go**

from one fucked-up lover to another. This one is special. She speaks my mother's language and has the gentle understanding and intellectual insight to love me for my genuine qualities. I really, really love Rosemarie. I will stop only if I am deadly exhausted and she finally grabs me and shouts in my face: `Pelegrine, damn it. Quit. I cannot give you what you need. I mean it. Please, go away.' Then I'll go. She has said half of the above already but not the rest. She doesn't want me to go away. What am I to do? I feel old, torn, sad and talented but undesirable. I want a partner, a lover, and a friend who sticks by me. A horse thief.

Channel 138

From Pelegrine's records, her poems and her diary, it became somewhat obvious that she replaced one disappointment with another. But it was also gradually becoming clear to her what her new predicament actually demanded of her. Rosemarie was all wonderful things that a person could wish for. But she could not clean up her attachment to Lawrence Sand, a man who, according to her, ignored and abused her in all manners possible. Yet she could not let go of him and hoped that he would return to his old self when he was an engineering student, traveling on exotic safari adventures with Rosemarie, inventing gadgets, making rare art but leaving her on their honeymoon in South America, stranded in a remote village after an argument--without a passport, clothes, a tooth brush or a dime. When Pelegrine heard this, she said to Rosemarie that she must have been a willing sucker, a person that must enjoy being treated like that because Rosemarie's stories were far from over. Amazing insights Pelegrine could offer to others but not herself. It is very likely she was such an astute clinician of the trials of human relationships because she was such an expert herself in sick connections.

Rosemarie returned from her honeymoon expedition what sounded dangerous, careless and life threatening. She was hitchhiking her way back to Latin American Civilization a woman alone with only the clothes on her back! But she continued to love him anyway and pursued Lawrence what by now amounts to eighteen years. Pelegrine hated it that Rosemarie spent all--and that meant all-- her frequent professor vacations hunting him, fighting him or wishing to change him. She continued to beseech the foolish disciple:

"Pelegrine, I must clear my affairs with him. Without that, you and I don't have a chance at all."

That in itself seemed reasonable and logical to Pelegrine. The only problem was that each time Rosemarie returned, the affairs were in the same state, in the same constellation and Pelegrine had to decide a course of action. Rosemarie was not.

Channel 139

One reason it was so difficult for Pelegrine to walk away from this gentle tiger was perhaps locked in a combination of triggers. For one, Rosemarie was a great cook, mothering type and a giving person. In other words, she embodied all the qualities that Pelegrine appreciated. But the way she was making love was something else. It was brand new, very unusual and very destructive.

It will be recalled that on their first night, Pelegrine held back not to go beyond the kissing stages. That wasn't easy. But she did it out of fear to ruin the preciousness of the moment. What she could not know was that it would take weeks before Rosemarie would allow a second kiss. Period. That was so, regardless of the fact that Rosemarie had allowed Pelegrine--upon Pelegrine's persistence--to spend a night in her house. A house with no beds. Only blankets on a hard wooden floor. But Pelegrine wanted to learn that experience, too.

They slept, side-by-side, naked. They touched only what Rosemarie allowed to be touched. That amounted to handholding, followed by quick good night brushes with lips that weren't allowed to linger. That was it!

Pelegrine would try and come-on to Rosemarie, who one night reluctantly agreed to another somewhat more extended kissing session. Her body betrayed her. Her cheeks got hot and her breathing heavy. The normal signs, indicating clearly that she wanted more. But the barrier refused to fall. She jumped up like lightening, ran to the bathroom and took a prolonged piss. Sometimes a shower even. Pelegrine could not believe something like that. What was that? Nowhere had she seen or read about behavior like this. She tried to rationalize and comfort herself,

"Good. At least, she must have gotten aroused. Why else would she be peeing or showering? At least, she is not frigid, even though she said she was. I had to laugh when I heard that."

Upon her return from the bathroom, she actively assumed a mother role and mocked,

"O.K. Little Pelegrine. Sleepy time now. Roll over like a good girl. Enough for one night."

And disappointed Pelegrine rolled over all right. But did not sleep till the early morning hours. The floor became suddenly hard. And her mind was confused as usual.

Channel 140

During similar nights, Rosemarie would go as far as touch Pelegrine, fondle her breasts timidly and let her middle finger wander down over the belly button, rubbing the pubic bone and, low and behold, one day, even entered Pelegrine's vagina. Pelegrine was in ecstasy, a heartbeat away from a stroke. Neither Browning's "Portuguese Sonnets" nor "J. Alfred Prufrock" captured this weightless moment where time stood still. Pelegrine almost fainted.

However. When Pelegrine eagerly was ready to return the loving, Rosemarie turned into frost. She sternly pushed Pelegrine back with an absolute NO.

Channel 141

Such incidents were to repeat themselves a dozen times, even when they were sunbathing in the nude in the middle of forest clearings or secluded meadows. Rosemarie was a super lover operating with natural talent and a lover's instinct. This was a woman, supposedly with no sexual experience. But an expert at the task! That fact once more proved Pelegrine's theory. The act of loving isn't learned in books. They only offer strategies but not the act itself. **That is in you. No matter how new.**

Nonetheless, Pelegrine was unsure about this one-sided activity. She was both repulsed and attracted. She was disgusted by not being able to touch Rosemarie. She was also appalled that she continued to let Rosemarie operate that way. She did not know what to do. But she did know that she was unhappy about it.

Channel 142

In the middle of March, Rosemarie responded with a letter and a gift. Pelegrine had been withdrawing, sulking and threatening to leave. Rosemarie gave her a silver ring with a little poem suggesting that this little ring could mean everything or nothing. It should represent friendship and love but not the binding confinements of such feelings--whatever that meant. Perhaps, Rosemarie was ahead of her time and knew of commitments that revel in freedom and limitless boundaries and absent restrictions. Perhaps, Rosemarie knew nothing?

Needless to say, Pelegrine flipped out over the ring. She needed so little encouragement to go flying. This silver ring really spun her. But Rosemarie's reply at this stage also demonstrated the state of their affair:

Dear Pelegrine,

I am really sorry that you are feeling bad. How much I wish I could help you. If you don't want to wear the ring, don't. I only gave it to you to tell you that I like you and that you are lovely. But you don't have to wear it. Put it in a drawer and, sometimes, when it rolls out, think of me. I don't want to hurt you. Please, believe me. But I feel so weak and inadequate. I want to be alone or with irrelevant people and concentrate on my energy. Please, don't suffer. Do something nice and funny. Go to New York City. The sky is blue and the air smells of spring. Forget me for a while. Forget me altogether. Don't make my problems yours. If you want to break or feel you have to, then do it. I would be so glad if we could have a casual cup of coffee together. But, I imagine, that's not possible under the circumstances. Please, do what you should and must. Don't be angry. But mainly don't be sad. Please. Please.

Channel 143

A postcard a day later stirred the embers:
I hope you feel better, dear Pelegrine. Here is a beautiful postcard with a meadow full of poppy flowers for you.

Channel 144

But Pelegrine was more than angry. She was trying to act and do what was best for her. She sent back an Emily Dickinson poem:

I can wade Grief
Whole Pools of it
I'm used to that
But the least push of joy Breaks up my feet
And I tip-drunken
Let no Pebble-smile
`Twas the New Liquor--That was all!'

Channel 145

Rosemarie was quick to reply:
I want to be your friend. Do understand me right? Please. Everything else can only be tragic and twisted. At least for the time being. Please, understand. Please, don't believe that you are having it harder. Please, come by this

evening, if you want to, for one hour or so, for wine and snacks. I will try to have heat in the house.

Channel 146

Pelegrine's eternal journal chronicles its record:

The situation demands--so she says--she is not free and thus unable to act. I should be content, patient and happy. I think she does not want to lose me but wants not to commit herself to me. She IS a Catch 22. Damned if I do and damned if I don't. One day, she suggests just friends, mother or sister. Then, 'One must not always want to have what one wants.' Shit. She is complicated. I am complicated. I think it's hard to pull back to 'just' friendship. When you play two sides at the same time, torment such as this is the result. What am I to do? Hang in there? Give up? Wait?

Channel 147

This is a journey into my private inferno. Maybe I can peel myself raw and find out what is wrong. Why are there always such mistakes when I love somebody? She loves me. She looks at me in a very unmistaken way. Then I don't know what's going on in her head. How can one love somebody and not want them, at the same time? I am behaving like an insane person. I cannot stop hurting myself. I think only of me, she says. Is that true? Last night I went there out of total madness. I was high. I had smoked a little. She barely let me in. I wanted to be loved or pushed away. Seriously. One or the other. I wanted action. I begged her to help me, not to let me in. Then it was too late. She did not send me away.

'For the last time.'

I hate my weakness and myself. Why did I even go there? So that she would not send me away? She is not intimate with me anymore. She has no more energy. I wish I had that problem.

Channel 148

Dearest Pelegrine,

You do me an injustice when you think that I am playing with you. Forgive me, please, but that is how I am. At least for the time being. You are hurting and insulting me, when you think that I am toying. Everything is controlled by your impatience. I really care for you. But I cannot suddenly be a different human being. If you are suffering because of it, these are the consequences that you must bear.

Channel 149

Dear Pelegrine,

You should know that my problem telephoned last night. He will arrive sometime next week. You should also know, that from now on I have to work a lot more, especially on my research. All this means, that we can see each other much less. Even though it hurts me to write this, I am also certain that it is the best solution. My personal affairs are all but solved. But who can predict when and if they will ever be. But you must live your life and cannot hang in the air forever. Please, don't think that I write these lines feeling cold and uninvolved. Maybe you would like to believe that to make it easier on you. Perhaps you are allowed to believe it in that case. For self-protection. But it is not correct. I am not cold and uninvolved.

Please, if you wish, you can come this evening. Around nine. I would be glad if you came. Maybe we could still go camping in spite of everything? Please, don't let your affection for me change into hate. I send you a tiny embrace.

Channel 150

An unbelievable back-and-forth tidal wave prolonged their pained relationship. Times followed where Rosemarie was opening up, once even lying completely and flatly on top of Pelegrine. She continued to give more of herself little-by-little, always just enough to send Pelegrine reeling. Rosemarie even went so far as to construct a long evening after a long dinner with Pelegrine AND Lawrence, the fox, who eventually intruded into the macabre theater of the two.

The married couple acted mean toward each other with razor-sharp awareness of Pelegrine's presence. Nothing was said which made the moments even more heavy. She had to sit between them in the car when all three had to go and fetch cigarettes because Lawrence had run out. Both insisted to drive Pelegrine home together, loading her bike into the trunk of the car because of the ice and mountains of snow that were ignored when she had arrived hours earlier.

Channel 151

The time with the husband and her beloved Rosemarie was strenuous and Pelegrine saw what an idiot he really was, what a self-serving bastard. He was a man using Rosemarie purely for his advantages. He knew she loved him. But he did not love her. He let her pursue him, nurture, provide comforts and perform slave-like chores. No wonder, Rosemarie tolerated the same behavior in Pelegrine. All people repeat themselves with others. Wow.

They owned a second house in M. Every vacation Rosemarie spent there. Every Thanksgiving. Every Christmas. Every summer. When the grass got hip-high, or the place too dirty with unwashed pots from his parties with other women friends, she went to clean. She went hunting without a rifle.

Rosemarie was there to fix it all. She flew thousands of miles so she could mow his mosquito heaven without an engine, but with a hand-pushed rotary contraption. She went to scrub and Lysol the infested dump of her hubby,

Lawrence, who refused to live with her in any of their houses. She paid all the mortgages and for the repairs of two separate households, in hopes that one day he would come to his senses.

Channel 152

On numerous occasions, Rosemarie had suggested that Pelegrine be with other people, classmates, with Yarrow, for example. Since she was also European, lived alone with four children, was smart and attractive-- like a model, said Rosemarie, Pelegrine should hang out with her. She urged and urged. But Pelegrine questioned why should she go somewhere else, when she wanted to be with Rosemarie. She would decide for herself, she thought.

When Lawrence came, he stayed and stayed, for weeks and weeks. Pelegrine withdrew, keeping to herself and began to forget Rosemarie, little by little. But with a lot of forced effort.

Channel 153

Yarrow had always been friendly to Pelegrine and was interested in a friendship. Only Pelegrine was disinclined and not ready for any distractions as long as Rosemarie was in her head. Yarrow once inquired whether Pelegrine had an unhappy love affair because she always looked so sad, pale and drained. Pelegrine was surprised that her condition was showing and instantly began to open up to Yarrow's perceptive inquiries. She started to tell her about this "guy" who had sexual problems and a "wife." He totally confused Pelegrine. He touched her but refused himself to be touched. Pelegrine was nervous because she wasn't sure if such aberrations even occurred with men. Weren't they famous for always wanting to grab all they could get their hands on? And here she was presenting an abstaining male, a voyeur with abstaining fingers. Yarrow sharply interrupted,

"What kind of man is that? All men want to be touched."

"Not this one."

"Well, Pelegrine, then you are crazy to stay with him."

"I know."

Channel 154

These talks marked the beginning of her friendship with Yarrow. Pelegrine spent lots of time with the wise woman who expressed a lot of understanding and compassion for Pelegrine's situation. She invited her for overnight stays and insisted that Pelegrine stop her contact with the "crazy man." Pelegrine was afraid to tell Yarrow the truth and the fact that it was a woman and not a man. She needed counseling for the insanity that was at work, regardless of the gender involved. She knew stupidity. It knew no gender. Therefore, the advice could be useful to her, regardless, she thought.

Another reason for her cover-up was triggered by Yarrow's obvious heterosexuality. Four kids, a thoroughly middle-class home in a picture-book suburban setting with station wagons, double-door garages, wide driveways, dogs and riding lawn mowers. She lived in a materialistic and status-conscious neighborhood that thrived on exclusivity and country-club mentality. They had historically no use for "queers, lezzies or fags." But since Pelegrine desperately needed an ear, she invented the disguise.

Channel 155

It worked. Even after Pelegrine began reading from her poetry and letter-log. Both women sat outside in the late summer air, wrapped in blankets when the evening fell, and Pelegrine would read and read and read, with Yarrow urging,

"Go on. Don't stop."

Pelegrine was clever and covered the pages strategically, changed the she's to he's and refused to give the book to Yarrow who wanted to see for herself and read the text.

"No, I don't want you to see it. I will read for you."

Yarrow's children were polite and hung around like moths, more or less, depending on their curiosity. Pelegrine did not mind them. But it was a little more difficult to talk when they were adamantly staying within earshot. The two girls, twelve and thirteen were equally curious of this intruding stranger as were their brothers, fifteen and seventeen.

Channel 156

Eventually, the subterfuge-story-telling became slippery and cumbersome and Pelegrine simply revealed to Yarrow that the mysterious heart breaker was not a man but a woman. Bang. Silence.

"I thought there was something strange all along. Because I knew no man would act that way. Believe me. I know men."

"Well, I did not want to lie, really. But I was afraid you would reject me outright if I had told you. I was desperate for some discourse on this issue. And you have helped me a great deal. At least I haven't seen him, pardon me, her, in nearly two weeks. And the longer I stay away, the more I know how important it is that I leave this hopeless relationship."

"But I want to know who exactly it is? Do I know this person?"

"Yes, you do. But I really can't tell you. Don't push me."

Channel 157

But Yarrow was not to be deterred from something she wanted to know. She never gave up. She was relentless and persistent like no other person Pelegrine had known in her whole life. And so under the strictest rules of confidence, swearing silence, Pelegrine told her who the troublemaker woman was--their mutual lit professor!

Yarrow was a trilingual linguist and knew Rosemarie well. She was now more than baffled. She was utterly shocked.

"And I thought she was such a nice, gentle and unobtrusive woman. I can't believe she behaved this way."

"Well, believe me, she did."

Channel 158

Thus approached the time where Pelegrine had a lunch date with Rosemarie. She reminded Rosemarie of her own suggestions to go visit Yarrow. Pelegrine told her she had done just that. And she could report also that she was definitely finished with her entanglement with Rosemarie.

Through her discussions with Yarrow, Pelegrine told Rosemarie that she had become convinced of her foolish connection and of the obvious hopelessness of a future with the married woman. Interestingly, Rosemarie acted surprised and sad and indicated petulantly that Pelegrine could have warned her. She also suggested that Pelegrine should have waited.

"Maybe. But I made up my mind. You are free of me, forever now. Free to mend your marriage. Free to be without anybody, as you wish so often. I will stay your friend, be discrete about our history and never will hurt you. I have told Yarrow about our futile year and a half. "

Pelegrine was exasperated and deeply saddened hearing herself say these words. Rosemarie sorrowfully accepted the decision and seemed to want a three-way friendship without openly discussing personal connections, however. There could never be a dialogue specifically addressing Pelegrine's and Rosemarie's special relationship. Never ever. Typical. Not long thereafter, she invited Pelegrine and Yarrow for a weekend supper.

Channel 159

Pelegrine began bringing clothes and personal belongings to Yarrow's house and she spent several days in a row there. Neither of the two women, both in their middle thirties, was aware that they were in the process of shaping a phenomenal event.

Yarrow could not get enough of the Pelegrine-Rosemarie poems. Again and again she wanted to have them read to her and eventually she wanted her own copy, which had ballooned into a three-volume prose poem. She became deeply touched by the sentiments expressed which she did not know women could feel for each other. She was convinced that the heterosexual world needed to be made aware of these powerful emotions, such intensities and ultimate beauty of their love, which most people assumed to be pornographic, hedonistic or destructive, instead.

Pelegrine agreed but was not convinced that her stuff was worth sharing on a larger scale. She remained forever modest sharing her writings. Yarrow coached courage into her but needed to do it often, because it wore off quickly.

During one story telling session Pelegrine suddenly found herself holding Yarrow's hand briefly, with their eyes interlocking and feelings crossing over between them electrically. Cold showers ran down Pelegrine's back. She could not believe that she was feeling this for the woman who was merely lending an ear, providing therapy and, of course, attention.

Yarrow's patient surveillance comprised the crucial component. A dangerous and dynamite psychological trick, which never failed to work on Pelegrine. Only she did not know that then.

Channel 160

Pelegrine immediately approached Yarrow, who responded negatively and assured Pelegrine that she did not share those feelings. That evening Pelegrine felt proud to have admitted her feelings so openly and so rapidly. The next morning Yarrow was different and acted friendlier toward Pelegrine and that became a clue.

"I guess your answer was not final then?"

"No, it wasn't. All evening I lay awake reprimanding myself for that stupid answer. But, knowing me, I always like to think about important decisions, at least one night."

Channel 161

That very evening Yarrow sent the kids to bed early and lit candles, put Spanish music on the record player and scattered comfortable pillows on the floor. Pelegrine didn't know how to act and sat paralyzed on the couch. She was always shy in making moves, especially the first ones.

But Yarrow helped as if she had done this before. She was another natural and honest human lover. She turned out the light and said to Pelegrine to lie down next to her.

"You want to kiss me?"

"Aha."

Channel 162

They became lovers. Pelegrine was not madly in love with Yarrow. She cherished, respected and learned to love her slowly. It was more Yarrow's personality, persistence and patience coupled with her astute perception that attracted Pelegrine to the pragmatic girl from H., a city known for its history of mercantile wizards and stoic, self-contained temperaments. Aunt Coco, the thin-lipped efficiency expert was born in the same city as Yarrow.

Pelegrine was disconcerted that she was comparing the aunt with her Northern ice lips, her harsh to-the-point mentality, and her often cold rationality bordering on indifference, to her new love. In the past, Pelegrine had occasionally struggled with northern tempers. Her fiery, explosive, overwhelming and uncontainable emotional personality sometimes collided with their clear-headedness. This somberness both, repelled and attracted her.

Perhaps she wanted to be involved with such temperaments in order to relax her own volcanic personality?

Her connection to Yarrow took place in August of 1982. In September she was ready with her first reports:

I have been with Yarrow since August. I came to her for rescue from Rosemarie and her perpetual preoccupation with her never-ending husband drama. He, finally, came here, and I still almost didn't act. The marriage had a right to be repaired. But it never was. His presence and the fact that NO changes took place and that I faced another year of suffering with occasional joy was too depressing.

I love Yarrow. She is different yet a combination of all that I had experienced before her. I don't rush into this life with her madly and with the passion that I feel when I don't think straight. I feel calm, happy and sure. I feel at home and comforted, loved and needed. For once, I can return feelings and get the same. This reciprocity is ideal and seems almost unreal I barely dare to believe it.

Her diction is superb like a stage actor's. I bathe in her language and word choice. There are four great kids with good hearts but adolescent dispositions. The juggling act of mother, lover and working woman isn't easy for her. I admire her but I also feel she isn't allowing herself to be herself enough. It is amazing how much people will demand of one another, especially if the giver is a SHE. And especially if that SHE is kind and indulgent. It is a real challenge for me to be by her side and be a partner and friend to her, a woman who has been giving and giving and, in the process, has become emotionally starved. I give her strength, support and affection. We wondered if we are each other's truly great loves.

Her story when she watched her mother die at eighteen, cut deep into my soul. I have never been exposed to a more moving declaration of love toward one's mother. No friend, no book has ever said it that way. My Yarrowlein loved her mother the deepest way possible. And her mother loved her just as much. I was allowed to share her most moving moment when she held her mother in her arms and watched her die after a long bout with tuberculosis. The story of her mom's dying made me feel very close to Yarrow. I will never leave her. We love each other. I have known her for two years, saw her in my classes but was unreceptive because I was involved with the professor. Now I am free of her and can breathe again. She helped me get free.

Yarrow told me that she had liked me for a long time but that I had been unavailable, distant and always busy. Since I sought her for emotional help, I really fell in love with my therapist. Three volumes of poetry resulted from my tragic and sad link with Rosemarie. I am my own living proof of Thomas Mann's and Nietzsche's postulations of suffering sublimating itself into art. Through my pain I have found a path to art and creativity. I understand other people's suffering better now. I am 37 years old and I am learning to recognice how little I know.

Channel 163

For the first few months, Pelegrine spent much time in Yarrow's beautiful house, which straddled big acreage and was connected to a waterfall in a park-like setting. Pelegrine commuted to her classes an inconvenient distance away. Her apartment expense became an extra burden since she hardly lived there. Yarrow had suggested that they see each other on weekends and carry on their lives during the week. Such a suggestion was unacceptable to Pelegrine who saw in it a cheapening of their romance. She was not interested in weekend-flings. And she suggested that she relinquish her town quarters and move in permanently with Yarrow whose house was large enough. It was strange that Pelegrine herself suggested this move because she remembered that Rosemarie once had advised Pelegrine should ask for a room in Yarrow's house that would be cutting both their expenses. This idea sent horrors up her spine-- four teenagers, noise and confusion:

"No way," she thought to herself, "would I ever consider such a move." Less than a year later, she herself requested what she actually had feared would not work. But perhaps love made her ignore the voice of reason?

Channel 164

During the fall semester she moved with all her belongings, storing most of them in the basement because Yarrow had all necessary household items, and most of Pelegrine's stuff was cheap student vintage. She shared Yarrow's bedroom and her closet. In the kitchen she blended her food with the rest of the household. Other than that, the usual five occupants and Mom's new friend shared the house. The children were not sure what to make of that close friend suddenly. But they tolerated their mother's wishes.

It wasn't long that tensions between the children and Pelegrine emerged. Yet they were hushed and squelched with countless bedside visits from Yarrow, counseling each child individually. Afterwards, often very late in the night, Yarrow came to bed to either a sweet night or a continuing advisory chat with Pelegrine. Yarrow became the empire for two teams, the connecting wire. Instead of bringing the troubles face to face, she just mitigated back and forth. She was the ambassador of five countries.

Their lovemaking had to be carefully orchestrated around a time when the children were absent. It was great when they visited their father on a weekend. But such a tiny holiday was often enough disturbed because there was, for sure, one child who did not want to go and see Dad. During the week it was a hassle also. Pelegrine and Yarrow had to be done with their loving exactly before three thirty in the afternoon. At that time the school bus dropped the children off outside their bedroom window.

And the nights. They, too, were often delayed with the customary lengthy evening talks. When the ladies finally went to sleep, they were frequently interrupted when the thirteen-year old had bad dreams and wanted to sleep with her Mommy. Thus all nights, all afternoons and all weekends were risky to express their feelings. One never knew which child might get up or even listen outside the bedroom door prior to entering.

Channel 165

It was difficult for Yarrow to appease her demanding children who had been used to having their mother all to themselves. And now this strange woman, so close to their Mommy and with new demands like:

Let the children help you more. The big hands of a seventeen-year-old boy are a lot stronger to shovel snow. The kids can fold their underwear themselves. They shouldn't drive your car because you are the one with two jobs not being able to afford to be without one should they crash into mailboxes like before. Make them help out more. Make this a democratic household with EVERYBODY pitching-in, not just the frail, 98 pound mother with a scoliosis bent spine and a heart valve defect.

Thus the children and Pelegrine built up their own quiet resentment for each other. The couple never had a honeymoon, never had a family declaration, or a family bonding leading to a set of rules that would work for everybody. They had only secret hours carved around Yarrow's outrageous responsibilities.

Pelegrine's emotional equilibrium was pushed to its limits. She flip-flopped from good days to horrendously bad ones. After she defended her dissertation and received her final degree, she continued to stay because she and Yarrow had established a connection. The children were never told what kind of connection that actually was but they probably suspected. They most certainly did resent the union but, maybe, the not being told, even more. Pelegrine had wanted a democracy but was afraid to reveal to the outside what kind of connection she and Yarrow had. She was always scared of rejection and these teenagers did not make it easy to become bold overnight, especially since Pelegrine herself was childlike, impulsive and not at all versed in family discourse. She wanted a family but did not know how to have it.

Channel 166

And Yarrow began telling her that she should help more with the work and pick-up the slack if the children were spoiled, willful and messy and lazy. Yarrow told her that way she would have more time for Pelegrine. But that went deep against Pelegrine's core and hurt her sense of justice. And her memory.

She remembered how her own mother was treated and allowed to cater to those that did nothing but demand and snap their fingers. Pelegrine never forgot that her mother was loving and never refused anybody who was adamant and pushy like a bully. But Pelegrine also saw that the gentle woman was taken advantage of by those that could have done the chores easily themselves, especially the boisterous, hunky stepfathers and healthy, unemployed "uncles." In essence, they took her mother away from her. In the end, Pelegrine blamed Elli for being so weak, blamed her for not dividing up her duties differently with some time for Pelegrine. It pained Pelegrine to see her own, beloved mother drained and abused and pulled in one direction, away from the child, forgetting to raise her.

Channel 167

It can be assumed that Pelegrine began making these subconscious connections when she saw how her one and only center, her beloved, Yarrow, was similar to but also the extreme opposite of Ellie. Yarrow did not demand enough help from her teenage children. She did not place added responsibilities on them. She maintained two jobs and catered to her big children as if they were five years old. They let her do all that because it felt good when one has such a devoted mother who denies herself a life. Thus she did not make time to be a mate and partner. Tensions developed between the women. Yet they were always nurtured by their tremendous love and the hope that when the children were grown, out of high school, at least, things would be easier. Yarrow would have more time to be with Pelegrine. Then Yarrow's fear of losing custody of the children because of her living with a woman, would no longer pose a threat.

Such logic initiated a prolonged back-and-forth of decisions and indecisions. A volley of pull-release. Pelegrine pulled back and then gave-in to Yarrow again. Back and forth.

Channel 168

With her advanced degree, Pelegrine stayed with Yarrow two years selling vegetables. At another time, when Yarrow was temporarily out of work, the women opened a maid service. They made a good team, charged twelve dollars an hour and finished the houses in four hours. Most ladies liked the idea of a double team. But when Yarrow found another job, she quit, and Pelegrine had to do the toilets alone. On her off days, Yarrow could have gone with Pelegrine who was terribly depressed cleaning by herself. Without her partner, the fun and the bravado were gone.

In a very short time, Pelegrine hated that work. Together it was like two educated charlatans doing housework to keep their bodies in shape, their pocket books modestly filled, but, primarily, their lives together in the same town. Doing that job alone made it what it was: dirty, tiring, demeaning.

Channel 169

Had the home life been more peaceful and nurturing, Pelegrine might have endured it. The work at the produce store lost its glamour also. At first, selling oranges and suggesting the right kinds of apples to upper class ladies was fun, a great relief from her recent scholastic intensity. There were no other jobs. She had looked and looked. There were only those that meant moving away.

Her professors were at a loss. To them she said that she was taking a break from academia and was writing poetry instead. By living with Yarrow she could afford to pay her 120 dollars a month rent. In the beginning it included food, but soon, bickering with the children had destroyed their connection on that level. Pelegrine began buying her own food, putting it on her own shelf in the kitchen.

Channel 170

Pelegrine has often tried to remember what it was that bothered her most in this relationship that started so smoothly. Yarrow never spent as much time with her as she had been accustomed from her marriage with Pontiac. Pelegrine thought that one-by-one, the four children would go their way within three to four years, would build their own lives and let their mother live her own. It took a long time before Pelegrine realized very late that the family was extraordinarily tightly knitted, bonded with lots of affection but held together with numerous layers of dependencies.

Channel 171

Here was a cluster family whose father hurt them deeply emotionally and whose mother, Yarrow, became a legendary matriarch performing both mother/father roles. In such a setting, there was no room for an additional relationship let alone one with a woman, and one like Pelegrine. The problem arose largely because one woman was doing the job for two while the other had no role at all. Pelegrine also realized that if she had simply put all her own needs aside and blended in with the new family by becoming a nurturing, Elli-type-giving-and-unconditionally-loving wife, she would have survived there. But such personality traits and behavior never were and, probably, never will be one of Pelegrine's characteristics.

For one, she is burdened with an overly developed sense of fair play, of justice to everybody, in addition to an extreme need to have a full-time partner. Had Yarrow and Pelegrine been open from the beginning, willing to take risks and face their partnership, had both demanded a restructuring of the existing family arrangement, their lives together might have had a chance to survive. Instead, they had painful battles with far greater losses than had they been honest with the people in their family. And so it happened, they went into hiding, kept the truth from the children and prevented a real family to evolve. Thus they created a phobic pressure pot where all participants exploded into isolated particles.

Channel 172

Pelegrine began brooding, withdrawing and suffering immensely. She became a wave sloshing in and out of this relationship like oceans visiting their harbors twice a day. Her diary becomes a helpful informant, reconstructing her journey into recovery.

Channel 173

In October 1982, two months after I welded myself to you, I am still around. We are gliding into winter. A yellow sun accompanies our mushrooms we gathered for our soup. There are fewer storms in the house because of us and sometimes they blaze exactly because of us. But we are blended into each other seamlessly into a tight love. The magic is intact. Comfort flows from one to the other. I love you as much and more than on the first day. I want never to leave you. I hope I give you enough. I love your little brown head next to mine. Your hand and feet slump down with their own special weight on me. I cannot love you enough. I can't wait for the time to be alone with you and only rare visitors interrupt us, where I will chop your wood and saw it to spoil you till it hurts. And where you will cook lentils and peas with me and pick me up when I slide into your arms, sick and stiff, almost unconscious.

Channel 174

Three months later:

Thanksgiving finally ALONE, completely alone. The silence in the house is numbing. I can complete my thoughts. I can start a sentence and finish it without interruptions. I can tell you out loud that I love you. You give me many roses and kisses with your blue eyes embracing me. We love each other quite strongly and our feelings have strengthened and are entwined forever. There is much coming toward us but we will stick together because we love each other. This is the first fall that I am not sad, especially like last year.

Channel 175

    Four months later:

Christmas. What will happen with me? I feel trapped. There are suddenly barriers. My problems have quintupled. But you are worth it. Your love does not suggest a **therefore**--it says **nonetheless**.

Channel 176

    Five months later:

Everything is O.K. again. You have held me up. Your letter opened my eyes. I am sometimes very childish. Thank you, my love. Thank you for your strength. I will learn to make sacrifices for us, too. Thank you for showing it to me. The kind of love that I have known till now had always been exclusively directed toward me. Now, I have to learn to love for the other person, for us. If I love you, nothing can come between us. Amen.

    We have two identical featherbeds. Our feet meet underneath and venture miles every night. I love your feet. They are sensuous and have pillow-like flesh like the inside of your hands, your mouth, and your lips. They are all oysters in September. I am honestly happy. I want to grow old with you. The wind is fierce today. I am afraid to blow away. But you will anchor us.

Channel 177

    1/2 year later:

Everything is still heaven. Last weekend, when we were finally alone again, we renewed our love. Today I went skiing alone. And I have new skis. I held conversations with you in the snowed-in chair lift. I told the snow how much and how diligently I love you. I never want to be without you.

Channel 178

    Eleven months later:

I am writing again because my heart is breaking. My beautiful darling sits at the shore of this lake and is consoled by somebody else. .

    I am accused of so much now especially being jealous of the children. She says I resent every minute that goes into child, house and yard. If I sat down there by the shore and participated in the moonlit talk under the stars, everything would be fine. It is always a question of my participation. I am so odd and such a loner. I want to be alone but also want to be dragged into company. Why am I so weird? Why do I always feel abandoned and discouraged?

    I know I am writing all this in anger, but you are hurting me. Your loving persona is gone and is engaged with someone else when I really need you. Your children can share you as much as possible next to your distant partner. I am loosening my ties to you. I am washing the European wedding band from my finger. Don't cry tomorrow with hollow eyes. Console yourself and seek comfort and diversion with those who are closest to you.

Channel 179

    The following day:

I am really stupid. Why am I such a creature that feels so easily enclosed and then breaks out in a fit of madness? I should buy myself a straight jacket. I am asking a lot of you. I really did not have a good reason, yet I whirled up our life with big waves, banging it against our love. I could have gone down there, joined the conversations between you and Rosemarie, adapted and participated. That would have been normal behavior. Foolish, lunatic me. I imagined that I was excluded from the cozy circle and my presence would be intrusive. I don't know what exactly was happening. Perhaps, I was jealous of the information you could elicit from Rosemarie, information she never divulged to me. I was afraid she would open up to you after staying so closed to me. I did not want you to put your famous getting-people-to-talk skills to work. I don't know. I want to be a threesome but tolerate a twosome only between you and me or between her and me but not between you and her. I wonder why?

I am probably intolerant because I have been dishonest with a partner once. Or am I greedy and possessive with my treasures? How will I arrange it that I won't trample our joy? I think I have a tendency to do that with my fervor. It is my urge to be active, my untamed blood, and my barbaric, aboriginal temperament--fiery, uncontrollable and needy. I know so much about human behavior, can identify symptoms galore. But if I am the culprit, I forget all insights and understanding. Am I an incurable egotist, a loner, damned to pursue an eternal search, never reaching my destination because when I do, I can't comprehend my fortune even when I am sitting in the middle of it?

Cassandra was cursed to tell truths which no one believed. Me too. I enfold a treasure but I am unable to hold on to it. Truth without wisdom is useless. My little Yarrow with your innate grace and gentility, I will love you while I write and think and read some more.

Channel 180

One year and three months later:
I still love you. Now there is snow and you. My butterfly cocoon, come and embrace my tree trunk with your warm, moist and busy love.

Channel 181

A few days later:
How long must I run amok, run up mountains, toppling down until I know I have what I want? Am I grasping for shadows and fogs? On some days I see the illusion. On some I don't. I want to make good my mistakes and not hurt you anymore. How can I make you happy and me content and fair? I want to understand you and see through your eyes what mine are missing. How can we meet and not lose each other in the process?

Channel 182

Pelegrine has difficulties relating these events to me. She is struggling with the recollections nine years later. She is appalled with the repetitions and the signs she chose to ignore which were visible early on, every time in each of her connections.

By using her journals to remember her journeys, she is directly confronted with her memories as she wrote them down with her own hands. She cannot run away from her own words. I give her biographical tranquility and tell her that it is never too late to learn and act differently. She has fits and outbursts at herself as she ploughs her way through her symbols and codes that reveal her self to herself. Just now she told me that she will never again jump into a relationship so quickly. She is also voraciously reading all available abandoned-childhood-neglect-and crippled-will literature. She sees herself in every chapter and preaches to her many semi functioning friends. Why was she doing this she asked her psychologist.

"To tell yourself, to reassure yourself what you have always known but kept forgetting."

Thus many people perceive Pelegrine to be "together," with both feet on the ground, courageous, independent, lucky and strong. Tough. Only Pelegrine knows that she gives such an impression because she has always suffered from existential despair. Close friends know, too.

Anyway, we better continue with her tales to come closer to the present, in hopes that Pelegrine can make better choices and not keep putting herself at the mercy of every helping hand that she reaches for and that accepts her grasp. Something must change. But at this moment, she is in the process of shaping these operating blocks. By the end of her story she hopes to have found a path.

Channel 183

    Good night my beloved sunshine. Please, never leave me. I have to complete the whole night without you. Why don't you wake up and kiss me?

Channel 184

    Sixteen months later:

There is no point to continue writing in here anymore. Our love is exhausted. I can't stand it much longer. You too. For example your nineteen-year-old son comes home the second time within six weeks even though he was supposed to stay at the far-away college till Thanksgiving. Coming from Canada is costly and, at this time, means missing classes. The moment we walk in the door, late in the evening, you leave and talk to him and return 3 1/2 hours later. Toward the early morning hours you come to bed, even though you have a nine o'clock class to teach the next day. Not to mention driving one hour through the snow to get there. That means getting up extra early. No talk with me either in the evening or in the morning. None. Only quarrels in the night. You threaten to get the police. And I fear a nervous breakdown. Doesn't seem to bother you. Even though I cry myself to death. Talking with your son about money, cooking him something to eat was once again, more important than your needed rest. But, of course, my behavior after two a.m. is then blamed for costing you your rest, sleep and health. Always my taxation is used, never the other. You say you cannot take me anymore. And I cannot take your extreme devotion toward your rather grown and extremely healthy and strong children anymore. Especially a nineteen-year-old college kid with his own car, who came home unannounced with a hitchhiker who also had to be accommodated. Your son then left and spent the evening with neighboring friends, leaving the hitchhiker your chore. You telephoned the son to come home at 2 a.m. You drummed him home and insisted that he take care of his stranger. That in itself would not have been so bad, but did you have to talk to him so much, so long when it was the worst time for you and me, especially since you had spent 89 dollars on phone calls with him within the last six weeks? Why must nobody wait? Why always I?

Channel 185

The day before went bad, too. We did not sleep lovingly anymore. A big space between us. My feet never found yours. All night long. During the day we had a million separate errands. You never want to do mine with me. But you don't mind if I accompany you. When you are finished then you have to drive all your kids to their friends. There was no dinner. You did go to the movie with me though, but not without a fight. An accident on the road. I wished I were the dead person. Halfway through the movie, we finally held hands. And then the above midnight ordeal.

Channel 186

I have looked for a place to live away from you, a refuge from your life. And I realize once more, for the third time in my life, that I must be on the move again. Oh, you, why did you say if I were deadly ill, then, yes, then, you would devote time to me? Why do I have to die so that I could have you? Is that not morbid and sick in itself? Is that not a slap in the face of the reality that we have?

I won't die, I hope. But you should have given us more quality time. Now we don't share anything. Only arguments. Only bad times.

Adieu. I loved you honestly and with all of me. It was not enough for you. Neither you nor I could do it right for the other. Both of us drew the shorter end. Please, forgive me if I am unfair, but don't forget that I loved you, that I wanted to live a life with you, but that I could not pattern it totally by your outlines. Console yourself with your diagnosis that I am a sick person and that you and your children are saved from me. And I had to save myself. Thank you for any material advantage I had from living here. I wanted to even it out with my "Mr. Fix-It" nature. That did not work. You said it was nice that things got fixed, but they had been dilapidated so long that you had gotten used to it.

This trait of mine also angered your oldest son. He had been asked for years but didn't feel like repairing faucets or leaky windows. This woman suddenly taking over his male duties that he failed to fulfill hurt him. And I thought that was an important issue to clear. Talk out in the open in a democratic council fashion, in a forum where we outline new living patterns. Where we delegate new responsibilities without telling them the whole truth behind those changes. The reality of you and me needed to be kept secret. But you did not want such a household conference that all healthy living communities need. You said things have been going well and that I should not insist on such drastic changes. And when I asked about responsibilities toward me, your partner, you replied: `Well, that is why I chose a woman. I knew no man would ever put up with this. But from a woman I expected more. I, at least expected her to pick up the slack and thus relieve me of some of the house and motherly work.'

And I ask, `Why should I be a slave to your lazy children? Make them do some of the work and reduce your chores. You cut back on what they expect of you. Let them help clean. Insist on it. You are thin with very little weight. You smoke a lot and you have a relationship. You need help from them.'

But you called me selfish and harsh. You called me jealous and wished somebody in my youth had done all what you do for your children for me. Because then I would understand your tolerance toward your lazy teenagers. And I was hurt because I did not think I was reacting out of resentment. I wanted to realign the household with EVERYBODY pitching in, not just you and I.

I am at the end. I have to start new all over again. Otherwise I self-destruct.

Good-bye my darling, my sweet, my excellent fucker. Every minute that I had with you was worth it. But unfortunately your appendages have devoured me. I am worn-out and feel drained and destroyed.

Almost every year recently, the fall season has become a burial month. I am paying for something. God doesn't love me anymore. He is punishing me exactly where I hurt the most. I am a crumpled leaf in the gutter. A window with no pane. A door without a house. A bath without a tub.

Channel 187

Seventeen months later in December Pelegrine went to job interviews. They had patched their life again. Pelegrine was repeatedly revolting and weeping over Yarrow's excessive generosity toward her family.

Yarrow's entire life was one big sacrifice. Her childhood and her young adulthood were characterized by unadulterated service to the wishes and needs of others. Pelegrine suggested that Yarrow work on her obsession to sacrificial behavior:

We both had horrible and very similar childhoods, Yarrow. Your past reminds me of mine. When I look at you, I nearly drown in my own memories of being a little girl. You not only remind me of that painful time--with you, I re-live it minute by minute. I cannot relieve my past. I must eliminate the cracks of my beginnings.

Channel 188

I am hurrying back to you, happy and with the speed of an arrow. I am miserable without you, because I love you so much, my blue eyes and soul, floating above me everywhere I go. The world becomes shiny and worthwhile only with you. I am cheerless without you but happy, at the same time, because in one hour I will be kissing you in the laundry room.

Channel 189

Pelegrine is constantly interrupting my writing. She is restless these days and uncomfortable because I am concluding her last episode, her last serious love. She keeps asking me how far I am. I keep telling her to let me write and get on with it. I told her this Yarrow stuff is more difficult than the other stories. It is still too new and not healed over with crusts and seasons. Perhaps

Pelegrine also experiences the discomfort that I am feeling while writing this part of her story. Sometimes she comes in and spends an afternoon in my study flipping through the manuscript, correcting spelling errors or tells me I misunderstood what she was telling me. At other times, and that is worse, she remembers another incident from her early years, and she wants me to stop writing at this moment, drop my pen and go back into the dungeon of the book. I tell her to be patient that it will all fall in place. I assure her that I will leave nothing out and she should hang in there and let me finish the journey of her discoveries.

Today she asked whether I knew what fantasy bonding is. I told her that making one's parents better than they are, loving a false image, covering up their real selves, heaping lies upon lies to make the present tolerable is what I understood that to mean. Of course, she was thinking of her own chronic infatuation pattern when asking me this tricky question. And I don't know that much about her psychology readings. But she informed me that she was having another one of her rumbling attractions, another one she shouldn't have but was watching its approach like a black cloud, slowly creeping up on a hot Virginia sky. She knows all the sign from the ripple in the leaves, to the curls on the water to the smell in the air, to the color of the eyes and the currents under the words. And she said:

If Manuela had not asked me to sleep on her futon, I would have never known that I had a problem. But lying next to somebody that I find attractive, smart, honest, consistent, straightforward and reflective, and talented and courageous and sweet and kind and unselfish but healthy and precious, is sheer torture. Especially if the other person may or may not understand what I am feeling, but especially if it is entirely possible that she does. I am on that familiar road again that I have been on since I was twelve, longing for affection. Now it may be lust.

I listened to her, smiling and shaking my head.

What am I to do? On the one hand, I would like to copy Manuela, say honestly and explicitly what my feelings are like:

'Manuela, I am interested in you. How do you feel?'

On the other hand, I must be afraid to be rejected or to stop fantasizing which is exhilarating just like when I loved the psychologist. In that case, I probably want to continue and say nothing and let her control the situation. That's it. I don't want to control it. I am leaving it up to her. And that is what is wrong.

Next week I am going camping with her and I would like to find a way to break my pattern of loving heterosexual, married women. My psychologist told me that it is O.K. to have feelings and to acknowledge them. But what one does with those feelings is a matter of choice. One must not necessarily act upon them. Now, that was total news to me, <u>the me</u> that never knew anything but to act, and act fast and get to the point. That's probably what Rosemarie meant when she said that she believed that one does not have to live-out all one's fantasies. I vehemently disagreed with her because I always assumed that one should do everything--in moderation-- but do it. And not hold it in if it wants out. That has been my perpetual license to seduce or indulge in the loves that caught my eye. And with my success rate, I did not have to learn moderation or the use of my brain. But now, dear friend, I am face to face with scientific discoveries and labels for my patterns.

I told Pelegrine to go on her trip, listen to her heart and be open and honest, take the risk, but get the festering out. A cleared air is better to breathe than an infected congestion. I sent her away and asked her to visit me next week. I had to go on with the story, sorting out her un-translated diary entries and figuring out her mess between 1982 and 1991. I had my hands full.

Channel 190

In January Pelegrine hit another low. And she writes:
It is all over now with us. It didn't last. Our love was not eternal. I wanted to be spoiled and cherished and not be squeezed-in, always misunderstood and

underestimated. I cannot go on living like this. You reproach me for not helping you enough. That is unjust.

I have reached the point that I don't want to do anything. Not even stay here. I have decided. I will reject any, and I mean any kind of connection to a mate. You say I dig my own holes. Maybe. And if true, just for that reason alone I must avoid relations. You say you love me. But only tailored to your measurements. My way of being is insufficient. But yours is, too. It is sad that we ran up this dead-end and believed so ardently that we had real love and a future with each other. You were my last chance. Since the last time with Rosemarie and now, especially since I have known you, I abhor getting close to a person. Maybe I have run out of will. I am exhausted from trying. It was too strenuous with you. And ungratefulness ends our dance. You are strong, matter-of-fact and convinced that I never understood you or really was concerned about you. That is low of you. I made such an idol out of you and placed you on a big pedestal. That explains why I can barely deal with the real you, your weakness and inconsideration. You are attractive and magic. But you are not willing to be free to do what's good for me. I must leave you even if it means my destruction. I am weeping as I write this.

In four weeks I will go to Europe. But before that I must move out and find a place to live. I have no idea where to go. I have lots of bad luck and more ahead of me. I don't want to despair. I have to wither away alone without letting others add to my misery. I am tearing you out of my heart like the others before you. Pontiac understood me. You actually do, too, but you want to change me too much. You ask for steps and leaps that I cannot jump. I love to love you but I am dying in the process. I never, never, never want to love another person like I did you.

I have become sick from this town. Everything is so harsh here in northern USA. The people are as cold as the winter. I will go away from here, from these humans that cannot part with their engagements. They cannot share. But it is expected of me. I am tired.

I have never been able to tolerate injustice whether to me or to others. I will be like that forever. I don't really want to die, but I could.

Channel 191

The pendulum swings to the rhythm of Pelegrine's clock. Four weeks later, the tune changes to love again.

I am having brain rot. I still love you like always. I believe I have a hormonal imbalance that slams me to the bottom of my senses. I must come-up with a control center by finding a particular activity or food which will calm me down during these times. Now, everything is fine and calm and we love each other tenderly. I am volcanic and emotionally unrestrained. I must not get so obsessed with the flaws of others. I must learn to put brakes on my feelings. I must not hurt others so deeply. I must slow-down my quick tongue. I just have to think of you. You love me in spite of everything. And I do you. I am getting sad when I think of my trip to Europe in March. I hate to be without you so long. I must go because Tante Josefa's age is bothering me. She is 86.

Your velvet eyes go with me in their blueness.
Your golden grasp holds my heart.
You throw bridges over the ocean to steer our dreams right.
I will be your oak tree and bedpost.

Channel 192

Highest caliber moments
Can only be captured
In split seconds
And only in a poem.
I invent my own language and
weld a golden rainbow from the sun.
Pure sadness never prompts a poem
only the joy that was and is now hidden behind the pain
can penetrate the paper.
I am sleep walking with words on the feeling
I have painted for my wall.

Channel 193

Today there has been no negative commotion. No bad feelings are creeping through the house. We are peaceful and loving. We are doing our chores. Visit each other and eat our meals together. You are succeeding to save me from the cliffs from time to time.

If you say you come in ten minutes, you come in 45 and I must not be sad. Every person must remain free for his own time. Right?

And now my aunt, Tante Josefa. I have forever wooed for her favor. All the people that were physically closer to her profited and I abdicated, instead. I have always fought for her approval and wanted love. She hates, loves and fears her son, all at the same time. He fathered two children with two different women in order to move me away from being an heir to his inheritance his mother kept removing from him daily. I was twelve years old and I played on her salon carpet.

'I will impregnate women and squirt children into this world so that you, my dear little cousin, who is uncomfortably close to my mother, will never inherit her wealth.'

Only today do I realize the significance of these cruel words. His first plunge produced a boy, in his thirties by now, a pampered, flatulating, fat Viennese spineless weakling who proclaims clichés, coated with smiley platitudes. He is clinging to his grandmother waiting for his future where he will be the universal heir. A magnificent irony, nevertheless. His father is still jealous. But now of his own son because my aunt has reduced his inheritance to the obligatory amount, leaving the rest to his little doughboy offspring. And now his own father is angered by him despite the fact that he fucked him into existence so that I would not take his place.

The second child, a girl from another woman, is a teenager now and not as dear to the aunt. The he-child charms her better. The she-child is gaudy and stupid. None of them want me to come visit the aunt because I have been around since World War II and once posed a threat to their money dreams.

When in reality all I wanted was to love my aunt and be loved by her. No more. No less. She was the only means that could have provided me with an opportunity to study and a chance to make more out of my life. But she did not hear me. And I had to go so far away to build myself a life and come back today to bid the old woman farewell.

Channel 194

One year and nine months later, in May, Pelegrine's record reads:
Yarrow and I are undergoing lots of strain again. I will never let her read my diary again. Our life represents one big stupid blur. We are strangers and live like two acquaintances. I haven't made love to her since February. I find it difficult to relax and forget everything while loving her. I cannot let go anymore. I am afraid of afterwards where everything repeats itself. I cannot write. Not even letters. I am paralyzed. I find no joy in anything. Not even sailing and tennis. I have to change my situation. It will kill us all, otherwise. I am sick. And she can't help me. Slowly, quite slowly I slough her off, leaf by leaf. The storm blows on and I flutter away. I cannot master the superhuman requirements. I can only withdraw into an autistic state. But that hurts her. And I want to save her from my reaction.

Channel 195

Still in May it was bad again:
It only goes downward. We live from crisis to crisis. I go substitute teaching and don't want to come home anymore. She is picking up dirt and is a passionate parent, performing duties with love and affection. That is how she expresses love. But she is wearing thin without knowing. Leaving us too much alone. And me! Why are we together? Only to be apart. Only to hope and wait. For what? Why can't my needs be met as do her children's? Whenever I mention my longings she says as long as I make such requests, she is unwilling to do anything. She does not perform upon demand. But why is she fulfilling so many

services of love dictated by her children who are not helping but taking and tearing from her? Doesn't she want her own life and feel a duty toward our union? I am part of it. How am I to perceive her love? How am I supposed to feel it? Why does she insist that my affections appear in the guise of patient sojourner, a permissive observer who selectively performs?

And how about her? Why doesn't she rest like them? Why doesn't she like herself more to take better care of herself? I simply cannot continue to watch her actions that demonstrate her belief that her children are the only beings worthy of such sacrifice and care? I could readily accept shared chores and duties and want nothing more than to assist her, but only if all parties are participating--not only us old ones. She doesn't want to demand services from the children unless they are rendered out of their own will she says. But since they are like most human beings and are not willing to perform non-demanded duties, Yarrow yields and insists that she must do the work herself. How can she afford such a position? Especially since she is sacrificing our love in the process? Her thin body, worked-out skin and my aching soul, they want to be catered to, caressed and held. Why doesn't she give us the time? She must take it from them. They are not little anymore. She is spoiling them and expects me to watch while she is collapsing, exhausted from indulging. She recuperates skimpily, wondering why she stays behind not getting ahead since she continues to gather pants, shirts and socks that are eternally spread before her so she can wash and sort to fold them, over and over.

I am even tired from merely writing this down. And since I am not picking up with her I am called selfish. I will NEVER clean after her big and pampered kids especially since their indulged home life has cost me a life of joy and belonging. She goes from rest to exhaustion before she comes to where I have been waiting for hours to share our love, our common culture, and our fun in learning. It can't continue like this. She doesn't really believe in our love. I don't see a future in this depressing present. I just have to find a place to live. And start all over again.

You, my love, you ask so much of me. You should get a memorial for motherhood paid for with a life of your own. You live through and for them only. I wonder if you will ever be on your two feet, taking care of yourself with a healthy distance between mother and offspring when you are in your 60's?

If you loved yourself more as an independent adult, not in the loving-to-control-your-children way, you would find more time to nurture us and I would get the feeling of belonging. I would be able to exercise with you, have hobbies we share and develop our brains. But how can I grow with you under these circumstances where you clean up banana peels, carelessly slung against the kitchen cabinets, thick and encrusted by the time you discover them at midnight while the culprits are sleeping; while you fold underwear for twenty-year-olds; while not budgeting the time better for important matters at such a late hour; while not letting the petty stuff go; while letting us expire. And you ask me to act grown-up, tolerant, undemanding and sweet. When you run without a rudder, steering for everybody but yourself. I am lost with you.

Channel 196

Later that year Pelegrine rented an apartment in the village, hoping that after she installed a telephone, allowing Yarrow instant access to her children, she would spend more time with Pelegrine. However, Yarrow rarely visited her and actually resented the move. And silly Pelegrine did not stay more than a night per week there herself. What a waste! In the evening Pelegrine could not stand to be away from Yarrow and she always returned to their common bed even if Yarrow wasn't there. Life had become one big torturous drama. By December Pelegrine was near desperation and exhausted from believing that all fault lay with her, that she was the sick one, the one that couldn't share. She contemplated suicide but wasn't sure if this self-indulgent family was worth her death.

Yarrow remained steadfastly dependent on the decisions, desires and plans of her children. Not until their activities where satisfactorily arranged, did

Pelegrine and Yarrow emerge as two starving adults hungry for time and fun that never came, because after the children were appeased, the two women were drained and spent. And instead of going insane, Pelegrine started composing curriculum vitae. She knew the only way out of this tragedy was finding a real job for which she was trained. Pelegrine had forfeited proper employment by never really looking for an academic job. She wanted to stay with Yarrow. Thus she sold oranges and apples and cleaned houses while waiting to enjoy the love that was never to be hers.

Channel 197

By Christmas Pelegrine had become a real existentialist, a survivor again. On a rainy day at an auction she bought a few acres of land in the Adirondack Wilderness. She built a primitive cabin with a woodstove. During the summer she had erected a screen house by attaching screen wire around four perfectly positioned trees, adding support with a fiber paneled roof and a door which she had found in the dump. She was a genuine Huckleberry Finn in a dwelling without mosquitoes.

By next year Pelegrine had accepted a teaching job as a university professor. Yarrow did not want to lose Pelegrine and also found a job within a four-hour driving distance. She was convinced that since she was with her children during the week, the visiting weekends were theirs alone. Yet her Christmas diary of that year tells otherwise.

Channel 198

A few days before Christmas, yesterday, on the 19th, one day after my birthday, I arrived at my snowed-in, barely accessible, partially winterized, very partially, 12x16 cabin in the Adirondack Park. Since my love is leaving me for Christmas and I am faced with a totally solo Christmas and New Year's, but especially Christmas Eve, I planned to spend it at my home away from home, at the place I usually go in the summer, never before in the winter. Too bare and primitive. No electricity, no water, no toilet. Items easier missed in the summer than in the freezing cold. But now! The chunk of ice in the stovepipe had to thaw allowing smoke to depart. The smoke out of my mouth never stopped.

After I arrived here, I got stuck in the snow immediately. I dug myself out with my hands, kept rocking the car back and forth till the tires grabbed a hold, entered the cabin, made a fire--no, took out the old sandy ashes and layered the inside with Southern fire bricks. Maybe this will hold the heat better. Finally, a flame but no heat for a long, long time. After an hour, I had become more and more despondent and discouraged, suicidally lonely, cold, hungry and sleepy with no idea what to do. To stay or to go back and camp-out in Yarrow's empty house, on the floor without furniture, while she flew away with her family to be with her European relatives?

At this point, I could no longer distinguish what was worse of all the disadvantages I was facing. I fell on my knees and prayed for enlightenment, some idea what to do. I decided to pack-up and closed my cabin, tried to drive out but got stuck again.

I rocked and burned the snow. Just before dark, I could reach the local tavern and order a whiskey. The bartender lady spoke encouraging words. I wanted to get warm before driving thirteen hours back home again. Another whiskey from a guest and another. They were watered, it seemed, and weak, but came together with conversations and reassurances that should I really get snow-stuck, a tractor would pull me out. Such talk and company gave me back my strength. Thus I decided to stay after all and weather it out, accepting an invitation from the bartender to spend Christmas Eve with the family celebrating at the adjacent restaurant which would stop me from burning my one and only candle. Which would save me some tears.

Channel 199

It was pitch dark by the time I returned to the cabin, set up my bed and froze all night because every two hours I had to add another fire log until I had to go outside and bring in more at 4 a.m. I wrapped a ski cap around my ears and hung on to the brief heat waves. After dozing into an exhausted stupor, I awoke with my feet ripping brutally into the antique army sleeping bag. The hours passed slowly making sleeping impossible. But feather spitting shortened the night. Next day I stitched the hole, shook-out the cabin, swept up a storm, cleaned the squirrel shavings and mouse shit, ate warm oatmeal and reached the point of peace to sit down and write these lines--exactly 24 hours later after a miserable start.

Channel 200

I forgot to mention the interruptions every half hour by my crying spells because it hurts so much to think of you and me, to think of you so far away from me. When this wound heals a little, I can breathe. I know.

Channel 201

Dark falls quickly to the ground and the black night beseeches every window. Went cross- country skiing, for miles through untouched snow resting on my eyelashes. My soaked clothes are hanging above the purring stove with hot air dancing in the cozy room. Slept an hour. I feel my grief sneak back into my stomach where it will sit down and give me cramps. I had two consecutive dreams rushing though my brain last night. Lit-up cars were driving around my cabin. Up and down the hills. I tried to shoot at them but nothing came out of the barrel, only corks tied to a string. I tossed the gun through the air back and forth screaming that I had a weapon. But the people were hollering that it was Halloween and cheered the night. I woke up in deep sweat.

The second dream delivered a sexy woman who laid her hands on my shoulders while hiking through the streets. Her grip became harder and her body walked nearer to mine becoming hotter with her muffled breath in my ear. I loved her sensuality and responded with my body walking slightly in front of her. Who was she, that strange, beautiful, soft, unknown woman with long hair and soft hands and tender skin colliding with mine accidentally until it could not part anymore? Unfortunately I awoke at the wrong time. But all day long I looked for breaks and tried to recall her image picturing how our rendezvous might have continued. I am still trying to reconnect to the dream.

My own real love has disappeared and is walking through her streets without me. I wish that a beautiful woman would fall from the sky just for me. Somebody who wants me the way I am, needs me the way I am, loves me and puts me at the top of her life because she is on top of mine. Where are you? How will I find you? Once upon a time her name was Yarrow but that lady has vanished, wishing that I stay alive and well and ready for her in January.

Channel 202

After midnight the entire one-room warmth was asleep. Cold icicle air awakened her in the morning. She did not get up right away but continued dreaming in a partial slumber until she climbed down the ladder to the matches, shivering and hungry. That was a special day because she had a two-liter bottle of warm water for her badly needed hair bath. An end to the itching and electrically charged locks. Her recently purchased kerosene heater burned the falling hair into smelly black gristles, mixed with eyebrows and lashes. At any rate, the whole room was wrapped into a burnt hair odor while a newly glistening head sat pondering solutions to a new task: morning shit in deep snow, sitting on ice protected by a giant winter sky.

Channel 203

Last summer she had dug a three-foot deep hole and built a wooden square box over it with a toilet seat mitered from three two-by-fours creating a triangular frame fitted precisely to her butt. This contraption constituted a genuine throne with her feet dangling in the air until she found a plastic crate for a footstool. There she sat, rain or shine, with or without an umbrella, performing her interior duties.

Except on a Christmassy December 23, she faced a new dilemma. She had to scratch away a foot of snow from the frozen seat before she could sit down. She could not get rid of the ice with just her finger tools and had to plop her warm behind onto the glassy surface and thaw it gingerly with her thighs. She slowly tried to free her numb behind frozen onto the toilet seat like a sponge tearing-up when wiping the freezer compartment in the refrigerator.

She had to shit regardless of the pain. It became a race between the naked buttocks, aching on this wintery surface and the hot and steaming, mile-long turd that could not be interrupted. An explosion of relief painfully crashed a snowy wilderness.

Not until melted nylon stocking-like ice seams were running down her legs, did the toilet queen enjoy her empty bowels, laboriously wiping her ass. She rose slowly and sank deeply into the returning footsteps, clutching her precious toilet paper roll under her arm. Her tiny wooden palace was hungry for fuel to give more heat, which had crept busily through abundant summer cracks.

Channel 204

Thus began and ended every day filled with routine jobs compelled by necessity--chores unknown to modern lives. But Pelegrine, never having really eliminated the hard memories of her childhood, knew burdensome life very well. She was an old friend to permanent cold and an absence of love. She had been trained in survival tactics. Why shouldn't she be a master? Every day she rejoiced when she discovered that she still knew how everything worked, especially when conveniences were catastrophically absent. Every minute she became a conqueror of difficulties, remembering also how she had always been uneasy when people wanted to give her one-sided presents.

She loved nothing more than to exchange favors with favors. She intuitively perpetuated a natural back-and-forth. She liked to accept help if she could reciprocate assistance in kind. Of course, no accounting was kept but in her relations, she truly enjoyed a natural harmony.

It has been a long time since Pelegrine has relished such dynamics in her life, not really since Pontiac. At this point, it is clear, that much time will have to pass before Pelegrine knows how to act upon this vital need. For quite a while she has been a torn person, going back-and-forth between reason and emotion, always being over-ruled and swept away by the latter.

Channel 205

On December 25, Pelegrine was extremely proud to have survived her first ever, totally alone Christmas, without a tree, without a present, without the presence of human being especially one that cares. For days and especially on this Christmas Eve, she tuned all Christmas songs to other radio stations. She was avoiding the melodrama of pain. She was artificially distracting herself particularly since Yarrow had punished her needlessly.

Yarrow's middle son, the nicer one of the two was killed the previous August by a car. The entire family was still grieving and was spending their Christmas in Europe to ease their devastating loss. The only problem for Pelegrine was that she was not part of the group grief. They did not need her. They needed only each other.

Pelegrine had a very hard time understanding why her best friend, did not need to be with her, but only her children. Yarrow had told her repeatedly that they were here first, had been around longer and required more care than Pelegrine. A hard pill to swallow. And on those occasions Pelegrine said,

"Why haven't you found another man, a father and companion for all of you?"

"Because no man would and could ever give what this family would require of him. Such men simply don't exist. The available ones are all too selfish and could never fit into such a role."

"And what about me? Why should I be better than a non-existent male?" Pelegrine asked.

"Well, that's why I tried it with a woman. I thought women knew how to sacrifice, to give, to give up and put themselves last, if necessary," was Yarrow's answer.

"Hell, piss and corruption. I'll be damned. I should do more than a guy? You must hate women if you expect such superhuman efforts. No thanks. No such shit from me."

Thus Pelegrine never accepted Yarrow's double standards. All she wanted was democracy. Yet Yarrow only wanted to continue the status quo of her miserable life that so many women and mothers suffer.

Channel 206

This particular Christmas manifested the height of their dilapidated relationship. Yarrow had waited till shortly before the holidays to inform Pelegrine of her European plans. She excluded her till the last minute to throw her a Christmas without family but for herself sought out to be with her own kin and blood. Pelegrine never did understand this need and such a choice. Such behavior to Pelegrine only demonstrated that she was superfluous and not good enough to be included. She wondered how she could ever feel like a mate when her partner acted with such self-centered independence. In their discussions Pelegrine heard only familiar accusations of being jealous and un-giving.

Channel 207

And in the winter landscape of New York, Pelegrine parried daily questions of why such a pretty girl is all alone at a time like this. The questioners were for the most part alcoholics, wife beaters, unemployed lumberjacks and toothless divorcees. What could she possibly tell them why she was as alone as they were? What did she have in common with them? Lack of good judgment? How was she to give herself courage when her sad eyes only envisioned her absent girl friend who found everything more important than Pelegrine? How could she continue to believe in Yarrow who was so full of good stories and reasons for all her misfortunes, late dates and missed appointments.

Pelegrine did not want pity from the winter strangers and none of their sexual advances, which invariably happened. She became angry at Yarrow for it was she who abandoned Pelegrine and it was she who made Pelegrine seem available to those lechers.

"Damn. Damn. Damn. What kind of monster would leave you alone at Christmas time?"

Only Pelegrine knew how this beast worked. She was angry and mad that these pitiful losers identified their loneliness with hers. She continued repeating Yarrow's words:

"But I am loved. It just <u>looks</u> like I am not. I am not really left alone. It just looks like it. But my love had important duties, important people to tend to. Gentlemen, I am really off-limits."

Yet nobody cared to hear that. Pelegrine herself heard the empty ring of these words. But she bravely repeated them when asked, every evening at the lonely restaurant bar. The question remained who was deceiving whom?

Channel 208

Nine days passed and Pelegrine cried only when she heard Vivaldi. His music moved her back to another time mingled with love and pain. The temperature had not left the minus mark in a week. Pelegrine's answers about the absent partner had become routine and slick. She began to believe her own stories. To fight loneliness in this remote winter, one could easily become a chain smoking alcoholic, she noted. To survive alone as a woman left behind in rural snows was damn difficult especially since men in such settings were waiting like avalanches for an opportunity to inch closer to Pelegrine and whisper seductions in her ear. She, who is moderately attractive with pretty eyes and a lovely smile, got a steady deluge of offers from men who were separated from their boring lives. Again and again, Pelegrine was telling herself that somebody once told her she was loved. She wondered how long she would have to tell herself these words? Every day it became more and more inhuman to repeat them, more unrealistic.

Channel 209

The great white silence enhanced by the extreme cold was balsam to Pelegrine's agitated nerves. She felt numb and mechanical. She took turns with cross-country or downhill runs, as long as they exhausted her severely. But she did not dare to venture out on the frozen lake. She liked to skate but since she could break through the unpredictable ice and actually drown, she realized that life meant more to her than she admitted. Her girl friend's parting flowers kept their first-day freshness in the cold cabin. Pelegrine wondered whether her friend's memory was as loyal as the flowers'?

Channel 210

On the 29th of December she was afraid for real. The temperature plunged to minus 25 degree. Pelegrine was wearing everything she had brought with her, five pairs of socks, two woolen scarves and multiple layers of thick and thin sweaters. The rug and the spare blanket were protecting her dog, Emily, who was practically lying inside the whistling wood stove. Still, in spite of the climatic nose-dive, Pelegrine afforded a splashing but refreshing shower from a makeshift contraption attached to the rafters, usually referred to as a solar shower bag with a release pin clamped to a hose allowing a flow of water at will. Even though she did not heat enough water, the feeling of being clean was heavenly.

Then she hopped on her skis and briskly slithered on brand new snow to the post office, four miles away. She stuffed newspapers into her parka and had sweated through the bulk thoroughly by the time she was back home.

She glanced over the white paradise and felt her eyes water. For some reason, here in this remote wonderland, she drifted into Austrian memories of cold, white and spectacular winters. Why, she marveled, did the past of pain come up this time to mingle with delight only to be remembered as pleasure when it really wasn't? Is that the effect of time, taking the edges off? She swallowed her tears and reprimanded herself harshly:

You crying little fool. Just like your Mom. Always on the verge of weeping when you are moved. That's why nobody likes you. People don't like crybabies. They all want hard, business-like, calculating humans, not somebody that can cry over freshly fallen snow! People like that are doomed to be left behind.

With these words Pelegrine got angry at her soft side and deeply remembered her mother who was even worse affected with emotional reactions. People marched daily on her mother's softness. Four husbands and numerous uncles had trampled on her. That is how Pelegrine became the protector of her Mom--the child-mother searching for her own grown mother for the rest of her life.

Channel 211

Pelegrine was strangely moved by her sudden insight of her mother's afflicted connections and her own unfortunate entanglement with Yarrow. Pelegrine felt similarly abused and ignored when the Yarrow family had no use for her. It frightened Pelegrine that as she got older she began resembling her mother's features and her misfortunes, as well.

Pelegrine's facial lines, hands, curves and their touch, body build but especially the psychological make-up took on contours of Elli. Every now and then, Pelegrine stared at her own photographs, struck by her resemblance to Elli. Pelegrine's unknown father genes must have overpowered, to some degree, the submissive Elli genes. The embodiment of the ongoing struggle between the rational and the emotional—the mother and the father opposites were apparent. What disturbed her was that her mother side began to overwhelm her father tendencies. Her prolonged and unhappy connection to Yarrow, and the fact the she was getting older, alarmingly disjointed Pelegrine's emotional equilibrium. She had read somewhere that the hormonal household will play tricks. She had hoped that this cathartic journey to the ice country would help her realign her bearings.

Channel 212

But one day, the cold had become unbearable, too cold even to perform the daily toilet routines. Instead she had to eliminate into a plastic bucket. The winds howled endlessly and Pelegrine was worried that the cabin would fly away with her in it. She could never get all her stuff together in time to evacuate, if one side of the building or the roof suddenly disappeared. The car was deeply snowed in and made an escape even more unlikely. If only the wind would stop, she mourned. Her entire newspaper supply was stapled over cracks and drafty holes, barely warding off such Canadian blusters. Thoughts like that and fears prompted Pelegrine to break camp, especially after the milk and lettuce had frozen inside the cabin, and Emily was unable to stop shivering under the entire supply of blankets and rugs. The cold connected Pelegrine to her memories but told her also to get going, to move on. She returned to her Virginia house, to her home she had bought in 1985 when accepting her job as a teaching professor.

Channel 213

Pelegrine was back where the water ran pre-heated in pipes for her convenience. She read somewhere that art is really translated by the artist from life--life as it is around everybody, but the artist restates the unnoticed familiarity, in such terms that others can also remember the essence, which moved the poet in the first place.

Yarrow rarely telephoned and Pelegrine imagined herself better coping without her. By the time January arrived, nothing really new happened between them except more of the same, periodic visits, a long distance relationship with children growing older and their demands larger. Mother Yarrow stayed involved, as always forfeiting her and Pelegrine's lives. But it would take Pelegrine many more years before she realized the devastating effect this crippling connection with Yarrow had on her. She would vacillate between trying once more and then giving her up again. Back and forth. And, of course, Yarrow was not easily shaken since she was convinced that they were perfect for each other as long as Pelegrine learned to solve her inner problems, maybe see a therapist, get well, become tolerant and acquiescing. Yarrow was convinced that she, herself, was not contributing to the problem. She only conceded, and that more than once, that she got out of the relationship what she had put in, which she admitted was half-hearted. She, therefore, knew, that she could not expect more from it:

"I know what my efforts have been. I know I did not contribute as much as I could have. I accept the consequence of a damaged relationship."

"You make it easy for yourself. What did you think I would do? Just watch and wait?" responded dispirited Pelegrine.

At least, in Yarrow's mind, her actions were forgivable, especially since she had remained faithful to her children and to Pelegrine. Yarrow was also adamant that she needed no therapists because the ones she had consulted after her divorce from her husband had told her she was O.K. and sent her home. She kept waving this verdict in front of Pelegrine's eyes that had begged her to enter couples therapy with her. But Yarrow insisted that she was well adjusted and that it was Pelegrine's insecurities and historic baggage that constituted their problems in their relationship.

Channel 214

It comes as no surprise that by January Pelegrine was suffering pretty severely from the nagging distance between them. She could no longer envision placing a kiss on Yarrow's lips. Pelegrine had gotten to the point of reading about sensuality instead of experiencing it with Yarrow. Pelegrine was afraid to have lost her passion for the woman she once loved. Entering each other's intimate space became difficult. Yarrow became more distant until she became only a memory to Pelegrine.

Channel 215

Their story was one of repeated nightmares that would stretch over nearly a decade and remains a testimony to human endurance and addiction—better called, stupidity. The two women visited and "unvisited," argued, made peace, argued again, ran away and found fault with the other on a regular basis. The end of January marked the year that Yarrow required distance and space for private grieving within the circle of her intimate family. This was also the year that so much was asked of Pelegrine and she could not deliver, the year that Yarrow remembers as a year of Yarrow needs and Pelegrine's inability to yield to them. This year marks the physical turning point of their emotional connection. Only they did not accept it as such.

Yarrow's demand on space and distance caused something inside Pelegrine. She was in much pain then, suffering to the point of dying in the cold, relentless snow by her cabin. She had never come in contact with a human being that demanded separation from a partner who was in deep pain herself. Pelegrine thought that couples are tested and stick together during rough times. They cling like vines to each other under a thundering roof. Pelegrine was convinced if Yarrow did not have anybody in the world, no children, and no relatives, that she then would eagerly need Pelegrine. Yarrow's methods were new and unusual and just would not mesh with how Pelegrine operated.

As a result, Pelegrine felt Yarrow slipping out of her life. But she did not want to believe it. Pelegrine also had trouble developing genuine feelings for new people who were slowly edging their way into their circle. Yarrow who never contacted her constructively only for arguments, was slipping out of her life for real. Yet, Pelegrine still wondered how Yarrow would play her cards and how she planned her future with Pelegrine who found herself still waiting for Yarrow's next move. At that time, Pelegrine was not aware that she had in effect given up control of her life, letting others take charge of it like her mother had. She had developed a most unhealthy pattern of putting herself in this position where somebody other than herself manipulated her life.

Pelegrine conceded to be calm and not aggravate Yarrow who was testing Pelegrine's commitment again, for one more year. Should Pelegrine pass the test, she then wanted to be together forever. That was the plan.

Wow. Another plan. Another test. Another gimmick to buy another year. Pelegrine sensed Yarrow's fear that usually saw herself as the only one who took risks or the only one who contributed real sacrifices. Of course, this logic was lopsided and did not bring them closer together.

Channel 216

By February, Pelegrine was struggling to write a film critique. It was hard since in the past, Pontiac had always helped polish and proof read her thoughts. With Yarrow, Pelegrine had not much help. Yarrow resented the time that it required and felt that Pelegrine should do it herself. Yet, Pelegrine needed help and lots of it, because she was trying to achieve tenure at the university and serious scholarship taxed her patience. Several of her colleagues had collaborative team efforts with their respective spouses, which made it a bit easier for some of them to climb the ladder of paper writing and publishing. In such cases, the couples' concerted efforts benefited both of them. Only Yarrow rarely got involved in such aid. The irritation with their separated lives eventually stopped any kind of constructive connection.

After she did not receive tenure since she hadn't published enough secondary scholarship and the Dean who hired her had encouraged the writing of original literature, he died in the middle of it all. His replacement was aligned with different faculty favorites and this alliance wanted no short stories, poems and original prose from his instructors.

Pelegrine realized years later, there had been only one person, and only one, in her life, who would have been able to help her play the academic game successfully. Only she possessed brilliance and foresight, knowing what was required to invest in a life together. That was Pontiac Wingo. Rosemarie also had the traits to have done it. But not Werra and not Yarrow. They shared a uniquely self-serving view and were unable to provide supportive input for Pelegrine. Pelegrine was terribly saddened and wanted to walk out of the world.

Channel 217

By March Pelegrine was hurting for her mother because her perpetual loneliness never failed to drive her thoughts back to her childhood where she missed another vital link--her mother. Whenever forsaken and in pain, the memory of her mother became alive and real again thus becoming the only part remaining constant in her life.

Mama

You did things I can't even do
and you lived from 1909 till now
and I live from now till at least 2009
and still will never have danced 48 hours non-stop like you
who won a teddy bear for your two girls
a bear that was much bigger than I
a bear I had to look-up to
until I was big enough to tie him to my boy's bicycle
which I couldn't straddle because I was too little
and the bike too big
but the teddy bear didn't mind
he liked the ropes that held him in place
while I pushed my legs through the cross bar
to reach the other pedal
with the bear sitting on my shoulders
on a ride down to the river where
he and I took a nap.

Channel 218

Memory Smells

In the urine I smell and remember my mother
The strong acid rancor pleases and repels my senses
Simultaneously
The stronger the smell, the more intense her image.

When I smell my underwear, I always remember her.
When my fingers have scratched my smelly armpits
Not after a shower but after soccer, I smell and remember her.
Is it because I remember her never washing my diapers?
Letting them dry on my little body till my thighs were red and raw
Until inflamed flesh housed new urine on diapers dried three times already.

The memorable odor!
on me...my mattress...my shirt...my hair and my nose!

And when she came out of those bedroom doors
always smelling like piss and body odors I could not comprehend
her smelly fingers which made me turn the other way irritated like I do today at my own smell in memory of her and my neglect.

I probably spent the first four years of my life in perpetual piss.
That's why that odor remembers for me every time.
Remembers the shameful.
How can I ever let anybody read the story I have to tell?
Won't everybody say "yak"?
And go away forever?
Why is urine my permanent friend and connector?
My only companion always with me?
Sometimes fiercely smelling
like vitamin pills mixed with mangoes
Sometimes faint and airy
like yellow chamomile tea.

Is this anal museum
My only true root
My only foundation
The only reality
That never failed?

Channel 219

Pelegrine wrote poems of this nature till, one day, she decided she had to reconcile with her painful past, had to make peace with her soul on some level. That helped her stop repeatedly writing about these horrible memories. She worked her way through it, poem-by-poem, memory-by-memory, until she reached the catharsis she longed for.

Channel 220

During her slowly progressing separation from Yarrow, the next summer an old friend appeared on the scene. Werra popped up suddenly and invited Pelegrine to join her to Tortola, a Caribbean island. Werra included the plane ticket and Pelegrine paid her half of the lodging. That trip proved a major experience. She missed Yarrow. But with her she wasn't going anywhere. With her everything was set in action haphazardly, the night before or not at all. Pelegrine always wanted to remain friends with all women she once knew. Werra was no exception. Friendships were extremely important to Pelegrine. They were her family most of her life.

Channel 221

In Tortola Pelegrine admired the landlady, Caesaria Todman. She was attracted to her blackness, her firmness and willingness to interact with one of her numerous tourist renters. This British Virgin Island experience stayed strictly within the parameters of poetry.

Tortola

Tastes like a mango from a garden called Caesaria only.
Flavors converge into one
but coconuts linger long after orange strings
have vanished into a new temptation but sinful.
Not a farmer takes her surplus bucket to the market
where unknowing tourists devour her haven and
her garden because
Puerto Rican superettes abundantly
supply foreign bananas with papayas to a paradise defied.

Pelegrine hiked over hills with goats and native people on one-way cemented streets. Occasionally she and Werra rented a Moke, a convertible South American VW Jeep. At other times, Pelegrine rented a bicycle and explored abandoned nooks and shipwrecked cabins on either the Caribbean or the Atlantic waters. She never before had the pick of separate oceans for morning and afternoon swims. In the evening when the two travelers went to the local hotel bars, playing calypsos on steel bands under golden moons, Pelegrine preferred to dance with native sons and not with Werra's white, decadent yacht owners. Pelegrine detested those people but not Rubin or Julian with their glistening necklaces and tailored shirts over narrow hips.

Channel 222

Julian, with tribal scars over his cheeks and an intense glance, rented sailboats to ladies with dollars and gentlemen with dough. He offered his companionship with a sailboat alone to an island called Jost Van Dyke famous for its desolate beaches and only his company. But Pelegrine feared his passionate intentions and declined but accepted a dance at Cane Garden Bay celebrating with steel drums July 1, the Territory Day.

At Brewer's Bay, Pelegrine met Brian who was camping and screaming after a coconut fell on his head. Brian was a graduate from the same school where Pelegrine was teaching. What a coincidence meeting him on an island?

He was an island hopper stopping at Mona Island only because it was uninhabited. Pelegrine longed to dare what he was doing. For her it was always too risky. She needed the protection of a second person, preferably male because most women where useless for this type of journey. Tough, courageous girls were hard to find. Brian befriended Pelegrine and she gave him and his stray dog, a lean, young and skinny, Tortolian Doberman-like mongrel, many lifts in the yellow Moke.

Channel 223

West Indian cookery attracted Pelegrine. She found that it was flesh forming, muscle and skin building, protective, regulatory and energy giving. Pelegrine tried to cook salt fish with Caesaria's instructions, adding Johnny Cakes and plantains to the *papaw* (papaya) au gratin. She loved the stuffed breadfruit, the *tanias*, and the sweet potato biscuits. The strange cuisine appealed to her as much as did the new and attractive people. She did not want to leave the mild air, the emerald water, the healthy food and the gentle natives. She wondered how she could return to waters with so many different greens, and salt water tasting--good for the daily two sips. How will she ever continue her floats, her kicks and glances at such colorful fish and coral?

On the day she bicycled to explore Nanny Cay, she buoyed in the green Caribbean salt waves, flushed with heavy winds. She observed four black boys starting a boat, which probably was not theirs. They could not control it well. They were beautiful and young and approached Pelegrine on the shore, inviting her to swim with them to the fish hiding in the wreck. She accepted and they took turns holding her hand under water, guiding her to their treasures. They climbed into the rusty flakes of the ship and slid along the edge deep into the yellows and blues, quietly mingling back and forth.

Channel 224

One of the older ones, probably sixteen, he gently pulled Pelegrine's bikini aside and caressed her with his fingers. He asked Pelegrine to guide his erection, which she just held. She enjoyed the almost reality more than what it normally is. They swam and followed each other till light rays from above enveloped their embrace. She was very excited and had a tiny, Caribbean orgasm above shimmering coral reefs.

Channel 225

All the chocolates in the world can't get the color of those bodies right, she concluded. The sounds of the endless calypsos everywhere, "when in boiling wedder (weather), hot, hot, hot, easy up...." Pelegrine lamented her leave taking ahead of time because she sensed an unfinished business with people and land. She hated to leave with fragments, without having known all there was to know, all the hearts, the suns and salt, before, during and after her daily swim marathons under the Atlantic and Caribbean waves.

"But well," she sighed, "some of it had to stay behind, a shadow of a friend. I could never truly become part of such chocolate colored brilliance, natural in its innate refinement."

Pelegrine, herself a genuine and indomitable nature girl, will be forever wild anyway wherever she lives. She will also never be able to stay long at set tables, only long enough to eat. Pelegrine took with her the memory of salt fish before and after mangoes, in the company of sweet Japanese peppers, mingled with basil from "de lady inside de blue shutters." Pelegrine did not want to go back to the Anglo Saxon Wasp world. One day she would have to come alone. And stay a long time.

Channel 226

It so happened that Rubin Prince, a tailor from Dominica, replaced the courtship of Julian from Cane Garden Bay. Rubin tailored his own shirts and pants. He had good taste and was a gentle, darling boy. Pelegrine had hopelessly fallen in love with the Caribbean rhythms, dancing till dawn after the clubs had closed. With Rubin she danced around rain puddles watched by a mirroring moon on hard packed clay, on real Tortola streets. Rubin was her entrance ticket to be the only white speck in the dark shuffle.

Werra could not understand Pelegrine's attraction to the real thing, to the people of the land. Pelegrine sensed that Werra was jealous of her interactions. She also had the uncomfortable inkling that Werra was still interested in her. It became obvious that Pelegrine no longer had such feelings for her, especially when Werra was up to her old tricks the way she acted way back then when young Pelegrine was so in love with her and had forfeited Pontiac and the stable life she was never ever to find again. The instant they were out at night, Werra commenced to flirt with elderly gentlemen, especially if they owned sailing vessels and maybe big bank accounts. The only difference this time was that Pelegrine was aware of the familiar pattern, which no longer affected her. She was only a friend to Werra, not a lover. It was ironic that Werra made a kind of pass at Pelegrine. She apparently never had understood why Pelegrine left her. Pelegrine realized to her astonishment that had she not removed herself from that woman, her agonies would never have ended.

It pleased Pelegrine to no end to tell Werra off. This time Pelegrine herself was flirting with people of her choice and not just Werra and it was Werra who was trying to hang on to Pelegrine. Werra, forever, excited two genders at the same time. Good thing that Pelegrine was free of that nightmare.

Channel 227

Parting time came closer and after several weeks of practicing little by little, it still hurt. Pelegrine could not stand to leave the calypso people, their blue-green waters and sun-sweet air. She swore that the chocolate city will never die for her, nor will her innocent and pure friend, Rubin, who sewed her a blouse in exchange for the money she gave him to buy ganji which they rolled in brown tobacco leaves and smoked in coconut jungles with his friends.

After the smoke, he slept with Pelegrine on the water reservoir all night. He gently moved his twelve-inch waist into Pelegrine who came so fast under his touch. She signaled that he had to ejaculate into the grass. And a gentleman he was. Unobtrusively and with a quiet elegance, he withdrew and with one quick, casual motion, he wiped himself. He hugged Pelegrine, swayed with her and wanted not to leave her. She knew it was a moment to be relished and could not go anywhere else. This guy was beautiful, physically and emotionally. He used to say, "likewise, myself," when politely replying. He was the best dancer, most honest, gentle and young, brief lover she had ever known. He spoke a paradise language, simple, direct and unequivocally sincere. Pelegrine hoped that nobody would hurt him or contaminate his spirit. He cherished his parents, especially his mom who had sacrificed much for Rubin to be a tailor in Tortola earning very little money but much, much more than in Dominica. She baked many loaves of bread in Dominica so that Rubin could go to Barbados for his training as a tailor. He always spoke about the depth of that gift:

"My Mommy still sends me packages of tannia, bananas and bread."
Pelegrine bought a pair of tennis shoes for his mother. She advised him not to immigrate to his dream city, Brooklyn. She did not know how to explain the type of hatred that was waiting for him there. Perhaps, that is why she only accepted two collect calls from him. She had to end his dream to be with her. He was young and needed to stay behind. He needed to make it there.

Channel 228

Because of such involvements, Pelegrine began recounting her sexual memories with men beginning in kindergarten.

The narrow, wooden, post-war bridge led over the knee-deep Fechela River. Pelegrine crossed it many times dangling her leather bag strapped diagonally across her body, with a red, badly chipped enamel cup and an aristocratically engraved silver spoon attached on a shoestring. Elli's monogrammed initials on the dainty spoon spoke of a time when she owned the whole set. Pelegrine confiscated this spoon for herself before all the uncles were hauling off the rest. She clanked it in rhythm to her steps performing her daily sojourn to the hastily erected post-war kindergarten barracks, smelling like a creosote and tar paper roofing factory.

If only the deaf mute everybody called "Stummerl" who had no tongue and couldn't speak, if only he would not block the narrow bridge with his body. If only he stopped hunkering there with his trousers wide open, dangling his dick and grinning toothlessly while grunting with joy. With one hand he held on to the bike--with the other he massaged his white contraption while stammering delight. If she spotted him in time, Pelegrine avoided the bridge and waded through the ice-cold water, instead. She still remembers the painful cut from the beer bottle slashing her big toe nearly in half. She left a bloody trail but escaped the obstructed bridge.

At other times, when she and her girlfriends encountered him in a safe distance, they were screaming ugly messages, sticking out their tongues and twiddling their noses, hurling insults upon the nasty man. Such memories of scary, lonely and close calls, have lingered with Pelegrine and continue to pop up in any penis encounter, especially the one with Frankie, Kati Schwert's, her best friend's, older brother.

Channel 229

At ten Pelegrine considered twenty-five-year-old men old and frightening. She recalled one day as she was looking for Kati. Frankie was home and beckoned her inside the kitchen. Suddenly he whipped out an enormous-looking protrusion. He begged the little girl to kiss it. Pelegrine stared and stared and was petrified with fear. She spun around and ran away as fast as her legs would carry her. To this day, she never told anybody about this. She was too ashamed. But she also stopped visiting Kati's home unless somebody else was there. She avoided being alone with the awful brother, no matter what she had to do. And to think that this man was married, had an imbecile son with a birth defect and a wife that resembled a retarded whore with big, red lips, fat hips and an inviting ass. Why did he need to molest little girls since he had such a hot number at home? After she was long gone and remembered this incidence in a safe detachment, there still were no answers to questions like that.

Channel 230

Anton was her first real boyfriend at fourteen. With him she learned how to kiss properly until one day she discovered, that he, too, had such a huge tube inside his pants. He and Pelegrine had been meeting in secret. That was customary back then in Europe. You did not bring your boyfriends around till they were seriously connected. They usually met at the tennis court fence. Both parties were clinging with their fingers to the fence mesh while staying astride on their bikes. There they eyed each other across the tennis courts. Nodding their heads in unison, they dashed away into the deep and dark forest beyond the castle ruins. There they exchanged their routine kisses. There was also a day when Pelegrine wore her first silk bras, discarded by her girl friend Helga who had developed fast. Anton removed this unnecessary piece of clothing with expert fingers. Since there really was nothing to grab, he just massaged her little nipples, adding to Pelegrine's wonder why boys liked kissing and rubbing non-existing breasts?

During one such forest encounter, he suddenly sat on a tree stump and Pelegrine kept ignoring the long sausage hanging from his opened pants. She looked everywhere but there. And he just sat and glared, saying nothing. Pelegrine was afraid again. She had seen such pieces of equipment before and felt the same uncomfortable nightmare in her heart.

She stopped following Anton into the woods after that day. She avoided him because she knew that sooner or later he would not just stay seated with his swollen sack. She did not know what was expected of her, but a sense of fear kept her from finding out.

Channel 231

Her penis "dates" can be counted on one hand, but not the million kissing encounters. She loved kissing and playing make-believe love games. There was Martina who lived upstairs. Both girls where nine years old and enjoyed their husband and wife game. Pelegrine lay on top of Martina rubbing her oversized doughnuts, hanging from both sides of her body when she was flat on the floor. When it was Pelegrine's turn to lie underneath, she suddenly peed a giant arch into the air. She was proud of her acrobatic accomplishments and Martina was in heaven. Then they went back to trading stamps, as usual. They never spoke about their game. They just played it till Pelegrine pissed. And then they stopped.

Pelegrine did not find Martina herself attractive. Only her breasts. They were magnetic like overgrown grapefruits. They were asking to be squeezed. Her big mouth was always open exposing the very yellow teeth and exhaling stinking breath. There was nothing appealing under her cheese-like skin and unimaginative, colorless eyes. Only her boobs. They were soft and divine.

Pelegrine was also an avid doctor player with the two boys who lived next door. The boys were very pushy with Pelegrine on the operating table. They always went straight for the operation on the hole, never tickling or using a feather to prepare for the surgery. They were clumsy and single minded. It was much better with Martina. There, Pelegrine could control what was happening.

It was actually a chore to ward off the boys since they wanted to play doctor every living minute of the day—even after they were finished playing. They had left the "hospital" in the haystacks, which were raised, on the fields like tepees to dry. They insisted on "surgery" when Pelegrine ran to the cellar fetching coals and wood for her mother. They were everywhere—always, always ready with their little, hard clumps—always pressing them on Pelegrine's behind. She permitted it for just a second but ran away quickly before they got a hold of her. This chase she would regularly win.

Channel 232

And then there were the movies. Especially X rated ones where people had to be eighteen. Getting into those forbidden films was one of Pelegrine's favorite pastimes. Some days she put on high heels, lipstick and a wig. On other days she crouched on her feet and wiggled her way between people's legs through the gate. She waddled her cowering duck walk until she found an empty seat. Only when the lights went out, was she safe and could stop moving from seat to seat. Getting into the theater to see an adult movie was a big chore but worth the trouble—of not missing "La Dolce Vita."

There was only one problem. What if she had to go wee-wee. She was a bed wetter and had to empty her little bladder often. She could not afford to go out to the official bathroom and be seen. Thus she simply let it flow on the wooden seat. She had to sit in the cheap front, unupholstered section and not in the rear of the theater in the lush and costly cushioned seats. It was harder to find an empty seat back there. She just sat in her warm piss until the end of the show.

One day the boy sitting next to her grabbed her little pinky during the picture. She allowed it and soon was holding hands with him. Furtively she ascertained how handsome he was and if worth all the trouble. He replaced Anton for a while because with him she could continue the kissing and brassiere games. He never paraded his dick. He was safe.

Channel 233

And it was safety she was looking for in her relentless, white-water, roller coaster relationship with Yarrow. Through her connection to this woman, she learned, at last, what she should have learned a long time ago: be able to live alone and not feel that it was wrong like Elli always said. But since they were an occasional couple, breaking and making up in turns, Pelegrine did not relish her solitude, as such. Yet these experiences contributed to what one might call growth. Pelegrine was not always so sure that her education could not have taken place another way. But by staying involved with Yarrow, Pelegrine's own ambivalence was nourished and did not help her become more decisive in her choices. It seemed like both women were reaching out at the same time, only to grab empty air coupled with their fears of what it takes to be committed. They were hoping for support and strength from each other, but got a bag of nothing instead. This failing relationship, however, did lay the groundwork for Pelegrine to learn more about life with men and women.

Channel 234

One day she took her mountain bike and discovered a wild life refuge, thirty miles south of her home. It was lovely, sitting in the sand and reading Anne LaBastille's *Woodswoman*, hearing only birds and waves. Thus she slowly forgot her craving need for people. Being outdoors under physical duress made her too busy to miss anybody.

She was actually preparing for her Hungarian and Czechoslovakian bike tour. At that time also, she was still burying Yarrow who, once again, could not make up her mind if they would spend their precious schoolteacher summer holiday together. Pelegrine recorded into her journal:

How long will it take that thinking of her will not hurt anymore? I feel I have made a big mistake in not stopping my unhappy relationship with her sooner. If she reads this, she will be hurt. We have always read each other's journals. It is becoming more difficult to say what I want, knowing she will read it. I guess, I must do it anyway. I am sorry, but my love for you did not work for us. I cannot understand now why it couldn't work. I stayed with you after I received my degree. I sold oranges and cleaned toilets, instead of looking for a real job. You and your demanding motherhood pushed me into suicide thoughts. Eventually I accepted a job away from you. You followed me to be in a one-day driving range. We visited until the weekends ran out of attraction, until they had burned us out. When your youngest child had finished high school you said, you would live with me. Then I heard you say when the child graduated from college you would come. Then it was when your enormous credit card bills where paid up. But you kept accruing more and more debts. I found too many screw drivers and wrenches in the snow. Nobody was in the habit of returning tools. It was easier to buy new ones. Thus the bills stayed big. You never wanted to finish your degree. It was easier to earn a pittance sooner but forever. You would not listen to me when I offered to support you. You would not listen when I wanted to give you my tenure and the security that goes with it. But I needed your help for that. I offered to put your name on my mortgage so that you could never be thrown out which you feared I would do. I know I have temper outbursts. But you also knew that I am reasonable right away again. All I needed was faith and support. I was working to give you that security.

    I always feel insane but pass for normal. Yarrow, I learned that feeling by knowing you. I am not blaming you. Maybe you did me a favor of making me aware of it. I just don't know what to do about it, except never burden anybody with my love again.

    I don't want to dislike myself. I am the best I can be. I will simplify as many aspects about my life as possible. Don't know where to turn or to go. Wish I could have 300 dollars a month as a gift and live in the woods. I just want to read and survive, be simple and use only essentials and stay that way till I die. Anne LaBastille did my thing but I'm doing my thing also. She is another

Thoreau, the one I've always been.

I, too, can chop wood and build an outhouse, not with discarded French doors. I build one with no help and wood from the dump. She gives me great ideas. If Anne did Walden II, I am not doing Walden III. I am doing what I have started before I heard about her. She is a scientist and free-lances successfully, has discipline and money. And guts and brains. I have some of it. I also must find a way to live in my cabin. I want the courage to give-up my job and believe in my good health and ageless age. I am in my forties now. Is that too old?

Channel 235

Too old for what? For trying to leave Yarrow? For interviewing a prominent author in the summer? For having a tempestuous love affair with that writer whose husband expressed interest in Pelegrine also—as did the daughter.

But Pelegrine had only eyes for Spinne who herself had a lot to gain by doing what she said she had never done before but knew how to sustain with engaging toes und the table, with illicit rubs and seductive massages behind everybody's formal back. Just like in the movies.

Pelegrine had a small research grant and a room with a Vienna view, provided by the mayor himself. Yarrow came along for three weeks, trying to mend their shredded relationship. It almost worked but debts called Yarrow home to a summer of labor. And Pelegrine had followed the track of a writer of her own post war generation describing common experiences. Pelegrine was attracted to the writer of a book she could have written herself. She liked the writer before she met her. They corresponded themselves into a prodigious summer.

Channel 236

Pelegrine had contacted the author and was awaiting the time before the first meeting. She sat in the city gardens, where as a little girl she had pushed the heavy Rondo platform, trying to jump and get a ride. Unbelievable that she would sit in the very same spot from thirty years ago. Odd memories arose in the perfumes of the roses. The adult child was back in a park for exciting reasons. The waif had come three thousand miles to interview a well-known writer. None of her friends and people back home believed she had such connections.

Pelegrine jogged along the Danube. It was two hours before the rendezvous. But she lost her keys somewhere among the tourists. Thus she could neither enter the rental car nor the room where she lived. It was ludicrous. Yarrow hanging out of the sixth story window, not being able to get out of the locked door without a key, and Pelegrine downstairs on the outside of the building, unable to get up there without a key—just like their life. No exit. And no entrance.

Pelegrine re-ran her path and traced her steps. She could not miss her rendezvous. Suddenly, she miraculously spied her keys under the same grape arbor where she enacted fairy tales as a child. Exactly there, she found her keys. Nobody would ever comprehend her double miracle—from then and from now. Thus her childhood grounds added the necessary magic to the mission that brought her back to gardens, thirty years after she had run through them barefoot. Today she ran, foreign and tourist-like in expensive running shoes, connecting absent years through lost keys.

Channel 237

After meeting the artist and falling deeply for her, Pelegrine received a familiar rejection. She went back to the park and lamented her affliction since age twelve. She wished to bury the infection that came upon her the minute someone she admired paid an ounce of attention to her. She wanted to kill the obsession to interpret every gesture, every nuance and every glance to be meant for her. Her hunger for attention at such times was truly pathological and it crippled her logical brain functions completely.

Her pattern sounded familiar like Winter and Moni. Pelegrine knew it all too well but failed to escape its magnetism.

Channel 238

She fought and fought. But this experience was new, something she had never encountered. After Yarrow left, she was empty and afraid. She missed Yarrow with habitual pain. Pelegrine did not want Yarrow to go. She anticipated excitement and returned to the source of her trouble while struggling with the reality of the situation. She wanted to see if she could shake the addiction, the obsession. But she wasn't sure if she wanted to win.

Channel 239

The mayor wanted his room back because the interview was over. The writer offered a bed. And Pelegrine volunteered to drive her everywhere because the writer had no license and wanted to visit Italy. Pelegrine readily obliged. She did not speak Italian and was content to live inside her dreams that were not happening. Instead, she saw and heard and learned a lot about Levico and Bassano, new landscapes and restaurants in ancient castles on steep hills and grappas by the river. Pelegrine paid and paid because the author was penny-less and hungry for new material. Pelegrine was increasing her debts as she was nursing her private fantasy.

Channel 240

She realized that a monogamous relationship with Yarrow would never permit such encounters. But then again, had the relationship been satisfying and consummated in marriage and commitment, would other attention givers have found her susceptible? Wasn't that the problem with Pontiac, too? Not enough time and activities together weaken and kill all bonds eventually. And Yarrow's intermittent appearances caused their toll.

Channel 241

And so it happened that Spinne stroked Pelegrine's neck one late night and inquired about her and Yarrow. What kind of connection did they have? Pelegrine did not want to talk about it but gradually volunteered to talk about her agonies and her eternal aloneness she had suffered with Yarrow over the years. Spinne listened and seemed to care but not enough to pull Pelegrine closer who trembled and wished for only a hug.

Channel 242

Elefant, Spinne's giant husband, was restless and got out of bed to piss, all night long. He stuck his head in the door, watching two women in the moonlight. Pelegrine rested on her stomach with her head in Spinne's lap who was caressing Pelegrine's neck--no more. But no less. Elefant was pleased and told Pelegrine at breakfast that he had never seen Spinne so attractive and sensuous. Pelegrine was confused why the man was talking to her about his engaging wife. She liked him all right but more for the daily bike rides, jogs and discussions about love and lust. He was a poet and Pelegrine's poetic self connected with his. Besides writing, he was a railroad switch worker, spending lots of time in a tiny caboose along the tracks. His humor and biting sarcasm came out in his bizarre tales. One could hear them on Sunday afternoon radio broadcasts. He was locally known. His wife nationally.

Channel 243

Spinne was famous and busy. Pelegrine, too, had visits to complete. It so happened that Spinne was to arrive in Vienna on a Monday. Pelegrine knew only the day, no time. That Monday morning Pelegrine went to the railroad station inquiring about the time of all trains arriving from Innsbruck that day. She planted herself on the cemented, guard stone that stopped the locomotives from rebounding. She awaited all arrivals, one by one. Late Monday afternoon, she finally spotted the only traveler of interest. Spinne froze in her tracks when she saw Pelegrine and appreciated her ingenious maneuver to find her.

Pelegrine met totally new people where Spinne was staying. They spent a night together on a double pullout couch. Spinne's friends, Miriam and Christoph, liked Pelegrine and invited her to stay as long as she wished. Pelegrine telephoned her hosts to tell them she was not coming home that day and would be gone for a while--not explaining why or for how long.

Channel 244

And that night was like another night twenty years ago, the one with Rita in California where she found out what being sexual and alive was all about. Spinne slowly tracked her fingernail along Pelegrine's arm, then down her hand and, eventually, slipping over to her rib cage. The finger slid up under her armpit and down to her hip. There it stopped and rested. Then the nail slid sideways to her spine. The girl's body lay motionless in anticipation. She could not believe what was happening:

"What does it mean when a woman travels with her index finger after having said vehemently that women don't interest her? These hungry heterosexual women always come around in the end."

Pelegrine broke out in cold sweat and followed the finger until she grabbed it and asked boldly into the dark night:

"Do you know what you are doing to me? You know I have loved you when I first read your book. But you have been rejecting me. And now you want me? Is that right?"

"I think I do. And I want it, now."

And that is how they commenced their non-stop love making, till noon when the friends knocked on the door, inquiring if anybody was ready to eat. The two really needed sleep more than food but settled for coffee since the living room had to be cleared for people who lived in it, for people who had slept and not frolicked all night.

Channel 245

The time that followed was identical to the joy Pelegrine remembered with Rita. Interestingly, she likened the experience to the one with Rita and possibly Werra, but not Pontiac, Yarrow, or Rosemarie. What linked these three people who essentially robbed Pelegrine of more than they gave? Rita, Werra and Spinne were older, sexually experienced women who were takers and not givers. They hurt Pelegrine because they never loved her.

Channel 246

Pelegrine savored her obsession with Spinne till the very last drop. They were sneaking around everybody and these clandestine components added to their thrill. Ironically, Spinne's and Elefant's long-time friends, Miriam and Christoph, both fell in love with Pelegrine at that time also. Miriam had once also loved Spinne who never returned any feelings to her. She just dished out rejection, flirtations and torture. But Spinne was affectionate and suspiciously flirtatious with Christoph. They had met at a health spa and who knows what they did during their underwater massages. Pelegrine suspected that the two had shared more than water.

At this time of the story, Christoph was extremely devoted to Spinne and Pelegrine, but not to his wife, Miriam. Miriam, on the other hand still doted on Spinne but especially on Pelegrine. Incidentally, Miriam also had been intensely involved in a six-month sexual fling with Elefant. But nobody was supposed to know. It was a secret. By now, Elefant had long dumped Miriam who lived in perpetual yearning for either Spinne or Elefant and now, even Pelegrine.

Pelegrine dodged all approaches from Elefant, Christoph or Miriam. She only wanted Spinne. Pelegrine returned their kindness but not their love. When Spinne had to return home, Pelegrine visited her own hosts briefly, removed all her belongings and was unable to explain her strange departure. For them, she just went out one Monday morning and never returned. It almost hurt them. But what could Pelegrine do? Tell them the truth that she was in heat for Spinne?

Channel 247

At home, Elefant just stared at his wife and told Pelegrine that he had never seen her glow that way. That same night Pelegrine rolled a joint and smoked it with Spinne and her twenty-four-year old daughter, Meta, while swaying to fierce winds on top of a mountain overlooking the city. Before going to bed, Elefant asked Pelegrine point blank,

"Do you want to sleep with my wife?"

"Yes," she stammered. She shivered in disbelief at her own boldness.

Channel 248

It was like in the movies. Elefant took Pelegrine's guest bed and she slipped into his. She made him swear that he would not come into the bedroom during the night:

"Promise."

"Absolutely."

And for the first time, with sanction, so to speak, she really made love, relaxed and passionate. She went down on Spinne who acted like she had never been in such ecstasy before. Pelegrine, too, couldn't believe she did that with somebody she did not want to marry. She thought she could only do this when being truly in love with someone special. But these truths like so many others last only until they are inconvenient.

Elefant admitted next morning that he had peeked. Pelegrine was furious. But he was so enthralled he said with what he saw. Consequently, he wrote a poem to Pelegrine, whom he himself wanted to love. But Pelegrine told him again, to cut out that thought. He was not in her books.

When Spinne finally rose, usually way after noon, he catered to her and she bossed him around. There were acute and intense eye exchanges and cryptic threats tossed between them,

"Don't. I warn you."

Pelegrine only heard bits and pieces and did not understand what they were talking about. Spinne asked Pelegrine if Elefant could stay in his own bed that night together with Pelegrine. Pelegrine did not know why she said yes. But she agreed.

Channel 249

Pelegrine stayed strictly on one side so that the wife lay between Elefant and her. Elefant got up and came to Pelegrine and wanted to caress her. She shoved him toward his wife and withdrew her massaged feet. She feared these people probably were into kinky stuff, more than she was willing to provide. She only wanted to be with Spinne, nothing else.

One afternoon, Spinne and Pelegrine were lying in bed when the front door suddenly opened. Meta was surprised to see her mother in bed still at three and, for whatever reason, in the guest bed. Spinne slid out of bed and Pelegrine stayed silently under the covers without being seen.

"Why are you still in bed? And why are you not in your own bed? Are you sick? Where is Pelegrine?"

"Asleep. Don't wake her."

But Pelegrine only heard about that conversation later and did not know what ingenious excuse Spinne invented. She hovered two hours under the covers daring not to move and was barely breathing. After near asphyxiation, she forced herself to act nonchalantly as if she had just risen from the longest, most deserving sleep. This was as a close call, closer than she liked. She hated confrontations of any kind and, definitely, not one of this nature.

Meta acted extremely friendly toward Pelegrine after this incident and began to vie for her attention. Pelegrine gently refused the affection from the daughter, encouraging friendship and sincere contact only.

Channel 250

Pelegrine's hot summer was savored to the last drop. When they drove on the Autobahn, they would periodically leave the highway, pull out a blanket, serve champagne and make love under the sky. When accidental tourists approached, they often had barely enough time to gather their clothes and act blasé.

They were inseparable and Spinne accompanied Pelegrine all the way to the airport in another country. She planned to visit Pelegrine while traveling on a lecture and poetry reading tour throughout the US, which Pelegrine promised to organize with sponsors and all. It was, after all, Spinne's actual goal. Pelegrine knew that.

Channel 251

By the time Pelegrine returned to the US, she had to deal with Yarrow. The encounters were hard and painful. Pelegrine expected the final severance. But Yarrow dug and dug till Pelegrine revealed the entire episode, minute by minute. And Yarrow could not discredit Spinne enough since she had been writing to Yarrow every week while the lovebirds were frolicking in Europe. Yarrow was thoroughly disgusted with Spinne and refused the silkscreen prints and perfume presents. She tore up the dedication Spinne had written—a dedication inside a personal copy of a newly published book of Spinne's poetry:

For Pelegrine!

Still looking at life through the frame of a too big boy's bicycle,
pedaling air—still sometimes
and still putting a bear to sleep down by the waters
wanting to be the cared-for-bear herself
with an unbroken tongue
finally healed

Pelegrine liked these words at first. But later, she didn't any more. They sounded cheap and not sincere.

Yarrow magnanimously forgave Pelegrine's transgression, yet their relationship did not improve. They returned to more of the same dramas, except now Yarrow would bring up Spinne in arguments. This woman served to drive home Yarrow's message that she had lost trust in Pelegrine with that experience although she had "forgiven" her. Whatever that was supposed to mean? Thus Pelegrine entered another wild-water rafting excursion in the River Yarrow.

Channel 252

Pelegrine hoped the following year that Yarrow would move to her town, live with her albeit poorly but together on Pelegrine's salary. They planned to accept part-time jobs for extra income. As usual, it did not need much of a dispute for that plan never to materialize. Yarrow accepted a full-time job, six hours away, instead. Another deja vue. They stayed horn-locked about this new problematic situation also. Absolutely insane. They both knew their connection had to end. They were destroying each other totally but slowly.

Pelegrine was tumbling through her days like a weed in the wind. She wept at odd places, even under water while swimming. She could not believe this was her life. She watched it paralyzed. She felt once more hurt again. She avoided contact with other people. She did not want to repeat herself everywhere. She avoided distractions and focused only on her fatal "attraction." It was not easy to reject normal distractions. It was easier to stay obsessed with the source of her pain. Thus time passed slowly without a glimmer of a hope, or a future worth living for. There were books, thank God.

Channel 253

Next summer she was cycling through Europe with Rico, Karla's husband. Karla was a student trying to patch her marriage, and Pelegrine, the "wise" mentor teacher-friend, gave advice she, herself, could not practice. She traveled through East European countries before the fall of the wall and Rico was a good but trying companion. At the same time, Yarrow was traveling in Spain, giving her daughter a graduation present. Pelegrine and Yarrow were hoping that they would connect somewhere in Europe. But hoping was all they did. Yarrow never helped to make it happen. She just made a promise. Accordingly, Pelegrine missed Yarrow in Europe and was disappointed again. This was one year after the Spinne spectacle. Pelegrine reluctantly visited the writer. Her cold and scarred heart took over by then because she had promised herself never to get close again.

Channel 254

Rico and Pelegrine visited Miriam and Christoph. He was thrilled to escort the travelers on his bicycle all the way to the Czech border. They relished their first night in a tent in Bratislava after they had cycled 49 miles. Pelegrine was tired and sun burned. The strange new people were friendly and curious. Pelegrine was still missing Yarrow but with less intensity every day. She was getting used to single experiences outside of the US.

Channel 255

Everything was different in Czechoslovakia. Even funny. What was considered important and what constituted a luxury never ceased to amaze them. Goods, which Pelegrine's world disposed of lightly, were craved here. Everything that the Western world was taking for granted was absent there. They hungered after ballpoint pens, Bic razors and panty hose.

In Trnava, Rico and Pelegrine were camping in a cemetery. When they left the graveyard to have a bite to eat, a waitress asked them to spend the night in her living room instead. Strangers picked them up, hungry for Kitsch and knick-knacks from the West. Everything Pelegrine was trying to leave behind and learn to do without, these people yearned for. They were generous, good-hearted, sad, resigned, all at the same time. They were obsessed with only one wish: to go to the Western world of glitz and glamour, to the big supermarket, to the endless credit cards, to the big cars, to the Roman decadence and destiny. That is what they wanted.

Rico and Pelegrine biked to Piestany. They had heard of the famous thermal baths and excellent massages. At that point they had completed 110 miles. They were relishing their incredible discoveries, eating cherries while balanced on the handlebars, accepting water from friendly people offering it from their windows. How long will people be that nice to people, Pelegrine wondered? Will cars, money and wealth remove us from each other?

Channel 256

Rico and Pelegrine had a fight and cleared the air for a better journey. He became more considerate, offered her the first sip from the one and only cup between them and not what was left after he was full. This incident helped them to have a respectful and generous journey. They biked through untouched countryside, camped anywhere because it was safe and free. They enjoyed fantastic meals and amenities available to them only because they were fortunate enough to be born in the West. Pelegrine became self-conscious of their shiny, Patagonia colored bikes and sweaters. Rico phoned Karla whenever there was a phone. Pelegrine silently wondered what Yarrow was doing. She was lonely for her.

Channel 257

The foreign bicyclists were not allowed to cross the Danube in a town called Sturovo. Thus they commenced to take the train to Budapest with their bikes in the luggage wagon. People in Hungary also were friendly and eager to take the two strangers home with them. But Rico and Pelegrine responded warmly and tried to convince the Hungarians that the very reason they were on bikes was to sleep under the open sky.

Wealth in Hungary was more plentiful and more western as compared to the gray and forlorn Czech world. Their history did not progress into a better one and kept the people cloistered in gloom and ashes similar to Pelegrine's post war life.

Rico changed into a considerate and thoughtful companion. Pelegrine became extremely fond of him—a feeling that lasted forever. His real self came through after she fell from her snazzy bike while completing a sharp downhill Hungarian curve in Ezstergom. Her rear pannier got caught in the spokes and the bike skidded across the highway with Pelegrine flying sideways into the air. Her gear scattered all over the road and down the shoulders. The traffic swished by and one carload of Hungarians shouted when passing Rico,

"Companion kaputt."

He hurriedly came back and searched for ice cubes in an iron-curtain country. He managed to produce a bag from a hotel and soothed Pelegrine's disjointed shoulder. She limped to a hospital, received x-rays without having to produce an insurance card and was sent on her way with bandaged arms and legs but an unbroken shoulder—all at no charge!

The trip was hard but they reached Tatabanya, a tiny village. A restaurant worker took pity on them again and took the bandaged foreigner and her companion home and insisted that they pitch their tents in the chicken yard. It was heaven that night to sleep in the midst of geese and chicken shit. The next day was just as great with a picnic by the wild river, enjoying their foot long Italian horsemeat Salami she had smuggled over many borders.

Channel 258

After the biking trip was over she sent Rico back home and continued her travels by car. She invited Miriam to join her on a trip to explore Yugoslavia and the Mediterranean Beaches. Miriam suggested nudist camps where people did everything naked. They ate without clothes in restaurants and only the waiters were dressed but not the guests. They sat on towels separating the plastic chair from the sweat. When the evening breezes were chilly, people put on T-shirts. They left their butts free like babies without diapers. Pelegrine was totally enchanted with this bodily freedom. She did everything naked: swim, shit, sleep, eat--day after day. She needed clothes only for jogging and when a slight chill hit the air. This experience was exhilarating to Pelegrine and she vowed to seek out every opportunity to enjoy air, sun and water with an unclothed body. She became one with nature.

Channel 259

Pelegrine also encountered her egotistical side on this trip. She wasn't sure whether living alone for so many years had taken its toll. She realized that many activities and events had to go by her instructions, and Miriam who had been a subservient wife and mother all her life, needed instructions on how to erect her daughter's yuppie tent, how one made coffee under the stars on a second-hand antique kerosene burner--not on a luxurious L.L. Bean original. Miriam had to be told that a woman can live self-sufficiently without a nagging husband. Pelegrine became somewhat impatient because she had expected more savvy from her, a woman who was adept at picking up road kill rabbits from the street, rush home, tie it up on a fence, gut it and skin it and serve it for a great tasting stew the next day. From someone like that Pelegrine had expected more know-how. Pelegrine was impatient with Miriam's inadequacies or Yarrow's absence. Who knew? It became more and more clear to Pelegrine that this was to become yet another summer without Yarrow. And memories of the absent mate discolored her present activities and undermined her joy.

Channel 260

It was fun to study people and their international genitals. They existed in all variations and positions. Some rested limp, some steep. Others were round and others were square or small or long or only a little lump. Some had hanging breasts or bell-shaped bosoms. Pelegrine became familiar with a million varieties of body parts. People glanced at each other for only a second before their eyes returned to an anonymous gaze behind neon-colored sunglasses.

Lots of wealthy Western sun worshippers displayed strong currencies behind bright privacy fences, brown bodies, and expensive tents. Naked windsurfers were gliding carefree through emerald Adriatic waves.

The band played old fifties melodies mixed with Cha Cha favorites Pelegrine enjoyed as a young teenager. Everybody danced with everybody including children on skateboards. The dance floor was a ball of color and Miriam had joined the long dancing tail with people holding onto each other's waists. Pelegrine eventually connected herself to the human snake and escaped her gloomy thoughts for a while.

Miriam was getting on Pelegrine's nerves. Miriam rose earlier in the morning to pick flowers and prepare a picnic with Turkish coffee on the blanket to please Pelegrine. She was touched by these gestures but felt uncomfortable because she knew Miriam was desperately seeking her affection. Pelegrine always resented people who desired her and she was not interested in the least. She never encouraged such behavior but some people just insisted with their persevering lust, kindness and never-ending attention. Since Pelegrine did not return these intense feelings but was reluctant to outright reject such admirers, she thus encountered a temperamental struggle, fluctuating from patience to outright explosion. She never could figure out why it actually repelled her to be desired by people she had not picked herself. She sometimes wondered whether others felt that way too, especially those whom she loved elaborately but in vain? She was sure that the homophobic people she had fallen for probably resented her the same way. Just as sure as did those who had said "no" but really meant "yes" and those who recorded the attraction and even responded briefly, but decided to get married in a hurry to make sure they abandoned this feeling. They probably ran away from Pelegrine, too?

Pelegrine became aware of a streak of cruelty in her when she was dealing with drooling followers like Miriam. It may have had something to do with the fact that Miriam was kind, gentle but stubbornly stupid, staying trapped in her miserable life. Pelegrine never felt patience for such human beings. She willingly counseled friends with unhappy lives like Miriam, but became furious with them, when they kept complaining but made no move to change their dissatisfying situation. She actually seemed to lose her respect for them and thus treated them like shit if they refused to change. After all, Pelegrine was a hero worshipper, not a saint. She liked strong people because she was well aware of her own flaws and limitations. Saints like her mother never got anywhere. Strong people like Tante Josefa did. Pelegrine had known nothing but struggle to make life livable. She could find little compassion for those who did not.

Channel 261

By November after that naked summer in Yugoslavia, Pelegrine was on her journey, still. Her tenure decision a year away. Her boss encouraged her, but her inner emptiness remained big and black, as before. She ardently tried to stop dwelling on it. She wished to learn better to know what she wanted, to avoid running into the same traps, over and over. At that point in her life she was certain that she liked women all right but also from time to time was dreaming about a male mate and companion. Women had let her down in two areas: the time they spent with her and the necessary commitment. Men were different. Few and only very special women could provide genuine masculine camaraderie. Whatever one calls such a difference, be it bold, adventuresome, easy-going--all those qualities she had a hard time finding in a woman. Women found too many excuses not to be straightforward. Pelegrine wanted to be a team with somebody and it did not have to be a woman anymore, especially after her ordeal with Yarrow. She was seeking an androgynous being where sexuality became secondary and human qualities primary.

Was the ordeal with women who hurt her really shaping her paths? People like Rita, Coco and Tante Josefa? Because as Pelegrine was trying to make it in America on her own, without parents, or relatives and with help only from foreign strangers, her most beloved aunt, Tante Josefa, started asking pointed questions during Pelegrine's next visit.

"What is this I hear from Albert and Coco that you are gay, queer and live a disgusting life?"

"I am the same girl that I always was. I am struggling to make it through school on my own. I am a university student and I work at night as a file clerk. And if anybody is reporting on my sex life, they must have been in bed with me. Otherwise they would not be so well informed. I have never broadcast my sexuality. I m shy and scared about that. I don't even understand it very well and I have no one to ask. Whoever is accusing me should be asked why they think they know. I have heard the saying, *It takes one to know one.*"

Tante Josefa completely shut down and threw Pelegrine out of her room. Pelegrine began to understand that maybe Rita herself was spreading this information to her family so that they could hate her. She suddenly knew why Uncle Albert and Aunt Coco rejected her. It was Rita who made sure of that. Pelegrine could not understand why all members of that Käfer clan, Albert, Coco, Josefa, all of them, why they let her down and never even talked to her about it? Was it such a sin to be like that? Why didn't anybody want to hear Pelegrine's side of the picture? She was utterly devastated when she realized that in this world, people, no, relatives, I should say, believe a one-sided smear campaign against one of their members. Little did she know.

Channel 262

Albert and Coco died. Pelegrine was stricken from their will. Her sister and her mother, each received 100 thousand dollars inheritance. Pelegrine's name was crossed-out on the list. Ten strangers received 25 thousand dollars each. And Rita Lange, their mutual bosom friend, received an amount that was initially 100 thousand but was altered to 200 thousand after Pelegrine was eliminated.

Pelegrine's fragile ego received its biggest and most crushing blow. It stopped her from ever identifying comfortably with the sexual orientation she had learned to discover with a woman called Rita. Pelegrine carried her private homophobia inside her, a fear of being discovered and disowned, again. She can only attribute that feeling of shame to the treatment that was to repeat itself when her mother's only sister and Pelegrine's beloved hero aunt, Tante Josefa died.

That woman, too, crossed Pelegrine from her million dollar will. And all that because Pelegrine liked both, men and woman. Women scoring probably higher on the emotional register. Her family made her hard life even harder by punishing her for such preferences.

Her Mama, Elli, however, never abandoned her because of that. But the other two big forces in her life, the ones that could have been instrumental in structuring a decent future for Pelegrine, her wealthy aunts and uncle, they slashed her heart and created an angry, insecure survivor whose ability to trust and unconditionally love have been severely damaged.

Channel 263

By November, Pelegrine's and Yarrow's entanglement was still intact. Their hour-long, tearful, long-distance conversations kept them both going in well-known circles. Yarrow started complaining about the money she spent for the phone calls. She seemed pre-occupied. Often she promised to call but never did. Pelegrine got angry with herself for sliding back into Yarrow's unreliable network. Yarrow also did not want to be with Pelegrine during Thanksgiving that year. She wanted to be with her children who were in college and whom the mother missed very much. Pelegrine hung-on, regardless. She had tried to end this relationship many times. But this time she wondered how much she still loved Yarrow. Pelegrine cherished Yarrow's gentle and forgiving nature, her caring and tenacious love. She disliked Yarrow's judgmental acceptance and rejection of people. Some could do no wrong and others she judged before they even spoke. Yarrow also was a superb fact-twister to suit her story. She became very angry and defensive when Pelegrine wanted to talk about that. Pelegrine began to see Yarrow's manipulative side. She was an expert at muddling-up issues and to confuse an opponent. That trait made her seem slippery and eel-like. And hard to trust. All these thoughts made Pelegrine act on edge, ready to be hostile and aggressive. As a result, Yarrow became an attacker and focused on Pelegrine's weaknesses. Pelegrine preferred open discussions and wanted self-examination and straight-forwardness for both of them. But Yarrow denied such talks:

"I thought you said it would be better if we didn't speak to each other at this point since everything between us is so volatile."

"But I told you I wasn't sure when I could leave from home. I had a meeting."

The truth was, Yarrow repeatedly had something more important to do than to visit Pelegrine. Since this happened so frequently, genuine emergencies were ignored since all excuses were lumped into one big unreliable bag of broken promises. Yarrow was the person who never tired of finding pretext, who was never on time, who never could make plans and stick to them. Everything happened in the last minute. There was no telling how many distractions were pulling her into ten different directions before she actually acted. One simply could not make plans with Yarrow. One had to sit tight and wait till she showed up.

Had Yarrow been sitting lonely in her apartment, with only books, fog, rain and weak sunshine to keep her Thanksgiving company, she would have tried harder to reach Pelegrine and even spoken to the answering machine. But Yarrow's silence, no return phone calls and the gray winter stillness of a love grown thin, have a language of their own.

Channel 264

One evening Pelegrine went shopping. She found evenings better because fewer cart pushers were plugging the aisles. She clutched her coupons in her fingers but never found the exact items to match the pictures. Pelegrine came home that night with eight shopping bags. But the ninth bag was a gift with kosher mayonnaise, herring and matzo balls. She examined the strange goods and was considering keeping them. But honesty is not as easily worn as a glove. One wears it because.... It was a little late to return to the store again at ten thirty at night. But Pelegrine drove anyway and returned the groceries not belonging to her. The manager beamed with gratitude. Pelegrine danced because she was thankful that she was good at heart and did the right thing...and not for the glory.

Channel 265

Pelegrine had heard that a crisis could function to reshape values and views. She baptized Yarrow's relentless ambiguity THE CRISIS. She concluded that being hurt never helped before. Yarrow never claimed authorship of disputes. She was saying over and over that it was Pelegrine's own doing, that things went awry. Pelegrine's heart was full of anger and feelings of misrepresentation and being maligned. And Yarrow continued to claim innocence,

"I had to do what I had to. You, Pelegrine, are the problem, really."
But for once and for all Pelegrine was determined to let go of the persuasive repetitions of the beautiful woman she so loved—let go of the perpetual self-deceptions that continued to stay between them. It was high time for Pelegrine to be her own woman-- to be solid and accept the loss of Yarrow. Pelegrine was worth loving, only she did not know how much. She learned there would be other things to find in life but first she had to love herself, accept herself and not give a damn what others think of her. She knew she was decent. The right people knew that, too. And Pelegrine pledged to herself:

When Yarrow's ceiling falls down on her again--and it will--you will reach a Pelegrine who, for once, will not respond with disappointment and rejection. I will accept your decision, which has always excluded me. I will remember that many other people had wanted to be with me but that I chose, not to be with them. So it wasn't because nobody desired me. The problem lay in what Yarrow needed and my response to that blue print.

Thus, Pelegrine determined that her ego could no longer depend on Yarrow's decisions. Pelegrine's self had to trust Pelegrine's decisions and never anybody else's ever again. This was to constitute the reshaping of her values. These were her resolutions as she approached the end of that year that was to bring her the death of her mother.

Channel 266

But before that death she was additionally violated. Pelegrine was in the big city of New York and the window in her two months old car was brutally smashed to pieces. Pelegrine was drained and out of energy to grieve over her first new car, ever. Every time she had made a major purchase, she was always on a devastating guilt trip because she was afraid to spend so much money. Perhaps she mourned her diminished independence because debts make people immobile. And the junk we call possessions make moving an expensive hassle. She could never move again like she did in her early L.A. days: Spread out one big bed sheet and let it hold everything. The rest stays behind. The Santa bag held the right amount of goods to own and was easy to transport in a convertible. Realizing that this was less and less possible, Pelegrine was remorseful and very unhappy after each material acquisition. The smashed window only plunged her deeper into the sorrows of ownership. She always maintained,

"The more you have, the more you have to maintain. More is not better. More is just more."

Soon after this encounter, Pelegrine went into psychological therapy, something she had wanted to try and numerous people had suggested.

Channel 267

     She was exhausted and slept for three hours after her first visit. After the second visit, Pelegrine was cooking, eating and walking around restlessly. She was sorry the sessions ended so fast. She had to leave at a point when she was emotionally highly charged. She stayed stirred-up for a long time. She liked the therapist, gave her poems, a short story and diary entries to read so she could catch the spirit of Pelegrine's patterns.

     Pelegrine talked a lot during these one-hour visits and, week after week, she hop scotched around in her history. From this woman Pelegrine learned that she had not been mirrored enough when little. She did not have enough feedback from Elli, which may explain her urge to express herself intensely. Oral diarrhea is what she labeled her urge to unload. It did not matter whether it was information she read in a book, saw in a film--she simply told it freely to almost anybody who wanted to know. The impulse was compelling and Pelegrine often was on a roll without restraint or caution. She felt like a demon had taken over and pushed logic and reason aside and let emotions rule. She continued to log her experiences:

     My therapy drains me more than I imagined. I also jog vigorously. I feel in great shape and less cluttered and maybe more open to my inside. I don't know if I like the doctor. She seems nice but I must be patient and wait to give her a chance. The good thing about this is, my thinking process goes on after I leave her. More constructive thought patterns are emerging. If only they would last. If only anything at all, would last. I have always wanted things to last and then undermined them so that they would end. Crazy. I guess, I want everything. Freedom and security. I am ultra sensitive to and get hurt by unjust criticism. I fear rejection more than anything. I want to learn to tell the difference between valid commentary and nonsense. I don't want to remain susceptible to opinions. I want to believe in myself, which I do sometimes, and then I don't.

Channel 268

After her third visit, Pelegrine's mother suddenly and unexpectedly died. *My beautiful beloved Mama is dead. I can't believe it. My reason to live is gone. I am afraid. She always was my ultimate brake why I never could commit suicide. My adored mother who loved me but could not nurture me. She is the reason why I am so vulnerable. She a child and me, too. We both never grew up. How does one grow up consciously? How do you know you are grown up—not jaded? I hurt. I could burst in two with the pain. I cry and I don't know what to do. I am so alone. Afraid. Not even with death I get any help. Always, always, everything by myself. All-important events I dealt with myself. Never with the solace of anybody. I am a wild thistle, a wild flower. I was forced to be strong. Tomorrow I have to go to work without having had time out for mourning like I have seen other people do. There never were proper periods of anything in my life. Always MUSTS. And HAVE TO'S. My stomach is revolting. Mama, where are you? Can you hear me? Maybe even see me? I want those myths of heaven to work for you. Then you could see for the first time in your life how I live. You could be with me.*

Channel 269

Mama, three days ago I received a letter which you mailed before you died. A letter from the dead. You wrote about your bleeding feet that were not healing. If you were alive now, I would see a death sign in that. Yarrow had already predicted you would die this year. I laughed at her because how could she know? And even now Yarrow is unreachable, as she has been when I needed her the most. I am forever and ever alone. Her phone is out-of-order says the recording. Probably forgot to pay her bill again. So difficult everything. Benjamin and I are mad at each other. He argued with me about the male mortality rate. He thinks their weakness is sociological. And I have read that to die eight years earlier than women has biological reasons, instead. He disagreed. And so we are mad again. He is my best friend but he is narrow-

minded. But usually he is extremely understanding of people. But now I can't tolerate his shallow thinking.

I hurt so and I don't know what to do. Help, help me, Pelegrine! I have got to turn to me. I only have me. If only I could have reached you, Yarrow. But now you are gone. And I will never reach out for you again. Only to myself. Good-bye everything, my original language and people.

Channel 270

Mamale died on February 1, at four in the afternoon for her. For me she died in the morning, for my little baby sister Zange in the afternoon. Now it is eight hours after her death and I have spoken with my sister. Mama is lying in the hospital in a coffin and a morgue. All night she will lie there.

Time is creeping too slowly. This is only two hours later. And I still can't stop crying. My dear, gentle Mama will be sleeping forever. A mild death. She suffocated but they called it "falling asleep."

Mama, Mutti, Mutti, Mutti! Never again a letter from you. Never!

Channel 271

Pelegrine's grief had not subsided two weeks later:
Still black. The pain is permanent. My stomach always in knots. Nothing is beautiful and worth living for anymore. Not even the sunshine. I hurt day and night. I go to work like a machine. I tricked myself into surviving. But I rush home to do Yoga since yesterday. Or I sleep. Or cry in my sleep. I will never be the same person again. Life is not important anymore. I saw a new therapist three times already. I like her better than the other one who had indulged me and read my poems, diary and the story of another impulsive interlude, a story that took place under the table. I did not feel I was in good and comforting hands. Cannot spell it out exactly but the chemistry between us did not help me. The new lady is more confident, more mature, less hip. She radiates more stability and just might help me find me. I wonder if that will ever happen? I just don't see how.

Especially since so much literature exists that suggests that the category woman has been socially constructed. And that women are diverse and that one's sex is not related to one's sexual preference or social role. And that sexual feelings and activities are not always best described in either man or woman terms. And the process of a woman identity formation is problematic not only because of homophobia, but also because of the blurry nature of sexuality itself. It is complicated because bi-sexuality itself can be viewed as either a lesbian cloak for someone who has difficulty coming out, or is unwilling to accept a stigmatized identity. Furthermore, a woman is often viewed as going through a bisexual phase in the coming-out process of lesbians. But I see my woman-orientation more as phase in my coming out, as a sexually androgynous being because I also believe one's sexuality is fluid and not a fixed component. It changes with age, opportunities and the right environment while being on the path toward one's claim to an authentic self. That is what I want—me and whoever fits into my picture—either a man or a woman. It doesn't matter. What matters is that the person connects with me from umbilical cord to cord, from psyche to psyche and will stop me from spending so much time alone, will stop my world-weariness.

    I like flexibility and define my sexuality by the way I live. There are many women who do not have sex and are not considered a-sexual. So what is their label? Labels are dangerous and, if applied too restrictively, ignore the fact that there are degrees of attraction in sexuality, and that those degrees are subject to change within ones lifetime. It all depends on the circumstances and the strength of the drive. We live in a complex world and to reduce everything to black and white, right and wrong, limits one's experiences to a simple duality. We are all a mixture of everything, a mixture of male/female traits in varying forms and can function best in a pluralistic setting. The either/or concept is too narrow. The range of choices is far greater than two, allowing for a rich and multifaceted human experience. To me being bisexual is as natural as being homosexual or heterosexual. If one level of sexuality is considered unnatural, then so are the other two. To me bisexuality surpasses sexuality. Being open and fluid rather than rigid and closed means that I can be attracted and emotionally bonded to any human being regardless of gender. By honestly acknowledging my desires which I may or may not act upon and by pursuing whatever makes me feel comfortable, emotionally, mentally, spiritually and physically will be my course of life.

Channel 272

Pelegrine was particularly depressed and sad after one of the sessions with the therapist. Her birth story, the bombing attacks and the back-and-forth between mother and child, Ellie and Pelegrine, became too much for the patient. Pelegrine cried during most of the meeting and did not stop afterwards. The pain she was feeling was very familiar. Pelegrine wondered how often she would have to continue to feel it?

Forever? Enough is enough? When are these pieces buried?
What will I do with my life? Exactly what will I have to change so that I can feel peace and quiet? Yarrow is my distant planet that is not with me. I think I have lost her. She becomes hostile every time I try to tell her about my pain over our separation. She says that one day she will be pushed too far and quit enduring. Then I will say 'So be it.'

She called it my obsession. I wanted to be a family with her and I have waited all these years till she finished raising the kids. That has been seven years now. I always wanted to live with her. But now she calls it an obsession. Because now she wants a career. She never finished her degree. She had been settling for 'abd', all-but-dissertation-jobs—second rate, low paid work. As long as she can land jobs like that, she will never stop using her credit card. She will have to go wherever there is money. She will never have time to finish her dissertation and receive her advanced degree. And I finished mine and wanted her to do the same so that we had a better chance of finding decent employment in the same town, maybe at the same school.

I was the one who objected to Yarrow's spending habits. I tried to help slow down the growing debt. I knew she was in a perpetual cycle that made her dependent on inferior jobs and kept us apart.

However, after the kids where out of high school the job itself became her career that kept her from being with me. Even though I had offered her room and board with both of us tightening our belts so she could write her dissertation and make us a marketable "couple." But no. She calls it my fixation wanting to live with her. I don't see my desire to be together as odd. I thought that was normal. I have to let go of her opinions. If she doesn't want to be my family the way I need it, I must be my own family. I am so confused. I never wanted to live alone. I can. But I don't like it. I want to like it. Maybe if I'll do Yoga all day long and continue that level of concentration during my other activities, it will be my private wonderland, my trance in the real world? I will focus on spots and on single thoughts till I forget intrusions and the environment. Will it work? Will my stress, my energy, and my hyper active me go away? My sparkle is flickering. I'll never be charming again. I have died and with it my 'joi de vivre.'

How To Go On

Clinging to students
flowers of children
and life with four legs
and tortuous winds
Kicking the sand
with an aching spine
and minimalist sounds

Dreaded nights and mornings
in sleepless company of dreams

No wake ups
but withered
uncaring
care

No money
no shopping.

No wants to maintain
only deaths
in graves filled with mothers
and lovers
grown weak and old
too soon.

I am eating funny, dull, old, unappetizing, unappealing remnants. Don't want to go shopping. I have no money. I don't want any money. I want to starve to death. I want to die. Fall asleep like Mama. I am so weak and already so old. I never will be a different person. I have no hope. Seriously. I am not lying. I have no energy. For anything. Please, let me fall asleep for eternity. Don't make me wake up. PLEASE.

Channel 273

Pelegrine drew a bizarre and surrealistic sketch of her situation. It was to punctuate her low spirits. Bombers and airplanes, baby carriages with hands falling out, eyes with smeared mascara, big, red lips, fat tears and a baby with a chain on its foot. It was probably her attractive mother, her birth, and her miserable memory of her earlier life that intruded into her consciousness and generated this gloom. She hated to go out these days. But when she did, she regretted it.

Horrible day. Four-car collision. I was stopped at a red light. The broken window ordeal barely behind me. But before the signal turns green, three cars behind, an idiot driver crosses over two lanes and collides with a pick-up truck pulling a boat. An American lady in a Buick gets pushed forward into my rear end. Shock, shock, shock all the way down my spine. And I had wanted to stay home. Now that I went out, I wish I had stayed buried. I am as low as one can get. There is no lower. And it is real for so long. And Yarrow makes me cry when I merely hear her voice. Why does she trigger even more pain in me than I already feel? Why? Why does she make me feel crazy, insane, and totally maladjusted? She eagerly points out my deficiencies. And even now when I tell her what I discuss with my therapist, she coldly insists that I should try harder and tell the truth. She is so rough, so cold and pushy. Why is she convinced that I am not telling the truth to the doctor? Why wouldn't I? If I am withholding anything, then it is without my knowledge. She could not just demand this openness anyway. What does she think?

I told her that my empty life is bleak and that I might adopt a poor and homeless child. She could only say,

'Good. Maybe for once you are thinking of somebody else other than yourself.'

This hit me like a bombshell. Does she think she is God? Only an enemy and a resentful person could say something like that. Other people reacted with positive and nurturing comments. They felt that my loneliness may be soothed with such an act. They could also see a connection with the loss of my mother, my end in so many ways, no children of my own, no marriage, no attachments, no roots—just me. It seemed a logical urge and strangers expressed kindness toward this notion. Only Yarrow refers to my seven-year isolation as selfish. She calls my wish of living with her an obsession. That woman has only harsh words. How stupid do I have to be in order to realize that Yarrow is not for me? Why were her words so powerful?

'You are the only woman I have and ever will love. There will be no other female connection after you. Sexually I really prefer men. I had the best sex with my ex-husband, the father who abandoned my four children. But my feelings are connected to you. I love you.'

I never quite knew how to interpret that last statement. Did she involve two compartments when loving somebody—sex and feelings? Don't they run in the same vein?

Sex had become unimportant between us. I had closed myself off from the daily disappointments. I thought my clitoris had atrophied. But in reality she had hurt me with her callous remarks. Yarrow is only good for herself and her children. As long as she keeps producing tears in me, I probably have no idea how deep-seated my anger and disillusionment with her is. It's deep and painful.

She just throws the ball in my court and tells me to get therapy.

Channel 274

The entries stopped suddenly and instead a drawing of knives and swords descending on a reclining body filled the entire page. But the next page registered regular text again:

Today I had a four-hour phone conversation with Yarrow. It was a good one. I wanted to call and bring her a less shattered me, so that she may not feel so lost and disoriented because of me. It is terrible enough that I feel as bad as I do. But disrupting her life and its balance because of my imbalance is wrong. And such a good self, a more sensible one, I could give her today.

Three days later:
I still feel more secure and not so down. My sister Zange telephoned me. Great surprise. We talked for real. She had a Catholic mass read for our Mutti. Her room at the senior center is still empty. The women wonder if she won't come out of the door as usual. Mutti had been preoccupied with death. Not too long ago a TV program on dying fascinated her. Several residents spoke highly of our mother. Mutti was intelligent and a good conversationalist who loved to read. She made weekly trips to the library and got new books to read. I love her so and will pass this love on to my life. I want to become whole and a loving person like her.

C.G. Jung is saying what I have been saying, my dear, dear Yarrow: action follows the strongest motive. The animus in the woman addresses the anima in the male. Does that apply to any two people, I wonder? I can see how this Jungian principle may work. Yarrow who has read so much more Jung books than I have, never speculated about my animus, my subconscious way of manipulating men. She always called me a flirt. But I am not. I am just doing what the situation requires. I am pleasing so that I can have what I want. In Jungian terms my mother's and my own behavior makes a lot of sense. Other opinions have always degraded this conduct or described it to be negative.

Letting Go

      Oh, how do I learn to discard
cardboard opinions
that harbor mildew
finding no residence
but in Salvation Army closets?

      Clean, clean, clean.

Let go of what you haven't worn in years
Let go of what you know hurts
Let go of what you know is better for somebody else
Let go of discarded dreams.

Make new ones

      Don't be afraid of change
Put furniture and things you can't part with
in storage
and live in the car
in a tent on the road.

      But do go on.

Channel 275

      Now is my spring break. It is early Friday, just past midnight, and Yarrow called me. She may have had plans to visit me because we are both having a break at the same time. But she speaks of too much work to do. Many times she had legitimate reasons. But they are repeating themselves. She never plans for anything. No life together because of no planning. I am tired of waiting for you. I am stopping.

Channel 276

Pelegrine started reading voraciously about all kinds of relationships and women psychologies. One book struck her. *The Way of All Women* called girls like Pelegrine boyish women. They are forever adolescent. They often seek partners who are mother or child-like. That certainly applied to Pontiac Wingo, Werra Weiß and Rosemarie Sand. All of them were a mixture of both. It is also true, such girls never work their problems out. They eventually go from person to person. They seek to be in-love. They hunt for the pinnacle and the thrill. They can't grow up. Their feminine side is undeveloped. Either their own mother didn't have it or they did not teach them the wisdom, the feeling, the feminine, the power of women. Pelegrine's Mom was sadly unable to instill any of that. She was more successful at modeling exploitation, powerlessness and abuse. That is why these boyish--not manly or masculine--youthful females are seeking womanly women to fulfill what they themselves are lacking.

Such theories seem to apply well to Pelegrine, for she preferred all her life to look like a teenage boy, the way they dress, act and relate to life. She has always looked younger than she was. Even now. And it is true she told me, she liked soft, gentle, mature, firm and womanly women. She disliked the men-like butch types but loved, especially those who came from a "normal" home with two caring parents. Those girls brought less emotional baggage into their relationships and were less likely to collide with Pelegrine's spot-welded repairs. Pelegrine-type women are projecting a kind of anima, an unfulfilled femininity. Thus, she is always searching for the fulfillment. Pelegrine became aware of her tendencies and went hard to work on becoming conscious of her reactions and hoped to learn to better articulate her feelings. She told herself that she must neither repress awareness of behavior nor the necessity to act. She desperately wanted to grow psychologically—at least past adolescence. She examined her relationship with Yarrow repeatedly. She tried to keep the requirements of a mate simple--someone similar in cultural and moral development.

Pelegrine remembered three months after her mother's death that she had once more assumed possession of a very private item that had belonged to Elli and only to Elli. This was not the diary but another important book called a *Stammbuch*—a personal anthology of friendship and memories.

In Germany the friendship book was widespread from the 16th century in bourgeois circles and among scholars and students. Its popularity also grew among craftsmen and artists. The primary function of a *Stammbuch* album is, apart from originally recording origins and genealogy, to record and confirm relationships across time and distance for posterity. Such entries include proverbs and sayings and best wishes. Depending on the imagination, degree of education and skill of the person writing into a *Stammbuch*, entries might also consist of drawings, engravings, embroidery, paper silhouettes, locks of hair, pressed flowers or the like.

With this book, one asks friends and relatives to write witty verses, or favorite proverbs, which they prescribe to the book's owner as a kind of prophecy. And then when one is old, a look through these pages remembers old schoolmates, family, friends and special encounters. But there is always only one owner of such a book.

However, Elli relinquished hers to Pelegrine who took a great fancy to her mother's blue, elegantly bound, velvet treasure. Here, too, the entries of Elli's family and friends had suddenly stopped. It was a repeat of the Elli-Pelegrine diary transformation. Pelegrine asked her own friends, aunts and uncles to write dedications to her. Ironically, that involved some of the same people for Elli and Pelegrine.

Again, everybody marveled at the quality of the pen and ink drawings but especially the stunning watercolor illustrations that adorned many pages. Because, once again, the left pages were prepared by Pelegrine's talented grandfather who had created this *Stammbuch* for his beloved young Elli. The companion pages were blank and reserved for the words from one's selected friends and family. This particular *Stammbuch* contained entries from Pelegrine's grandmother to her nine-year-old daughter, Elli. There were messages from Elli's lovers, from relatives and best friends. There were even poems from the time when Pelegrine and Zange were school children themselves writing their personal dedications to their mother.

Thus, it was eerie for Pelegrine to "own" her Mom's book. It was wild to see her own verse composed as a ten-year old child in still unshapely and wobbly letters written to her beloved mother.

It was even stranger that Elli ended up writing into her own book as a mother to her child, Pelegrine, where once, a few pages earlier, Pelegrine, the child, had written a dedication to her mother. And her sister, too. She once had written as a child to her mother. Elli. And later was asked to write in it again. But this time she had to compose words to her sister, the new owner.

Funny. One treasured book, with two separate owners in which each one becomes each other's devoted contributor, inside one and the same document. Zange writes to her own mother and then to her sister. Two mothers--Grandma Käfer writes to her daughter, Elli. And Elli later writes to her own daughter, Pelegrine. Two mothers writing to their children. But only one child receives two-way entries in her mother's repossessed book. Only Pelegrine!

Pelegrine has strange feelings whenever she traces the true chronology of this book. The merger of her persona with that of her mother's touches her. Taking–over her Mom's personal books was an act of unconscious imitation. Pelegrine was stepping in Elli's footsteps. She resembled her mother even more than that. She was equally ambivalent and could not easily make and stick to her decisions. It was always hard to make lasting commitments. It was also hard to be mean and tough and not waver.

Channel 278

Another time Pelegrine had asked Elli to write down her memoirs for later when she wouldn't have her alive any more. Elli wrote only twenty pages. Then after her death, Pelegrine ripped-out the twenty pages from the composition book, stapled them together, and, once more, continued writing her own life into her mother's unfinished book.

However. She could no longer confiscate stories from her mother. She had to capture her own life in her own book. Pelegrine had acted as a custodian of her mother's intimate memories for the last time. She never would have to continue Elli's partial life. She never would have to complete Elli's jobs.

Elli's life lies bundled and complete in more than twenty pages. It lives inside Pelegrine's thick memories.

Channel 279

Four months after her mother's death, Pelegrine drove camping to the Outer Banks of North Carolina. She was living in the dunes again. Her tent was up and the sun was setting orange. Her coffee was dripping and the psychology doctor told her to become dependent on herself, center herself, so that she would know what she wanted.

At 10 p.m. the same day, she still felt great. Full moon. Pelegrine stood on top of a high dune and stared at the stars for a long time. She swayed to the moon. It was divine. She didn't know what her problem was. So lucky. There were couples here and there in the distance. For the first time in her life, she did not envy their togetherness. She hadn't spoken to a human being for two days. Pelegrine registered by putting 30 dollars for three nights into a silent envelope. Only her dog Emily could hear her mumbling to herself. She was not lonely. Why not? Is this going to last?

Pelegrine saw the distant whitecaps in the moonlight glistening against the shore. The fierce wind brushed her warmly and also the big, fat bug candle. She could not end it and crawl into the sleeping bag. This was not a night to leave lightly. She wondered why she felt so good. She promised herself to record her feelings every day. Pelegrine wanted to know what it was like to know what one feels. She planned to report her findings to the doctor. Why did she think about her so much? Her face appeared constantly.

Channel 280

  Night not so good. So windy and small biking tent kept flapping around my face all night. I have never slept in such a tiny tent in such heavy winds. Got up at 7. Put up the old Eureka Timberline tent. I want to sleep tonight. Made it to the beach with the small folding bike and the attached cart on wheels tied to the seat with an umbrella and floppy beach chair wedged in. Emily and I looked like Mr. Faulkner's Snopses. I didn't care. My invention served my purpose.

  Every day I own the secluded part of the shore. My travel aids allow me to go quite far and burry myself in total isolation. I wear no top and enjoy the breeze. Water fine and strong. No pain, still. Bugs keep biting my legs. Otherwise, I am still silent. I am not even speaking to Emily because she is passed-out in the sun. Why won't she go in the shade I made for her? The umbrella flew away three times which is now propped-up sideways with cords attached to a giant, abandoned driftwood sculpture. And it works. Nobody is here, except one man thousands of binocular yards away. He is reading and doesn't bother me.

  Still June. The first day is over. So much wind. I am camping in a semi-primitive way. I haven't done this in ages. I am wearing the same tank top for the third day and as of this morning no underwear. The beach is often empty and I removed the bikini top and bottom gradually. At the end of the day, I just slip on my cut-off sweat pants. My burned body loves the fleece. My dinner is over and the one dish is washed. I am smoking a cigarette. The sun is still out at 7 pm. And so is the wind. This breeze is a major deterrent to do a lot of things the way I usually do. I don't walk around the picnic table unless I have to. Little pieces of paper towels are tucked in the cracks for wiping this or that and my fingers. I feel chills but that must be the sunburn. I burry my umbrella and beach chair in the dunes. They will be waiting for me tomorrow, and I don't have to drag them back and forth every day.

Quiet and peaceful Thursday. Spoke to odd people at the water faucet. Small talk about the dog. They were surprised that I am alone. Why?

If only there were more shade. Trees or a roof. Now that I don't have a chair here at the campsite, I spread out an old coat I had in the trunk and I am sitting leaned up against the car for my back. Not the best chair. But it works uncomfortably. I took Emily into the cold shower, which had a rope dangling to be pulled for water. She hated it. It was nearly impossible to hold her in place and pull the water and, with no third hand, rub the water and lather over her. Then I tied Emily's leash to her collar and to the shower rope. Thus, I could foot-operate the invention and, voila, I had two free hands. Emily had to part with the salt

Sunset Moonrise

A cherry moon hides
behind the hot gaze of the sun.

An orange sunset hides
behind gray clouds.

But the simultaneous *moon to my* pink right
breaks a thick blanket mist
interrupting nothing.

8:30 is not always too soon to go to bed. A thunderclap woke me up at three in the morning. Crawled out of tent and secured things. The bad weather disappeared with my sudden headache. And at 7, the hot sun beat me out of sleep. So, I changed campsites from #40 to #36. Now I have shade. I don't have to haul everything so far to the table. Advantage of shade outweighed all drawbacks. I dragged the whole tent, bedding and all, over there. A second person and I could have hoisted the freestanding tent onto the car top. But I could only lift and drag. I am so hot and have a perpetually sweaty upper lip. I don't care. By 10, I was on the beach, as usual.

Angry sea and an almost storm in the night made it hard to find hidden umbrella and chair in the dunes. I also got my period. Great! What a day! I stayed on the beach for seven hours. I dropped a pealed banana into the sand. I washed it in the ocean. I swallowed the gritty bite. I never put on my top the whole day. When hikers come this far, I only drape a towel over myself. I am getting bold.

But now I nearly choked. An old, ugly man appeared out of the dunes, looking around wildly. Then he disappeared as fast as he came. And he reappeared twenty dunes farther to my right. He sat on the beach, took his pants off and was totally naked. He went up to the water. Stayed two seconds and came back to put his trousers back on, sat down and scratched his head. A little while later, after I had read two pages, he repeats the identical scenario. He undresses, goes to the water, and feels it. And gets dressed again. This time he exits into the dune after passing me first. Weird.

Emily never pays much attention to passers by. But this time she flickers her teeth and growls at the exhibitionist. Strange. Now I am obligated to watch the dunes behind me. He probably has been back there watching half-naked me. Shit. I don't have time for that. The ass. Why doesn't he go into the water and swim? At first, I almost admired his guts. He was far enough away from me. He meant no harm. So it seemed.

My damn period. My stomach has been hurting all day. Spent mostly in umbrella shade. Fear of burn. The wind burns, too. Friday night isn't over yet. 9 p.m. My cramps are still with me. Damn. I am enjoying tonight's hardships more. I lit my lantern. At last. Now I have table space to write as opposed to my knees. Opened a bottle of wine to free cooler space, and I've got to drink it while it's cool. My body is burning. How much heat will the wine add?

I see nobody at all. My site is secluded, nestled in a valley of trees. The physical hardships are indescribably hard. Every step a chore. I am primitive as dictated by my reluctance to move. A good test for my patience. I can't get mad at anybody. I don't have energy to be angry. I am gauging my moves better, so my rope won't split when humans come to test it. Will that ever happen? Only car doors slamming in the distance.

Heard my phone messages today for the first time. Before I left, I caved-in and bought a machine. Only two messages. One from the car garage and one from you. The doctor told me all my answers lie inside me. I wish I could hear them better. I am patiently trying this camping alone, without anger, using the time to find me more. Yesterday I tried Yoga in the tent. I don't know if it worked but I managed to zombie into a tranquil quiet. Then I fell asleep listening to Eartha Kitt. The hot white sun burned me awake at 7. Tomorrow I will have shade. Perhaps I'll sleep longer. The hissing noise of the lantern is unpleasantly loud. I just glimpsed the pink or is it a rosy orange moon between the trees. All night he looked into my face. Today my tent lies low for the moon and the weather. He looks like a paper lantern right now, bright and red. Such a color! What a lucky dog I am. Remember it, Pelegrine.

Next day much better. I could sleep till 9. With shade over the tent, the dog and even the table. Thus, I made coffee. On the beach, I rode my little bike on the hard packed sand at the edge of the water and Emily was happy to be back. She rolled over and skidded into a long, diagonal spiral slide, right in front of my front tire. I laughed and nearly fell over her.

I lay in bed last night hearing a "Bob White" and cried a quick tear. I felt the trickle on my chin. Thoughts about Mama still stab me. When will those stop? I miss her forever. Not physically, because I never had her anyway. But the reality of being truly motherless hurts. When she lived, she loved me in the distance. She knew my temper, my goodness and me. I am like her sister, Josefa: stubborn, sentimental, moody, unpredictable, full of energy and smart. But also good-natured, soft and pliable like my mother. I am still both of them. Their child.

Making decisions requires that I think things through. And I must have been too impatient to do that. Maybe that's why I don't decide willingly. I must try a new tactic. Take each decision that comes toward me and contemplate the in's and out's for at least a day and then decide. But <u>do</u> decide. And stick to it. Only change, if the same process was involved that forced a new decision and revision. Each time follow the same process. Weigh the pro's and con's and then go with the feeling AND the logic. They both must meet, given time.

I experienced precisely this decision-making process when switching campsites under the most arduous conditions. It was truly painful and it didn't pay off till 48 hours later. But it did. It would have been so easy just to stay, complain and suffer, and be spared dragging that stupid tent with all its contents to the car and to the table four times, the distance of a football field in desert heat. But that torture brought Emily, the cooler, the food and me what we sorely needed: shade.

Probably a raccoon took my bag of oranges, apples, onions and bread. I found pieces of food scattered far apart. That poor animal hauled the heavy fruits a long way, before it could enjoy the only thing it really wanted, the bread. Finding my fruit was like hunting for Easter eggs. A happy dog is sprawled out next to my knee. Last night I showered with my salty bicycle. The salt water acts fast and noticeably. The couple waiting for my stall, flipped out when this strange woman exited with a dog and a bike.

Channel 281

And, lo and behold, the naked man returned. When she got to her spot, Pelegrine wondered why she encountered a makeshift, plastic beach wall propped up on supporting sticks.

Here he is, this time undraped behind this wall, prancing naked to the shore, standing and staring into the surf for interminable seconds, returning to get dressed immediately. The same ritual. Then he walks past me along the shoreline and disappears into the dunes. He carried a plastic bag with a pair of binoculars. Now I know. He has been peeping behind the dunes, discovering my furtive topless escapades and then felt compelled to parade his body briefly before mine. That has to be the explanation.

After he had left, I walked up to the dunes and chased him with my binoculars, watching him get into an emerald green station wagon and drive off. I felt eerie because I also saw him helping a man open his car with a coat hanger. The naked dude was helping somebody? Perhaps he is part of the summer staff? But how can he be, looking scroungy, spooky and acting odd? I don't run around sneaking up on single boys, scaring them with my nakedness. I hope he doesn't find my camp spot. Every time I see dunes that "move," I become tense and instantly engaged in a mission, abandoning my precious refuge.

Channel 282

Pelegrine explored the island. She hiked to watch the ferries come and go. She discovered the fire station that sold 5 dollar fried fishplates. She shared a picnic table with sea gulls. Noisy, tanned and over-weight families were stuffing themselves. Pelegrine dismissed the familiar pangs that often crept up when she found herself sitting alone and solo in settings were families, church groups, crying babies and unruly dogs dominated. Pelegrine knew she had to fight this discomfort and not let it cripple her sense of accomplishments. She told herself to dump such fears and negative emotions.

"You have got you. And that is a lot, you surviving bomb baby, you."

Channel 283

My God. Words are too slow to capture all that has happened to me today. Another pair of males had arrived before I did and took over the improvised wall. I see a man and a dazzling 5 year old, blond boy. Both nude. Hmm.

I tried not to let that bother me and change my own ritual. I slowly removed my top and got ready for my day in the sand. My breasts had tanned *so dark that my whole upper body was one single dark brown lump. After a while, the boy came over to play with Emily. Jesus. What now? He must be foreign. Perhaps Swedish. He never answered to anything I was saying. He accepted grapes I gave him and volunteered his name, Maui.*

Gradually he became friendlier and began to play in the shallow surf with me. We were on our tummies and rolled over like dolphins. We frolicked on all fours pretending to be dogs. At one point, I was using gestures, speaking very slowly, pointing to the naked man and asked if it were his Daddy. But no answers from Maui, except an enduring fascination for Emily and me. After about an hour, the presumed father put on neon-yellow shorts and asked if the child was bothering me. I said no and learned it was his nephew, not from Sweden, but from North Carolina with a speech impediment. He was learning to speak at age 5. I was relieved that he actually understood English. I assured the man who himself was the son of a now 70 year-old Cape Hatteras mother and a far away, Australian father, that the beautiful boy was no trouble. He left us, removed his fluorescent pants and continued his sunbath.

Channel 284

The nudity of both man and child was disturbing to me since sexual situations have always traumatized me. When I think back of my childhood, to the boarding school nuns, to the exhibitionist scaring me on my way to kindergarten, and back to Frankie's big organ, I still don't know how to deal with any of it, really. I have had only one real experimental involvement with Archie Woodruff. I am not so sure that counts. I have loved a few ladies, but I never fully grew up. And when this partially developed woman is challenged with sexual situations, she is at a loss about what to do.

Channel 285

My brain worked overtime. I struggled with the double standards this society imposes even on innocent children. Maui could not know why I was uncomfortable with his and his uncle's nakedness while I was braless. If I were in Europe, I wouldn't be nearly so concerned. But here. In North Carolina. All by myself. Always responsible for me. Foreigners always judging me, not really understanding that I myself liked to be free and liked to live and let live. I have enjoyed becoming strong and bold myself to find the courage to go naked when it is not a publicly offending violation.

I compromised, as usual. I put on a long T-shirt and covered myself from their eyes.

Channel 286

When I lay back down on the blanket, Maui sat on top of me thinking I was a horse. I pulled him off and went into the water for a swim. He was impatient and insisted that I would return to the blanket. But I preferred the chair. So what did he do? He just climbed into my arms, cradling up to me like a baby. I stroked his sunburned back. He was exceptionally affectionate and seemed to miss a mother.

Channel 287

But little Maui continued to surprise me. At one time, he sat on the blanket while I was lying next to him. A person strolled down the beach past us. Immediately, little Maui placed a large empty beach bag over his genitals while stretching the rest of the bag over my resting head. I thought that was funny. He displayed shameful behavior while covering my head that did not need it. But why cover anything? What went on in that little mind? At one moment so free and uninhibited—the next so inhibited and 'normal'? Already showing signs of duplicity operating under cover. In the dunes?

Eventually, the uncle joined us and told me more about him and his family. At that point, the boy had fallen asleep in my arms, curled-up, sucking his thumb. I asked the uncle about the boy's mother. I wondered if he was seeking affection and contact. I learned the parents were divorced and that they take turns looking after Maui. Everybody has him a week. This was the uncle's week. For one day, it was my turn.

Channel 288

On a Monday in June of this summer, I am sad. The Canadian couple I had befriended was leaving tomorrow. Lovely people who also enjoy the simple camping and backpacking pleasures of life like me. Outer-Banks soul mates found in the Barrier sands around the Island winds. After my prolonged, one-sided Emily conversations, I talked non-stop to people. They enjoyed my tales from this beach with my gentleman dune peeper and my deaf baby boy. They met the electrician who returned exactly at the moment I was in the water without my clothes.

Channel 289

For a long time he stood planted on the beach while I floated and gloated till I got cold and waved him a gesture to move on down so I could get out of the water. He told me later that he thought I wanted him IN the water. So, he took off his pants and joined me with only his Fruit of the Loom separating us. I scolded him to take off his clothes also and swim naked if that's what he wanted or move on away to let me get out to get dressed. I had come here to enjoy myself and not be scrutinized by a chicken man curtailing my freedom.

Another man joined the scene. I had spotted him with my binoculars sunbathing in the nude also. He stood on the shore watching the scenario.
The men were eying each other, wondering what would happen next.
My electrical admirer didn't seem encouraged to join me. He left the water and vanished into the dunes and the temporary visitor walked on to his sunspot. I ran like lightening to my blanket, put on my bathing bottoms. I was furious at the

peeping coward who viewed nude bathing that way. Wanted to watch but not join. I can't believe I wasn't scared of him.

Channel 290

A flash thunderstorm interrupted my journal writing. What torrents flooded down on my tent and Emily! She dug herself under the tent floor, under my body, lifting everything up. I was shaking inside the tent, and she shivered underneath me. I barely removed the sticky wet sand off my feet as I rushed through the zippered door. Then I myself became a little dog-ball like Emily, curled in the middle of my tent, trembling with her. When the inconsistent storm pretended to stop, I darted out the door again to fasten loose items and rush back in because the storm was not done yet. So much water, so fast. The tent seams leaked in places and I toweled-up the puddles. All my stuff on the table I had covered with a tarp was flying in different directions while being washed and drowned. Emily's hunk is pressed deep under me below the tent floor. Where could I put her? I am helpless in here. Why did she choose that spot? Now it's pounding even harder. How many storms am I watching come and go? I had heard yesterday that during one such hurricane storm last week, a man was picked-up in his tent and dropped into the mud of the Sound 60 feet away. Why do I have to remember that now? Lightning, please, don't hit me.

Channel 291

Story after story, after story is the story of my life. I can't keep up with my stories anymore. The storm turned out to be a hemorrhage of 6 storms in all, from 8 p.m. till midnight. One stopped, another one rolled in. I was so scared but Emily was more so. I was inside shaking and she trembled outside because half her body stuck out from the tent and was pounded by rain. I covered her with the tent floor more and protected and warmed her with my body heat. She shared hers with me, separated only by the nylon of the tent. Emily nearly broke my heart. She was always frightened in storms. The wild sounds of the loose tarp did not help. I never have dogs inside my tent. Never. I like it clean and I do not like to slave to get it that way. The inside of the tent was the only sanctuary away from the relentless sand and never ending sand spurs. Emily could never come in there. I could never get it sand-free. When living that wild, the tent becomes the ONLY place free of sand and grit. I don't see how people can give-up that one clean spot after wallowing in sand all day long, day after day. At home, she is an outdoor dog, with limited access to the easily cleaned kitchen linoleum. I raised an outside husky with thick fur.

Channel 292

Neither one of us slept much that night. I realized my 4-year-old Emily was still a baby. When the sun finally rose, we were too sleepy to get up. I dragged out the damp bedding, laid it in the sun, plopped on it, and slept in the dune. Then I remembered the Canadian couple and went to their car and wrote a note offering to fix coffee for them. Their night was surely just as wild. They were outfitted for on-foot back packing and had only minimal equipment with them. They were delighted at the notion of coffee. I was thrilled I could please them. They stayed and chatted and then had to leave for home. We were compatible beyond belief and vowed to go on a wilderness trip together, one day. I was sad all day because they were gone.

Channel 293

The commercial fisherman was called Harold Gray. He was also a sun worshipper and had discovered my preferences with his binoculars. He is now my sunbathing partner. Remember the electrician's exit? Remember there was another passer-by? Well this man turned out to be Harry, who said that he was aware of my predicament in the water not being able to come out without my clothes. He wanted to bring me a towel but he didn't know if Emily would let him. That moved me. I thanked him for the thought. Now he has joined me and is sharing the afternoon. I made it very clear to him that I had no sexual interest in him. After I explained the word, he answered that he had a monogamous marriage. Thus, I received a sunbathing buddy.

We take turns watching both directions while the other is dozing or dreaming. That way we could warn each other when beach strollers were headed our way. I remember once I had drifted off. He simply just came over and put his towel over me, saying he didn't want to wake me. Two old ladies were approaching. I told him how much I appreciated his chivalry. We are both Sagittarius and one devil catcher had met another. An unforgettable scene shall forever imprint this connection in my mind.

Channel 294

We were looking at birds with our binoculars. We saw an osprey, a bird much larger than a sea gull, dive down into the ocean in a straight line, pick-up a small flounder, get up into the air and fly right over our beach. Suddenly, the bird dropped its prey into the sand about 100 feet away from us. He circled for a while but could not do a land dive and retrieve his fish. That would break his neck. He probably couldn't see the sandy fish anymore. I said to Harry, 'Now, it's my fish. The bird brought me my dinner.' And so, we went in search of the fish, which was hard for us to see, too. The 100 feet turned out to be more. But Harry's eagle eye spotted the flounder in the sand. He washed the fish for me with the ice water from his cooler. Half an hour later, the fish was frying in my pan. Harry promised to bring me a blue fish tomorrow.

Channel 295

Eight months later I received this card:
Dear Pelegrine,

We visited the aquarium recently in Baltimore and, watching the flounders hovering over the seabed, thought of you and our summer adventures at the Outer Banks `Flunder fliegen nicht jedem in den Mund!" (Flounders don't just come flying into anybody's mouth.) Seriously though, we wanted to wish you all the best for the year ahead and hope that we'll continue to keep in touch, albeit sporadically. We had such good exchanges in the summer and it would be good to do that again, should it be possible to arrange. Greetings to Emily, too. Ian and Judith, your camping friends from Canada.

Channel 296

I am learning to know what I want. I miss my doctor. This week I won't see her. She is probably not even thinking about me. I wonder what she would have to say about all these events here? Should I let her read them? But I don't want to love her. I need to discuss this with her. Will I have the courage to tell her? But she needs to know, so she can help me get rid of this lifelong tendency that I have had since I was 12 years old.

Channel 297

Progress

My tanned eyes are tired
and my heart is heavy
My head is on my arms
and I want to enjoy what I have
and not cry over the absence.
    *All this in **June**.*
    *In **August***
I am back in my Adirondack cabin
the first time since that turbulent
Christmas Eve, two years ago.

I am treating the outside walls for
fungi, mold and rot
with overwhelming odors
staying with me still
after swimming off my sweat

I am reading, re-thinking and
remembering while co-existing
with squirrels and mice

I am reading my old maps
drafting blue prints
and trying to heal
childhood wounds…   by myself…   for myself.

Channel 298

You did not show up. I try not to be angry and not overly hurt. If I am to draft new maps, other people's old patterns, must no longer evoke the same old feelings in me. I must change for me, even if you stay the same. This is a good experience for me. It forces me to face my anger and its source and lets me choose new answers to new patterns.

The silence here is unbelievable. I can hear myself think and breathe. In the small lake I hear the echoes of my cough, my splashes and Emily's first voluntary swim and thunder in the trees. I am my defective universe wanting to be whole.

There is a chair, empty. From time to time, I fill it with people I have known. I carry-on would-be conversations and realize that I would never think my solitary thoughts or ponder my feelings or marvel at the rain drops in the orange sky, were my room filled with the presence of another wounded being. Solitary confinement is the only way to reach understanding. Too much time is spent in action and in idle chatter. Well, well, well.

Channel 299

On a Saturday in August of the same year of the turbulent June, you appeared at 3 p.m. and stayed till 9:30 p.m. I had you all but six and a half hours. I am trying to be happy about it and not negative. The visit was great. Like old times. As long as I don't harbor resentment such as 'Why didn't you come as you said,' and ruin the precious moments that are allowed, I am fine.

Channel 300

I was scared three times. Really scared. Once I sat outside, looking up and by the sand pit, 50 feet away, stood what looked like a wolf. Last night I heard such a deep howl, never heard before in my life. Coyotes sound different. A painful, piercing scream. I let Emily sleep inside. Shortly, the mousetrap went off, merely stunning the little beast, which I then had to kill myself. After days of aggravation and mouse shit all over my things, I get jittery.

I burned piles of trash, fiberglass, paint cans, rags and tampons. Black smoke. Went close to stir the pile. Escaped in time before a loud explosion shattered the air. Sparks and fire-cracker-like swirls fizzled around. Sounded like a big shot gun. That kind of forbidden fire one definitely doesn't stir and poke.

It was getting dark. I wanted to transfer a few more logs to the woodpile. Suddenly my nose nearly touched a spiraled circle of something. I thought the loggers had left some heavy rope coiled up. I looked again and perceived four little darting tongues and one thick, fat red one, lunging at me. Snakes! Babies and mother, all curled-up in one round rope-like ball. Wonderful and cuddly. Except freezing terror for me. My face so close and I almost picked up the rope. I just watched the yellow squiggles stretching over thin black bodies. I concluded they were harmless. They were king babies. I only wished I saw yellow diamonds instead of stripes. Red tongues. I went to get the camera, shakily attached the flash. Couldn't focus. Was too dark. Took pictures anyway. Turned out great. The ball of rope was rapidly disintegrating. Little snakes peeked out everywhere. What a sight. I even squatted with the flashlight talking sweet. I wanted to co-exist. I did not move the rest of the wood. I was afraid.

Channel 301

The lantern acted funny, too. Loud, explosive hissing flames. Barely gave me light to write. Today I had my share of explosions and shock. I did not want to blow-up while messing with the lantern. Only one tiny candle left. Otherwise, the day was great. Three swims. Crossed the lake in rubber raft with

Emily sitting in the middle. Long ride with me paddling fiercely because raft developed a leak. Both ends rose to the sky because Emily and I sank into the center. Oh, well.

On other days, Emily swims so much now. She is no longer afraid of the dark Adirondack Lake. She swims side by side with me, in tandem. When I notice her getting tired, I grab her four legs, hold them tightly bundled, treading water, giving her a rest. Sometimes she heads for the shore herself and takes a break. Because her crazy human mother swims big distances and doesn't seem to get tired. Hmm.

Caught no fish. Lots of snorkeling in the mud. I always feel afraid when I look around under even shallow water. The illusion of being trapped in the deep frightens me. Even underwater films make me uneasy.

Sleeping in the sun. Biking for newspaper. A beer at the motel while waiting for the phone. So much sunshine in one day. Almost unbearable.

Channel 302

When Pelegrine returns to her peopled life, she hears that every one of her friends spends different summers. She knows nobody who does a solo trip like that. They enjoy Pelegrine's movie-like tales. She doesn't mind entertaining them but does not want to end-up feeling sorry for herself. Because she does so much alone and never sees another model to help her enjoy a single woman's vacation after vacation, Pelegrine struggles to accept herself and get to the point and actually relish her freedom and strength.

Channel 303

Because they loved me, they stayed with me. I tested their patience. Their love pulled me through. I wanted to be well. I wanted to be happy. I have always wanted to be happy. Who doesn't? I always wanted to have a relationship. I once married a wonderful girl. I thought that would be good for me. She was a wonderful woman. She seeded the literary me. Pontiac Wingo.

And we had ten happy years together. With Yarrow, I had eight stormy years. But I realize we both made mistakes. I thought my connection to her would change me. But nothing changed me. I had a problem. She had a problem. A big problem. And I think I made a lot of people very unhappy. I know she loved me. I regret the most of making her unhappy. We caused each other much pain. But I had to get on and I am back where I started, where Uncle Albert and Coco left me in the mouths of Alfred and Rita. I have made peace with my tormentors. I embrace the moment. I no longer live outside my time, my yesterdays and tomorrows.

Channel 304

I feel less depressed. I look forward to getting up. I can cope with me. I don't feel guilty with what I have. I am beginning to find out who I am. I like it. They call it recovery. Very fashionable now. I entered recovery wanting to recover. Because I was so unhappy and so miserable. Anything was preferable to the state I was in. I saw several therapists. I started a practical exercise program, watch my fat intake, and listen to my second voice, the one that warns me regularly. I had to express and destroy a lot of emotions that I never faced before. I had to get real. I had to do things for myself differently.

Channel 305

I finally live alone. I have never lived "alone—alone." There has always been some kind of family, dysfunctional or not, people, roommates, lovers, and entourages of sorts. I was never good at confronting people. I had to learn to tell people what I thought and felt. I had to learn to rock the boat. I got a dog. Emily and I get up in the morning and start the day together. And my life has gotten better. I have learned to enjoy helping other people. I have learned to be there for somebody. I have never stopped trying to be a decent human being. I always was, but I didn't have confidence and trust in me.

Now if I feel bad and depressed, I call some one to chat with or I go out for a walk. Or I put on music I like either in my ear or on my system and sit on my stationary bicycle and then jump on my trampoline. I do something to change the trajectory and shake up my sludge. I never communicated that way before. There are so many people who have the same problems and they don't communicate because they don't think people want to be there for them. Anyone reading this, it is O.K. to ask for help. I didn't think it was because I thought it was a sign of weakness. But it is a very spiritual thing to do to ask another human being for help.

I was an emotional carcass. I was dead. I would always deflect a compliment. I never could accept one. But now I am accepting. Yes, I have done some great things in my life. And there is a lot more to do. I have got my love of life back. I had lost that. I am human. I am not perfect. And perfection was something I had always striven for. We are all flawed. Once I realized what my flaws were, I could do something about them. I can accept myself now for who I am. And that has taken me more than forty years. I have peace of mind, for the first time in my life. You have seen me when I was happy, when I was troubled, when I was oblivious. And it shows that I am heading for another level of peace. There is no inward battle going on anymore. Whenever I falter, I listen to my heart now and not only my head.

Finally, I have stopped writing about sad stuff. About my bits and pieces. I remember other people's journeys in my words. I have gotten good at being alone. I am no longer a deer running across a field changing course depending on the glares of circumstances.

Epilogue

I still don't know how often I will have to repeat myself before I am actually able to put a stop to my own repetition. I have been looking forever for a trainer to train me. I want to have learned from my mistakes. But as long as I stay attracted to awe-inspiring people who give me attention, as long as I raise them on a pedestal and make them into heroes, as long as I insist that these people love me, I am short changing myself.

My Pelegrine story ends with high hopes in the American West. I go there all right. But ten years later I know that I have not learned enough lessons about being connected to people.

I deeply admire Nadja Salerno-Sonnenberg who shares my passion about life. I also adore the Dutch shadow boxer, Lucia Rijker, 1997 lightweight world women's boxing champion whose isolation gave her the ability to stay focused in the midst of the biggest chaos and threatening pain. I want to channel my Nadja self into a centered Lucia-type being.

I don't know what lies in front of me. But I do know that my continuous alienation and existential despair must lead to the burial of my primary pain and eventually un-poison my water supply, letting me float and fly freely.

§

Ten years have passed since I first unraveled my life and tried to restring it, hoping that it would make more sense. While I am putting on my final touches, I also realize that change is slow yet possible. I look into my own mirror once more and see the same person with the same heartbeat, the same mechanisms, with so many things the same, which I hoped, would have changed. The only thing that has changed is that I am twenty years older, a little smarter, a little the same and a little new. I am glad that I do not have to talk about my past anymore. I am finished with my shavings.

When I look back at my characters, I also see how the situations that were not good for me, unfortunately, also have not changed. I still speak with

Yarrow over thousands of miles away. And just today I realized, as I put the final touches on my "Pelegrine":

You, Yarrow, are now THAT age which I was predicting and wondered how you would be at this time. And, guess what? You still live in very close proximity to your now very grown children. You are raising your six grandchildren now! Your explanations are, as always, superb, but the same. Back then it was lack of income that prevented you from having a life with me. And now it is the same. You can't leave your kids because now they pay the way and you still need the money. Wow! Only the employers have changed, not the propeller of your reality. I guess, my instincts were telling me a lot back then but I refused to believe them. You never really wanted a room of your own, a life with a mate like me.

Sadly, the same is true for Rosemary. She never cleared her table either. She never won her husband back but never gave him up either. She is an old woman today, living a lonely bachelor life that I wanted to color and cheer-up. She also still speaks to me from very far away and her voice continues to sound tender and caring toward me when I hear her. But a life together was also not meant to be.

And just yesterday I heard Barbara Walters talk about her tumultuous life and numerous marriages. Her book reveals her failures and triumphs. But one concept she articulated perfectly for me at this stage of my life:

*Whatever you get yourself into, be it marriage or love, if you have a **heavy** feeling in your stomach, **DON'T DO IT.***

I did have those heavy feelings each time before I connected myself anyway, against my heavy heart. I overpowered those prophets and did not listen.

I will listen better!

I am, moreover, afraid of what will happen when I invite my friends to read this book. They have been waiting eagerly for years. And I always dodged and beat around the bush and heard myself saying, "Well, I tell you, after you read this, you will not want to know me anymore."

"But why?"

"You will see."

And now is the time that some will, finally, see. And I struggle from day to day. One day, I don't care and on another, I care again of losing some. But if I really have arrived where I say I have, then it must not bother me if they all see me and know stuff about me that they have wondered and suspected but have never been told. I am very private about my personal life. I hate labels and I am afraid to be labeled now. But all my apprehensions because of the expected brouhaha because of my proclivity of who attracts me, must be put to rest. I guess, I will have to walk the walk after I did the talk.

You must know, that I have rewritten this story several times. At one time, I disguised all personal connections heterosexually because I wanted a safe story. But then my narrative would not have helped me examine my nightmares and discard them. Thus I had to tell it the way it was and let my life flow through me and consent to live in the present moment—allow me to drop what Deepak Chopra calls the heavy suitcase of unreal time and illusive judgments. I continue to practice the trick of dropping the past and live NOW because the only time on the clock is now. I am enjoying this exploration because I am exhausted from the race about my past and the fears of what people will think.

And I also know that I have come a long way struggling with my sexual identity. And I am truly thankful that a scholar like Lisa Diamond was born and expanded the Kinsey studies on gender and human sexuality and enlightened us that "female same-sex sexuality is a dynamic system," meaning that it is a highly fluid and situationally responsive system, which can often undergo abrupt changes depending on the circumstances. In many cases, it is difficult—if not impossible—to predict its long-term course based upon initial experiences. She and I are convinced that there is no point in a woman's life at which one can look back at one's past and current behavior and say, "Okay, I know for sure what type of attractions and relationships you are going to have for the rest of your life." In fact, my journey has been and still offers such testimony.

But my ultimate insights from my journey to my source, have brought me distance and space. I simply had to go through my troubling memory by using it without it perpetually using me. By going through it, point-by-point, episode-by-episode, I reached detachment because I succeeded to step outside this memorized person I was. I wanted to re-create my life in stages, regurgitating it one more time, so that I could bring about detachment and, finally, walk away. Thus I have shaped a freer life because I am no longer polluted by past experiences, which I had also created. Since I know this process, I can walk away from my constructions just like any artist can, and be able to enjoy a less frenzied, peaceful me. And, in order to get there, I had to step outside myself, unravel my myopic history of discontent to gain a larger perspective. By riding my old waves, I stopped myself from drowning in them. My old engrossed ego had to let go of taking it all so personal so that I could be free to breathe and live. Thus by shifting my focus, I could become a more cheerful, optimistic and content being.

Right now I am in the middle of another voyage inside another book which begins as a cowboy on a cattle ranch later catapulting me into colorful Central Mexico where I am experimentally and prematurely retired, welcoming yet another adventure as a single woman living on a shoestring in the 21st century.

I want that one to be a journey of courage and of observations. It is only now that I am brave enough to be who I am and not mind being alone. I do not have to follow prescribed paths. I have found purpose and know from Nicolas Ray that there is no formula for success—only for failure: trying to please everybody. I no longer look to others for acclaim, approval or validation. I have become my own purpose by choosing not to look outside myself any more for authentication of my values. I have all I need.

Carpe diem, Pelegrine! You have realized that you have an extraordinary life because you are an extraordinary woman. You are to celebrate yourself for who you are. You are to be happy. That is an order. **The End**

www.ingramcontent.com/pod-product-compliance
Lightning Source LLC
Chambersburg PA
CBHW022106150426
43195CB00008B/286